AND GOLIATH

AND GOLIATH

**The Littlest Navy SEAL's Inspirational
Story About Living Your Biggest Life**

by

**David Brown
with Robert Gettlin**

Library and Archives Canada Cataloguing in Publication
Brown, David, author
And Goliath / David Brown

Issued in print and electronic formats.
ISBN: 978-1-990644-99-3 (paperback)
ISBN: 978-1-998501-00-7 (ebook)

Editor: Phil Halton
Cover Design: Paul Hewitt
Interior Design: Mohammed Tahir

Double Dagger Books Ltd.
Toronto, Ontario, Canada
www.doubledagger.ca

TABLE OF CONTENTS

Foreword. i

Chapter 1 From the Ashes 2

Chapter 2 Bring the Fight. 8

Chapter 3 I Want to Be Under the Sea 17

Chapter 4 Confidence 28

Chapter 5 Quitting and the Fear of Failure. 31

Chapter 6 UDT/SEAL It Is 44

Chapter 7 You're in the Navy Now. 56

Chapter 8 BUD/S Screening Test. 66

Chapter 9 Successes, Failures, and Focus. 75

Chapter 10 BUD/S 85

Chapter 11 Symbolism and Setbacks 95

Chapter 12 Haze Gray and Underway 103

Chapter 13 First Phase Redo 108

Chapter 14 Beyond Impossible. 117

Chapter 15 Hell Week: Up to the Breaking Point. 124

Chapter 16 Hell Week: Tijuana Mud Flats 133

Chapter 17 Just UDT. 143

Chapter 18 I Want to Be Under the Sea II 147

Chapter 19 He's No Different Than the Rest of You. 154

Chapter 20 Forging the Indestructible 160

Chapter 21 Final Night Surf Passage. 169

Chapter 22 My Trident. 181

Chapter 23 Highs and Lows. 192

Chapter 24 4th Platoon and SEAL Team 4 203

Chapter 25 Into the Unknown, Into Success 213

Chapter 26 Rape, Sexual Abuse, and Autopsies 221

Chapter 27 With Only a Sling and a Stone 231

Epilogue 244

DEDICATION

The events in this book happened over a lifetime, and the following contributors helped make some fuzzy memories clearer. Without exception, every man on this list would make the ultimate sacrifice to protect the other. LLTB

BUD/S Class

George Coleman	115
Tony Gumataotao	115
Steven Heinze	115
Ken Rice	115
Mike Ireland (RIP)	114
Chuck Pfarrer	114
Robert Ross	116
Siegfried Webber	121
Mike Detraglia	106
Mike Baker	113
Terri Hopkins	82
Vic Muschler	---

FOREWORD

What makes a young man decide to face the challenge of becoming a Navy SEAL?

What sparks that difficult journey, and what makes some candidates succeed where so many will fail?

The truth is—no one knows.

The first step to becoming a Navy SEAL is a course called 'BUD/S': Basic Underwater Demolition, SEAL training. BUD/S is regarded as the toughest military training in the world.

How difficult is the challenge?

In an average year, 800 men and women will climb Mount Everest. The number of men who graduate from BUD/S training each year is classified, but I can tell you it is a small fraction of the number of climbers who summit the world's highest mountain. Let's say it's a very small fraction.

Despite the Navy's best efforts, no tests can reliably predict who will pass and who will fail. Most aspirants are winnowed in BUD/S' infamous "Hell Week," a merciless 24-hour-a-day combat simulation and endurance test. Classes will lose as many as 40% of their candidates in the first few hours; by the end of the week, another 20 or 30% will quit or be forced to drop out with serious injuries. The cut has been made.

A few of the injured, a select group of determined souls who have impressed their instructors with grit and determination, may be given a second chance to "roll back" and restart training—from the beginning. These "roll backs" are the hardiest of all— and David Brown was one. He started in my training class, 114, was rolled back with an injury, and graduated one class later with 115. There is no greater testimony to a man's fortitude.

But Hell Week is only the beginning. Following that test come five more months of demanding and technical instruction: diving, land and underwater navigation training, and demolitions, combat first aid and hyperbaric medicine, maritime sabotage, hand-to-hand combat, and the intricacies of small unit and guerilla warfare. Nor is the challenge of BUD/S merely physical—many buckle under the academic coursework. After six grueling months, the 150 to 200 men who started a class will normally be winnowed down to a couple dozen. The few who graduate together will be forever bonded, but even still, they are not yet SEALs. Only after another year and a half of advanced (and classified) training will BUD/S graduates earn their place among the smallest and most elite units of the United States military—the operational SEAL Teams.

David and I were classmates in 114 and later, teammates at UDT-21 and SEAL Team Four. Everyone called him "Brownie." It was his moniker and callsign. He had entered BUD/S at 18 years old, just barely a man. Standing 5'3" and weighing a mere 110 pounds, his quest seemed beyond ridiculous to ordinary people. But in the attributes that define a SEAL, there is no "ordinary." The community of Naval Special Warfare is a rigid meritocracy; a SEAL's personal and operational reputation is everything. David was respected by his teammates as a brother and was known as an Operator who could be counted on. A SEAL can earn no higher accolade than the esteem and trust of his teammates, and David had both.

Every SEAL will tell you that the job is all-consuming. Though deployments will take a SEAL around the globe, a SEAL's world, ironically, can feel like it's getting smaller—not larger. Inevitably, a SEAL's group of friends becomes the small group of Operators he works with. A SEAL trusts his life to his teammates on a daily basis, and they, in turn, put their lives in his hands. It is an exacting profession. Eventually, it can become difficult to relate to others outside "The Teams." Many SEALs can feel isolated in this world. The attributes that made them what they are make them different from other people—not better or worse, but separated and profoundly different. Sadly, the unique burdens of a SEAL's life can eventually take a toll not only on the individual but on his loved ones and family.

Brownie's life has been one of perseverance, tenacity, and achievement—from childhood adventures to love lost and found, to BUD/S, the Teams, an exciting career at NCIS, and then a steady climb to the top echelons of Federal law enforcement. *And Goliath* is Brownie's story of BUD/S, the Teams, and what comes after—the good and the bad, a story told with candor and courage.

Chuck Pfarrer
New York Times Best-Selling author,
screenwriter, film producer, and former
SEAL Team Six squadron leader

AND GOLIATH

*"You're wasting your time," the Navy recruiter said.
"SEALs are all muscled up strong guys. You're way too little. I
mean, be realistic; you'll never make it. Forget about the SEAL program. Pick something you can do."*

In the Bible story of David and Goliath—a lesson of courage, faith, and overcoming impossible odds—a small shepherd boy bravely volunteers to fight a giant Philistine. The king's entire army fears the giant and warns the boy not to fight. Despite the warning, David arms himself with a sling and smooth stones from the brook. With a fearless heart, he approaches his rival. The Philistine, mocking David, attacks the boy with a spear and shield. David instinctively dashes toward the battle line; clutching his simple weapon, he arms it with a stone, slinging the rock deep into the giant's forehead—killing him.

And Goliath is a story of determination and persistence, and finally, a triumph over impossible odds. It has endured for millennia because it reveals the seed for success.

This is my epic struggle to slay Goliath.

1

FROM THE ASHES

Stars are phoenixes, rising from their own ashes.
Carl Sagan

Speeding south on California Highway 49 in the early dawn four days after Dina's death, my trembling hands gripped the steering wheel as I unconsciously navigated through old mining country. The gas gauge's incessant glowing "E" nagged, causing me to swerve into the first station and creep up to the pump.

Fumbling for my government credit card in the glove box, its contents spilled. Frustrated, I spun to exit my seat, only to be roundly returned, tearing a hole in my freshly tailored trousers. "*Shit, what the hell?*" Grabbing my hip, I discovered the seatbelt caught the pistol grip of my Glock 9mm…as a lefty, my safeguard was always strapped there. After extracting myself from the tangled mess, I stumbled out and began filling the tank.

Returning to the car's confines, I sat as still as a corpse, staring blankly through the windshield at the lighted "ICE" sign above the convenience store freezer.

"Pop!"

The nozzle handle signaled for my attention. However, lost in my thoughts, I remained oblivious to this cue and mechanically shifted into drive before accelerating without a second thought.

"Bam!"

The noise echoed from behind the car. Shoving the transmission into park and bolting from my seat, I encountered a crowd gathering, their eyes wide and their mouths agape at the sight of the jettisoned hose and nozzle lying on the concrete.

"My God! Did I do that?" I stood silent and embarrassed in my unsightly wrinkled business shirt, a hole in my trousers and tie askew. How could some idiot—not someone like me—forget to return the nozzle? In my low, I became that guy.

A kind man perhaps in his mid-sixties, wearing bib overalls and a sweat-stained John Deere hat, walked up and put his hand on my shoulder.

"Are you all right, son?"

No, I wasn't. But words were impossible. I was too ashamed.

How did this happen to me, a former Navy SEAL and now the Special Agent in Charge (SAC) of a federal law enforcement program? I was so pensive I couldn't pump gas.

I wasn't a screw-up. I swear. I was always on time, never made mistakes, and, for God's sake, never failed or quit.

Two years earlier and on top of the world, after being promoted to SAC before my fortieth birthday, the price for my achievement was now coming due. After zig-zagging my wife and daughter across the U.S., the Pacific and back in my determination to achieve "success," everything I'd worked tirelessly for evaporated.

Sheer willpower enabled me to graduate from Basic Underwater Demolition/SEAL Training (BUD/S) class 115, joining the tiny handful who served as a Navy SEAL. Operating in the military for years, testing my body and mind on missions worldwide, my experiences hardened me to stay focused, unwavering in the goal— pushing forward in the never-ending evolution to complete each mission every day.

And then came a moment in the military when my compulsion to strive for undefined success wasn't enough. Leaving the Navy for a career in law enforcement led me to the top of the organization as the SAC in Sacramento, CA. There, I intended to build my dream retirement home on twenty-eight acres in the Sierras and live happily ever after.

Mary, my wife of twenty-one years and high school sweetheart, had other plans. She'd grown tired of my work schedule, relentless travel, and now me. After our daughter graduated from high school, Mary made her move.

In the kitchen of our rented house, I demanded, "We're missing six thousand dollars from our checking account; what the hell happened to it?

"I withdrew it to buy a Harley Davidson motorcycle," said Mary.

"What the hell? You can't take six grand out of the bank to buy a motorcycle without telling me!"

Angry, I stormed out and walked two miles into town to cool off. After an hour, I called her on my cell phone and left a message, "Come pick me up, I'm in front of the Nevada City Library." A short time passed when a man in a battered red Toyota pulled to the curb and rolled down the passenger window.

"Are you David Brown?" he asked.

Stepping back, I brushed my left side, feeling for my Glock. *Shit, I forgot it back at the house.* Twenty-five years of jailing people gets you many enemies, and this guy appeared fresh out of prison. Searching for cover, I said, "Yeah, why?"

He parked and approached me. As he began to extend his hand, I cautiously did the same. But instead of a handshake, he produced a legal document.

"Your wife has filed for divorce," he said. "I'm Mary's attorney. She's been planning this for months. You've been served, David. And by the way, the money she took from the bank was to pay me, not to buy a motorcycle."

What the hell do I do now? I had few options as he got into his car; I leaned into the open passenger window. "This sounds odd, but can you give me a ride home?" I asked.

He smiled and laughed: "Sure, get in. I'm a lawyer, not a jerk."

Saddled with her demons, Mary wanted out. A retirement chalet in the foothills was my dream, not hers. So, she booted me from the rental property and took nearly every dollar and possession I owned. It was a price I was willing to pay to end the failed marriage.

As a former Navy SEAL—some say a certified badass—I'd been through much worse. On those difficult days, I'd say to myself, "I don't need anything or anyone. Give me a K-bar knife, and I'll survive alone in the woods. I don't need worldly possessions or people."

I wasn't born the smartest, tallest, strongest, or best-looking, but I possessed something priceless—unbounded persistence and determination. My traits took me from certain obscurity and a life of mediocrity to achieving the improbable—some say the impossible.

With money running low and nowhere to turn, I had little choice but to sleep in my truck. Arriving early to work, I'd freshen up at the restroom sink and put on my stoic demeanor as the omnipotent boss in command in a demanding and precise occupation. The façade I presented wasn't fooling anyone.

Before long, problems at the office began to snowball. My frequent absences led to a bungled multi-agency search warrant, and I was responsible. Within days, I became the subject of two internal investigations, and my job was on the line.

Still, I'd been through worse and recalled the pain and torture of Hell Week and enduring the twenty-three weeks of SEAL training. I was "Brownie" to my former SEAL brothers; I never failed and never gave up. But even a badass needs an escape plan.

Then I met Dina on a dating website and was sure my luck had changed. On our second date, she asked, "So, where do you live?"

In a panic, I couldn't say in my truck, so I said, "Nevada City," which was partly true.

"Oh, we should go there sometime," she said. "It's nice in the foothills."

Now what?

I couldn't lie, so I said, "Honestly, I don't stay in the house I rented in Nevada City; my soon-to-be ex-wife lives there. I'm sleeping in my truck until I find a place." Her eyes and mouth opened wide, and she grabbed my hand.

"Not anymore; you can stay at my house. I have plenty of room," she said, smiling. Like an angel, she took me in, and over two months, I envisioned my future as bright again.

In July, I went with Dina to see her oncologist. Sure, she had told me about her breast cancer when we met, but we both thought it was in remission. That day in the doctor's office, I learned a lot about cancer, chemotherapy, and hospice. Still, nothing—not my SEAL training, my lifetime of overcoming physical and social barriers, or my challenging missions around the globe—could prepare me for what was to come.

Like a horrific car crash, it happened so unexpectedly. On a sunny, blue-sky morning in late August 2003, I stood helpless as my beautiful Dina passed away. She lay in her bed on white linen sheets, surrounded by her family in the home she loved. She was gone, and I was again… alone, homeless, and broke, but mostly brokenhearted.

Defeated, I was metaphorically cast into the woods with nothing but my K-Bar. I always thought I was prepared for this situation but never expected to be in it.

Dina died on a Thursday, and on Monday, I was on my way to work because that is what SEALs do; they complete the mission.

Whenever a SEAL was killed, teammates met at the Casino, a dirt floor bar in Virginia Beach, and had a beer keg in his name.

Afterward, we'd go on to the next mission the following day because that is how we were trained and bred; it's in our very being, our DNA.

There were no raised glasses and brave shout-outs to a fallen hero that morning in the gas station as I stood pathetic and helpless while a group of customers gawked at my vulnerability. Lifting the nozzle off the ground, I returned it to the pump. After thanking the man who put his hand on my shoulder, I got in my government car and continued my drive.

On the ramp to Interstate 80 from Auburn, the fog in my mind and in the valley began to clear. My thoughts flew back to BUD/S and the Teams.

Thousands of miles away on the other side of the globe, we parachuted out of aircraft at night and into the black ocean. Racing our rubber boats onto foreign beaches, we carried out classified missions without the thought of injury or failure, always knowing that no matter what, we would survive. I understood that my options in the most challenging days of being a SEAL were no different from now, decades later.

White knuckled, I gripped the steering wheel. As the sun in the rearview mirror breached the mountain peaks, I stood on the battlefield, ready to confront the ferocious foe feared by all.

Goliath.

2

BRING THE FIGHT

We are nature. Our every tinkering is nature, our every biological striving.
We are what we are, and the world is ours. We are its gods.
Your only difficulty is your unwillingness to unleash your potential
fully upon it.
Paolo Bacigalupi

At seven years old, I discovered an essential truth—I possessed the power to reject the lie that I was too small and weak to achieve my dreams.

My realization that I didn't have to live according to the world's predetermined rules began on a rather typical afternoon at Grant Street Elementary School. At 3:30 p.m., the end of the day, Ms. Plumbo, our proper second-grade teacher, sporting her best bouffant hairdo, rose from behind her imposing oak desk and issued her daily command: "Class, line up for dismissal!"

"Line up" was the ritual order for me to go to the back of the classroom and stand by the cloakroom door at the end of the single-file line. That place was so familiar that I was conditioned not to think about it. At least not too much. The back of the line was for the littlest student, me.

Jumping up to assume my assigned position, two monstrous hands clutched my shoulders and shoved me down. Slammed into my seat, I gazed up at the biggest kid in class. His red hair mop-topped a white, round, freckled face with glowing green eyes. My menace, Albert Kita.

"You're not going anywhere, shorty pants!" He was twice my size, so I dared not make a move. He hated me, and I didn't know why.

In our little coal mining town of Wilke-Barre, Pennsylvania, my friends and I measured distances in units of corner biergartens and neighborhood candy stores. Albert lived two biergartens and a candy store away, a space that seemed so far it was as if he hailed from a different country.

Declaring war, the red-haired bully made school our battleground. As he shoved me into my seat, he laughed, "Go to the back of the line, shorty pants!" and walked to the front, where the big kids went. Lowering my head, I sulked past the desks to the cloakroom door to my given place.

Since kindergarten, my teachers trained me like a dog to go to the little end of the line, and we lined up for everything—lunch, recess, gym, library time, dismissal, you name it. My conditioning was so complete that from elementary school to the military, upon hearing the "line up" command, I ritually went to the short end without consideration.

But for me being small was normal, everyone in my family was. My father topped out at five feet four inches. My mother made it to five feet two inches. My brother and my sisters are about the same or smaller. The tallest I would ever grow would be five feet four inches as an adult—practically a giant in my lineage.

Not yet five years old, my mother graciously sent me off to kindergarten. I remember her saying, "Let somebody else chase him around for a few hours." According to all accounts, when left alone, I'd climb up on the highest object in the room and jump off pretending to be an Army paratrooper or international spy in pursuit of something. My lack of fear and common sense often put me in the family station wagon with my mother, racing to the hospital emergency room, where I'd be bandaged, stitched, or splinted.

From my first day of school until high school graduation, I held the distinction of being the littlest boy and sometimes the littlest person, but I didn't think it was all bad. Sure, I got teased, picked last for dodgeball, and ignored by the girls. While the jeering and name-calling always stung and made me angry, I learned to ignore it. Most of the time, I was carefree and saw myself able to run faster, climb higher, and fit into places others couldn't. And everyone got harassed for something—the fat kid, the skinny kid, and even red-haired Albert Kita was picked on somehow.

But being little meant being bullied, and Albert was the number one bully in our class. After he pushed me into my seat, and with all the girls laughing, I realized I needed to do something.

After lining up as usual, we walked single file down the school's main hallway toward the massive front doors. Once we crossed that threshold, it was every kid for himself, and I was without the teacher's protection. His big, freckled face waited beyond the entry, ready to pounce. I'd never been in a real fight before, and my sight blurred as tears filled my eyes. All I could do was run away. Clearing the doors, I took off.

"Where are you going, shorty pants?"

Never looking back, scared and crying, I ran down the dirt alley behind the school, past the backyard fences, and onto Market Street. My street.

Some towns are designed, and some develop over time. Certainly, Wilkes-Barre was built for the convenience of miners to drink, and a biergarten on every corner made it easy. My grandfather, Herman Brown, was a miner and hated it. He immigrated from the Netherlands in the 1920s to escape the mines, only to end up underground once again driving coal cars in Wilkes-Barre. A little guy like me and my dad, and a tough-son-of-a-bitch, so I'm told, Herman survived more than thirty years hauling anthracite to the surface. His ability to endure years of physical abuse in the mining industry was a testament to his tenacity and toughness.

That afternoon, as I darted away from school with my nose running and tears streaming down my cheeks, I sprinted past biergartens and candy stores until I burst through the front door of my father's business, Lee's TV Sales and Service. My dad was a hard-working, self-taught television and radio repairman. When not in the store selling, he worked in the back fixing things. A natural salesman, he could sell anything to anyone and loved every word in every conversation. But I wasn't searching for my father.

Flying by the ornate wooden console televisions stacked two high in the showroom, I reached the tall counter. There sat my mother, Jean, a fiery Irish woman, a fighter short on patience and quick to anger. She took no crap from anybody, and while never graduating from high school, she could produce a sentence more devastating than a heavyweight's jab. Seeing I was out of breath and with tears rolling down, she scooped me into her lap.

"What's wrong?" she asked. "Why are you crying? What the hell happened to you?"

Her eyes flashed in disgust, her lips pursed, and she shook her head as I sputtered out my story.

"Oh, no, no, no, no! Nobody's going to pick on my little boy," she said. Taking my hand, she told me to make a fist. "If that boy or anyone else bothers you again, you ball your hand up tight, like this, and punch him in the mouth." Having me practice, I hit her hand as hard as I could.

"Like this?" I asked as I punched her hand repeatedly until a smile came over my face.

"Now, don't let anyone pick on you," she said. "You show'em. Pow! Right in the kisser!"

"Yeah, pow right in the kisser," I repeated with a laugh.

Unable to understand at the time, that moment of tears and anger on my mother's lap in my father's store helped change the trajectory of my boyhood. The experience ingrained in me a trait that became vital to why I would be successful in life. Not that I sought to get into physical fights with bullies, but I realized that things worth having are worth fighting for.

The next day, Albert continued his bullying. But instead of shrinking in fear, I thought about what my mother taught me. "Pow right in the kisser!" The final bell rang, and as expected, Albert waited for me by the front door, but I didn't run; I walked through Grant Street Elementary's institutional metal double doors and past my nemesis. Shocked that he did nothing, I turned and walked away. Then he shoved me from behind.

"Hey, where do you think you're going, shorty pants?" Albert laughed out loud, "Ha, ha, ha! Hey, I'm talking to you."

Ignoring him, I kept walking. Another shove. This time it caused me to fall forward, skinning my hands and knees and scraping my favorite Buster Brown shoes on the blacktop. With him towering over me, I crawled away, got up, and ran, stopping in the dirt alley to make my stand. Planting my feet, I turned to find an out-of-breath, red-headed fat kid closing in. Holding my position as he came to push me again, I clenched a tight fist, wound my arm back, and landed the most brutal haymaker punch I could muster. Pow! Right in the kisser! Precisely as my mother taught me.

The blow stopped him in his tracks, and he gasped as his lips quivered. Not knowing what to do, he reached out, picked me up like a toy, and tossed me against an old wooden garage door. Slam! I tumbled to the ground. Enraged, I jumped up and threw a right cross to his jaw. He stood stunned, held his face, and cried, "Why'd you hit me?"

Holy shit, it worked! I learned the word shit and many other curses from hearing my parents yell them daily. Of course, I didn't dare say any of those words in front of my mother and father, but standing in the alley, having just socked Albert, seemed the perfect reason to say shit and much more.

"I punched you because you pick on me every day, and I hate it!"

Albert stared down at me, but suddenly, he wasn't a menacing monster.

"I'm messing with you," he sulked. "I won't push you if you don't punch me."

In his pleading, I contemplated my next move. "Um, okay, so we don't have to fight anymore?" I asked.

He shook his head from side to side. "No, no, we don't. Let's go." He reached out and put his arm over my shoulder like a buddy would do.

We began walking down the alley, leaving behind the small crowd of kids who'd huddled to watch our rumble.

Cocking my head up, I asked him, "Are you Okay?"

"Yeah, but you sure can throw a punch! Where'd you learn to fight like that?"

"My mom," I said; "she's a tough son-of-a-bitch."

He laughed. "Your mom? Boy, remind me not to get your mom mad at me."

During our walk home, we talked about school, girls, and the candy store across the street from his house, which he invited me to try. "They have the best Sen-Sens, ten for a penny!" he said. In those ten minutes, we began to become friends. Albert and I couldn't have looked more different, but we were alike; we just didn't know it. It took a physical altercation for us to find that out, a lesson I never forgot.

Once I learned that if I landed the first punch, I'd win the fight, it became well-known that if you messed with me, you would end up with a sore lip and a hurt face. And let me tell you, a reputation for winning fights is as good as, or better than, getting into one. So, I used it to avoid most of them. But, thanks to my mother, I was always prepared to take that swing if I had to.

Still, as the littlest in class, I was an easy target. Some people can't help themselves by picking on others they believe can't or won't fight back. Luckily for me, my adversary usually got more than they bargained for. But I didn't always win because losing is part of life, and in fifth grade, I was knocked unconscious by a bully in a playground brawl. After coming to, my friends dragged me home, fearing the worst.

After another station wagon trip to the hospital that turned into an overnight stay, I returned to school with a black eye and a solid reputation—a reputation as the little guy who stood up to the menacing giant. By not backing down, I made the other kids feel like they could stand up for themselves too. My aggressor was expelled, and I became a playground hero.

Once my mother encouraged me to stick up for myself, I refused to flee from bullying and would stand my ground despite my age and size disadvantage. But this built-in trait supported by both my parents was not aggression. I fought only when necessary to protect myself and others and, later in life, to be successful.

Of course, the ability to control this tendency is the difference between a positive and a negative outcome. The bully has the same fighting propensity as the hero. The hero, however, resists hostility and learns when to engage and when to hold back on the fisticuffs.

Also, thanks to my mother's influence, I showed little deference to authority figures. Not that I disrespected those in charge, but I never considered anyone as better than or superior to me, regardless of their age or size. This propensity didn't evolve; it sprung from me like a jack-in-the-box.

Wrongly accused by a school patrol monitor of jumping the lunch line, my fourth-grade teacher, Ms. Carr, summoned me to the front of the class, intending to make an example.

"I'm going to show you how our justice system works, Mr. Brown," she said.

She called it "open court," but it became Carr's Kangaroo Court, where I was indicted, tried, found guilty, and sentenced by her—my punishment: a trip to the principal's office.

From bullying by a student to bullying by a teacher, I stood before my prosecutor and judge. Gritting my teeth and clenching my fists as she conducted her twisted version of classroom adjudication, she reigned behind her immense oak desk, the ultimate symbol of elementary school authority. Defenseless and ashamed, I fumed but dared not slug Ms. Carr. That is when I realized she held no power over me.

With my legs crossed and squirming, I said, "I have to go to the lavatory."

She responded, "Make it quick, David; we are not finished here."

As I dashed from the room I thought, "*Oh yes, we are.*" Running down the hallway, I flew down the stairs and out the school's double doors, bolted down the alley, and headed home. Disgusted and fed up and searing in contempt, I stomped over the threshold of my father's store.

Having lit my mother's short fuse with my story, she intended to provide a remedy with more than a simple note or phone call. The incident triggered her fighting trait, and someone at school would have to pay.

In no time, she and I were in the principal's office. My mother was so upset I could see spittle flying from her mouth as she sternly voiced her concern that I, in a panic, raced home in the middle of the day. Shaking her finger at Ms. Carr and the principal, my mother proclaimed my virtuous upbringing, to tell the truth with honor and integrity, not to mention being raised a proper Catholic boy, for whatever worth that held.

Slumping in her chair, the principal turned to my accuser, who managed only a few words—"I'm sorry, Mrs. Brown, it won't happen again."

Discovering the confidence and ability to defend myself, I began to protect the defenseless. I stood up for other school kids who were teased and bullied. I took on a sense of duty to act for those who needed help.

Why a person would stand up for those who need defending is eloquently summed up in Colonel Dave Grossman's acclaimed book *On Combat*. Grossman employs the analogy that in society there are Sheep, Wolves, and Sheepdogs. Most humans are sheep that want to be left alone to live their lives. Then, there are the wolves, those who prey on the sheep. And finally, there are a few Sheepdogs. While the sheep don't particularly like the Sheepdog, the Sheepdog instinctively protects the sheep from the wolves.

In this paradigm, the Sheepdogs of society naturally confront danger and fight instead of run away. They volunteer and are the protectors, our police, firefighters, first responders, and warriors.

Like my great-grandfather Pieter Braun, I was a Sheepdog. Born in Nieuwenhagen Limburg, Netherlands 1871, he was a decorated soldier in the National Army of the Netherlands, 2nd Infantry Regiment, 2nd Battalion. Pieter was also little. Listed in his military record as 1 meter 619 millimeters in height, or about five feet four inches, Pieter hardly presented himself as an imposing figure but stood out as fierce and courageous, and like my great-grandfather and the Biblical David, I embraced my Sheepdog obligation.

Given the direction and opportunity, I took those common family traits, clenched them, honed them, and used them to seek success.

Why does any child take a specific path, with some moving forward and actualizing their potential? We don't have a crystal ball to see the future, but there are ways to determine one's probability of success. Recent advances in behavioral genetics and psychology enable more accurate predictions of individual strengths and weaknesses that correlate with life success.

Is it nature or nurture that makes us who we are, and can the answer unlock the door to succeeding?

3

I WANT TO BE UNDER THE SEA

Don't be pushed by your problems. Be led by your dreams.
Ralph Waldo Emerson

When I was in grade school, I often dreamt of flying off from our backyard's eight-foot cement brick wall. Standing atop the wall, I'd lift my chin, concentrate, and begin to rise like a bird. The neighborhood's yards, fences, dogs, and trees whizzed by underfoot until I lightly touched down. Dreaming you can fly is common among young men. Dream experts profess that the manner of flying is essential to determine the meaning.

Flying like a bird in dreams symbolizes optimism, a new start, and a free spirit. It also means you have inner strength and empowerment. You have removed all negativities in life and are limitless. Taking my dream literally, I endeavored to make it happen.

Sneaking into my dad's shop early on a Sunday morning when I thought no one was near, I rummaged through his tool caddy, searching for a utility knife he used to cut up the television shipping boxes. Slithering into the dark, quiet workroom and past the broken, dismantled televisions, I snagged a roll of electrical wire off the workbench on my way out the back door to the cardboard graveyard.

The perfectly angled containers stacked high displayed the "M" for Motorola. With a flick of my thumb, I exposed the blade and began my feverish effort to carve out my flight enablers from the discarded heap. Cutting up one side and down the other, I created the fantasy wings in minutes. Now, to the launching area.

Climbing on our aqua-green station wagon's hulking chrome bumper, I dragged the hastily carved cardboard over the back window and onto the roof. From there, it was a short hop to the top of the wall separating our house from the neighboring convenience store. Pulling the roll of wire from my pocket, I cut lengths, running each section through holes in the cardboard, making loops and handles.

With my wings fastened, I prepared to glide over the driveway to a soft landing next to the neighbor's grapevine. With complete confidence, I stretched out like an eagle about to take flight. As I leaped into the air with my chin up and chest out, my flimsy cutouts folded, and I careened into the dirt face first with a thud and in a cloud of dust.

Gasping for breath and spitting blood, I jumped up and thought, *"Shit, Mom's gonna kill me if I have to go to the hospital again!"*

With my front teeth intact and only suffering from a split lip, skinned knees, and palms, I could fabricate lies to get my minor injuries past my mother, but the wire ligature marks on my arms presented a problem and would take some explaining.

Unexpectedly, my mother came flying out the back door. She'd seen me sneaking around and followed me outside. In a panic, she ran towards me.

"David, what the hell did you do? Are you trying to kill yourself? You better not have to go to the hospital again!"

With her unblinking eyes as wide as saucers, she scooped me up, examined my chin, opened my mouth, and moved my arms up and down like testing the joints of a Barbie doll. Seeing the wire marks, she panicked.

"You could have cut your arms off! Now get into the house so I can put iodine on those cuts."

"Iodine! No!"

Wanting to fly was an obsession. Careful thought wasn't one of my natural talents, and I was open to trying anything, dangerous or not.

No challenge seemed too big for me, with danger acting as a motivator. We begin to develop our personalities when we are very young, and I demonstrated plenty. As we mature, our inherent traits and character reveal who we are. Why we become the way we are is a product of genetics and our surroundings, and *heritability* is a way to measure which has more influence.

Heritability is a measure that reveals if a trait is more likely inherited, like height, or is a result of our environment, like the language we speak. The higher the score, the more likely the trait is genetic; the lower the score, the more likely the trait was developed from our experiences.

In his book *Blueprint: How DNA Makes Us Who We Are*, behavioral geneticist Robert Plomin writes, "Genes are not destiny, and heritability describes what is, not what could be."

My experiences revealed my inherited traits. At the same time, my family and surroundings left lasting impressions. The number of influences is immeasurable, and the memories are locked in like a chapter in this book. Missing some of those experiences may not have affected my future, while others would have assuredly altered my path.

My parents' successful business enabled them to buy a summer cottage at Harvey's Lake, sixteen miles from Wilkes-Barre. The story behind picking the right little house became family lore.

We loaded the five of us into the station wagon and began the journey. Melanie, the oldest and second mother to us kids; Leo, six years my senior and my role model; Bonnie, two years older and a regular source of headaches for my parents; me; and lastly, the baby, Wendy-Jo, pushed and shoved our way into the hot car.

My mother, sporting her latest wig and carrying a bag of snacks and a pack of cigarettes, followed. My dad, with his dark hair slicked back, usually smoking Kool menthol, locked the back door to the TV shop and joined the wagon's mayhem. As we drove, we passed the large, stately lakefront homes and boathouses only to turn away from the water and onto Baird Street. With a kid hanging out of each window, we drove up the hill to the cottages in our price range.

As the story goes, the kids shot from the car and ran across the grassy front yard of the first possible summer haven. Whoever was assigned to watch me didn't. While the rest of the family stood admiring the cottage's curb appeal, I bolted from behind the massive Chevy, disappearing into the shadows.

With her mother-bear instincts, my mother sensed me missing and said, "Leo, where's David?" She got both my father's and brother's attention in a single quip. Was that her strategy or panic? The family's interest shifted from the cute cottage to thoughts of, "*Oh my God! David's lost in the woods.*"

As luck would have it, my brother spied me sneaking up the washed-out dirt road and laid chase. Dodging the ruts and roots, I scurried behind a large walnut tree, keeping still as the family followed in pursuit. Within minutes, the gaggle caught up, everyone calling my name, running in circles, searching under every bush and around every rock.

Frustrated, my father, knowing my penchant for causing my mother great anxiety, called out, "David, come here now and stop screwing around! You're scaring your mother."

Popping out from my hiding place and with a huge smile, I said, "Here I am!" Steaming and with fire in her eyes, my mother grabbed my arm.

"You son-of-a-bitch," she screamed in anger and with relief. "Don't you ever do that again? You scared the hell out of me!"

The family stood silent, and my mother calmed down as the situation shifted from me to a small dwelling peeking through the woods. Gazing at the tiny house as if it were a framed Thomas Kinkade painting, my parents fixated on the weathered "For Sale" sign affixed to the barbed wire entangled post.

The setting seemed perfect; green grass and hovering branches shaded a screened-in porch. Crossed white birch limb railings and slate front steps adorned the entry. The double-shuttered single-pane windows would offer a cooling breeze on hot summer nights, and the immense stone fireplace would provide a comforting blaze in the winter, a place to toast marshmallows and make memories.

And we did, with blow-out parties thrown by my parents, where relatives and friends filled the yard and the house with food and alcohol. Family water balloon fights and garden hose duels that ended in the house were common. My parent's fun, crazy habits rubbed off on me. Their zest for life made a welcome impression that's lasted my lifetime.

In those days, we all ran around the neighborhood with toy guns, playing cowboys and Indians, carrying pocketknives and a handful of firecrackers. But I couldn't do it alone. I needed a mentor, and Leo taught me how to survive in the wild, or at least in the woods at the cottage.

I admired everything about my brother. If he liked it, I liked it. He played with rifles, pistols, and knives, and so did I. He loved spy movies like *James Bond, The Man from Uncle,* and TV shows like *The Avengers, Speed Racer*, and *Johnny Quest*. I listened to all his music (and still do) and tried to copy what he did in school. My father taught Leo how to throw a knife and shoot a BB gun and a .22 rifle, and Leo gladly guided me.

During the summers at Harvey's Lake, my brother and I pretended to be adventurers and survivalists. Spending our days in the woods, we hiked and scouted animals and shot tin cans. We climbed hundreds of trees and planned secret attacks on our neighbors.

Dressing in made-up military uniforms, we'd low crawl through the brush, up and over the neighbor's garden wall. After throwing rolled-up sock grenades onto their patio, we imagined we were German prison camp escapees who would sneak back to our three-tier treehouse to award each other medals for bravery.

Leo fed my appetite for action and adventure and allowed me to develop essential skills. I could shoot a soda can off the burn pit wall from 20 yards in no time.

The debate about what influences a child's development has been raging for years: nature or nurture. Supporters of the nature theory insist that genetics determines not only physical traits but also personality. Supporters of the nurture theory say physical traits are inherited, but that is where the genetic influence ends.

A study at the University of Edinburgh found this: "Genes play a greater role in forming character traits—such as self-control, decision-making, and sociability—than was previously thought." The study of more than 800 sets of twins found that genetics is more influential in shaping critical traits than a person's home environment and surroundings. Psychologists at the university who experimented say that genetically influenced characteristics may reveal how successful a person will be.

Scientists may argue that my brother shaped my personality through our childhood experiences. We both, indeed, pursued Sheepdog careers. He was a paramedic firefighter. But even as I admired and took great interest in Leo, I developed my own ideas, desires, and traits.

While in grade school, I discovered my love for scuba diving and the ocean, an odd thing considering I grew up in a valley in Pennsylvania coal country. Watching every television episode of the *Undersea World of Jacques Cousteau, Voyage to the Bottom of the Sea,* and *Sea Hunt,* I marveled at the sea life and the futuristic devices they used to explore the depths.

I wanted to scuba dive badly but needed to earn that reward from my father. He and I agreed that he would buy me a scuba tank if I got all As on my final third-grade report card. Try as I might, I ended up with two Bs, and I got nothing—well, almost nothing.

Tommy O'Brien owned and operated Harvey's Lake Diving School. An old salty merchant marine, he turned his hobby into a profession. Relying on his know-how, he taught two generations to dive without a single accident. At least, that's what he told people.

As a consolation prize for my good grades, I received one lesson with Tommy.

The summers in northeastern Pennsylvania are short, with swimming weather between June and August. The warm air temperature lulled the unsuspecting into the stunningly cold lake water. On one glorious summer day, my father pulled me aside while the family vacationed at the cottage.

Grabbing the car keys, he said, "Jean, I'm taking David for his scuba lesson." His stoic demeanor and matter-of-fact movement reflected his attitude that *he*, head of the household, made a command decision.

Concerned but understanding, my mother reminded him, "Okay, but keep a close eye on him. You know how he is." With that, I grabbed a towel and sprinted to the station wagon before anyone changed their mind.

On the drive to the other side of the lake, thoughts ran through my head of doing backflips off a boat's edge with my scuba gear like Jaques Cousteau did on TV. Talking a mile a minute, I explained how it all works to my father as we winded down the two-lane lakeside road.

"The deeper you go, the more pressure is on you, and you're weightless. Oh my God, I will be floating underwater, like I'm in outer space!" I said.

He turned, glaring at me, and in a spooky voice, said, "No one knows how deep Harvey's Lake is. Many people drowned here, and their bodies were never found. Don't get freaked out if you see a skeleton or dead body down there."

"What? A body? No way! You're trying to scare me."

Steering off the road into the dirt, we arrived at Tommy's school. Quite the character with his beer belly hanging over his tiny speedo-style bathing suit, he reminded me of an older, out-of-shape Lloyd Bridges.

On cue, my father started a conversation and talked to Tommy for what seemed like forever. "He loves scuba diving," my dad said. "I don't know where he gets it from."

Tommy snickered; summing me up, he said, "I have just the scuba bottle for you." I couldn't manage a full-size steel cylinder at eight years old and sixty-five pounds, but he had little tanks for kids. He went to his homemade wooden rack and picked up a beautiful yellow cylinder attached to a black fiberglass molded backpack. At that moment, nothing could take the smile from my face.

Putting the tank on the ground, Tommy said, "If you can pick it up and carry it, you can dive today."

Struggling, I lifted the device.

"No problem," I said with a nervous chuckle.

Rummaging through his locker, he grabbed a dive mask and spat into it before he handed it to me. "*Yuck!*" I thought, "*Why the heck did he do that?*"

He sneered at me and winked. "When you're in the lake, you can rinse the spit out," he said. "It keeps your mask from fogging up."

Next, Tommy gave me a set of fins, but they were too big. Panicking, I fretted that I couldn't get in the water without them. "Do you have a smaller pair?" I asked.

Tommy's face contorted. "No, those are the smallest I have," he said. Pausing, and with his hand on his chin, he continued, "I know. Put your socks back on and try them again."

"They fit!" I said...well, they kind of fit. But I wasn't about to say they didn't.

"Now for the dangerous part. Don't hold your breath underwater—inhale through the mouthpiece. Breathe slowly in and out. You got that?" Tommy asked.

"Got it!" I said.

"Now, suit up!

After attaching a hose and regulator, he opened the tank's valve and pressed the button on the mouthpiece, and air shot out. *Pssst!*

"If you get water in your mouthpiece, push here, pointing to the front of the regulator, and the water will come flying out."

Standing perfectly still, my mouth agape, I watched his every move and ingested every word. Walking to the small sandy beach, tank on my back, fins, and mask in my hand, I got in the lake.

In today's world of lawsuits and liability, most people have at least a half-day of instruction diving in a pool followed by a week of training to become certified as an "open water" scuba diver. It took

Tommy thirty seconds and a few sentences to teach me, an eight-year-old, to conquer the depths alone.

Fear never entered my mind. I was too young or ignorant to understand and never sensed the real danger. I carried a cylinder of compressed air on my back and was about to enter a frigid lake and dive for the first time by myself. I should have been terrified.

People fail at things, but some don't even begin to try because they fear the unknown and unfamiliar. They won't persist because they lack confidence. Understanding *why* you can do something establishes a base for you to stand on while battling those fears, and from that foundation comes confidence.

Standing in soggy socks, I rinsed Tommy's spit from the mask, sat on the rocky bottom, and put on the fins.

"Okay, now get that regulator in your mouth, roll over on your belly, and float," As I did, he yelled. "Don't forget to breathe!"

My face hit the water, and I stretched my legs and arms, becoming suspended weightless under the surface. Breathing and floating, breathing and floating, I remained motionless staring down, fascinated by the pebbles and sand only inches away and beyond the thin glass. With each breath, the bubbles rose around my chin with the audible "pssst" of air.

Tommy tapped me on the shoulder, "Okay, now stay in the roped-off area." And with that, I began my voyage to the bottom of the sea.

"*Stay in the roped-off area,*" I thought, Ha! He doesn't know me very well.

Off I went, diving deeper with each pass in the confines of the small, designated swim area. The adventure got the best of me, and as I swam away from shore and into the dark depths, an image of a sunken boat appeared. I surfaced to see my father and Tommy at the school talking, not paying attention to me, so to the wreck I went.

The depth's pressure caused by the immense weight of the lake produced a "squeeeeal" and pop inside my head as the air in my ears equalized. Stunned and pausing for only a moment, I refocused on my quest to reach the sunken remnant.

Above me, the surface faded in my descent, and darkness beneath gave way to the sand where the wreck rested in its watery grave. Suddenly, a hazy thin stratum like a sheet of liquid glass separated me from the sandy bottom. Showing no deference to the eerie phenomenon, I continued diving deeper until I pierced the haze.

Holy crap! On the other side, the cold awaited. Unwittingly, I had passed through a thermocline—a transition layer between warm water at the lake's surface and the much colder water below. My view of the boat was unobstructed, but with no protection from the temperatures other than my shorts and socks, I began shivering and curled up into a ball to keep from freezing.

Sinking like a stone, I panicked and turned from my sunken target, kicking and following the bottom to the shallows.

Breathe, breathe, breathe! I was confident that if I did as the speedo'd old mariner directed, I'd be ok. As I surfaced, he stood on the shoreline. *"My scuba diving days are over,"* I thought because I went outside the roped area and dove deeper than given permission. An ass whoopin' was surely coming from my father.

"How'd you like it?" Tommy asked. "Fun, isn't it!" I couldn't believe it. He and my father were so distracted talking that they had no idea how far or deep I went.

Standing in two feet of water, my lower lip quivering, I said, "It's cold, freezing. But I love it."

"Well, all right, get back in there until you suck that tank dry, then make your way up here, and I'll give you your dive patch." After another ten minutes underwater, with each breath becoming more difficult, my air was gone, and my first dive was over.

Back at the dive school, Tommy took my tank and said, "You're an official scuba diver," as he handed me a small round cloth patch adorned with a diver's image that read, "Harvey's Lake Scuba School."

In the years following, I made my way down to the wreck alone, braving the freezing temperatures. The old wooden cruiser, reminiscent of the *SS Minnow* on *Gilligan's Island,* lay still, long ago stripped of anything of value. Its purpose was to entertain divers like me, permitting us to explore its cabin and hover over its bridge, wondering about its past.

On my later dives, I pretended to be a Jacques Cousteau team member searching the depths for artifacts and to my father's chagrin, dead bodies.

Becoming more confident and tolerant of the cold water, I logged another five dives by ten years old, alone with my soggy socks as Tommy and my father chatted for hours shaded by the dive school awning.

Some suggest adversity builds character. The reality is that adversity reveals what character traits already exist. The basis of everything you are or ever could be is contained in your DNA. As Plomin writes in his book, "DNA is the blueprint for who we are." But what does that mean?

Many people perceive a world and a lifetime that will prevent them from reaching their potential. Our daily experiences are bound to reveal the blueprint of who we are. But we need to be open to those events, ready to live and to learn.

4

CONFIDENCE

Man often becomes what he believes himself to be. If I keep on saying to myself that I cannot do a certain thing, it is possible that I may end by really becoming incapable of doing it. On the contrary, if I have the belief that I can do it, I shall surely acquire the capacity to do it even if I may not have it at the beginning.
Mahatma Gandhi

Our success stories begin at birth. All that happens through childhood, our teen years, and after we leave home helps determine if and how we live up to our potential. That is why I have yet to reveal my Navy SEAL story.

I learned two life-changing lessons during high school that paved the way for my successful journey. Without these two milestones, my life would be completely different.

Every tale that leads to the Teams is unique, and certain personal traits are essential. The distinguishing features are the stories and circumstances in which confidence, perseverance, and determination are expressed.

By the time I was a teenager, my father, who ran two businesses while concurrently concocting get-rich schemes, rarely came out of the basement. He and I weren't going fishing or throwing baseballs in the backyard. We pursued our own interests as I disappeared into the middle of the family pack. When not tending to her youngest, Wendy Jo, my mother was occupied fending off the flocks of boys forever chasing my sister, Bonnie.

Being the fourth of five kids doesn't earn you much attention, particularly if there is no reason to get attention, but I needed confidence in myself and what I did.

In his examination of the academic performance of twins, Plomin made a closer study of confidence or the faith the children had in their ability to do well. The twins were given a standard IQ test at age seven, then again at age nine, and were tested academically in three subjects: math, writing, and science. Next, they were asked to rate their confidence in their abilities in each subject. Plomin and his researchers also factored in reports from teachers.

When all the data was cross-referenced and analyzed, the research team was struck by two findings. First, the students' self-perceived ability rating, or SPA, was a significant predictor of achievement, even more important than IQ. Simply put, confidence trumps IQ in predicting success.

Second, the researchers found that much confidence arises from what's in our genes. They separated the confidence scores of the identical twins from those of the fraternal twins and found the scores of the identical twins to be more similar. Plomin's research suggests that the correlation between genes and confidence may be as high as fifty percent and more closely correlated than the link between genes and IQ.

Therefore, confidence likely comes from an innate character trait linked in some way to our genes. An inner belief that you will succeed at a particular task and understanding why you can be successful increase the probability of making that happen. No one can give you confidence, and no one can take it away.

No one told me to walk out of elementary school when I disagreed with my third-grade teacher. I decided that. Applying my mother's encouragement to defend myself when wronged, I could, without a doubt, question a student's integrity and the teacher's methods. Her influence activated a predisposition already inside me. In that situation, truth won the day, reinforcing the lesson and how to apply it, not with my fists, but with my actions.

Perhaps I inherited these traits from my tiny but tough ancestors, which enabled me to take my mother's teachings and make them my own.

Building confidence at an early age is essential. I don't mean everyone gets a trophy or the playing field is level. Confidence is built through experiencing difficulty and setbacks and overcoming them through effort, learning, recovery, and achievement.

There are aspects of life that aren't fair. Every person has attributes over which they have no control—for example, being the littlest in school.

And we live with these attributes our entire lives. Do adults six feet three inches tall have more confidence than people five feet three inches tall? Maybe. Yet, a person's physical size doesn't reveal personality traits. Society admires taller people, almost bestowing them with unearned honor and success. Scientific studies suggest there is a perception that taller people are more intelligent, more trusted, earn more money, and are even more likable than short people. This perception is primal and unwitting.

Of course, too much of anything is never good. I thought I could fly once, and I was confident I could. What I failed to do was to understand why I couldn't. Confidence alone doesn't always win the day, and self-reflection is often the missing element to understanding that every person has limits and that no one can be or do everything they desire.

5

QUITTING AND THE FEAR OF FAILURE

Mediocrity doesn't just happen.
It's chosen over time through small choices day by day.
Todd Henry

Weighing eighty pounds and standing four feet ten inches tall, I decided to try out for the ninth-grade football team.

Like most kids my age, I played neighborhood football. We'd make phone calls and see how many neighbors arrived on the grassy field behind the VA hospital. Forming teams with whoever showed up; size didn't matter. Sandlot football may be different from the organized high school sport, but armed with confidence, a burning will to overcome, and certain of my ability to compete against anyone, I was sure to be in the starting lineup.

Suiting up with help from my teammates, I stood at eye level with the numbers on everyone's jersey. With my shoulder pads nearly as wide as I was tall, my pants tied tight around my waist to keep from falling, and my knee pads hanging to my shins, I headed from the locker room, ready to play.

Carrying my helmet and water bottle, I climbed up the bus steps; my pads banged back and forth along the seats like a pinball machine. With a side-eye glance, the head coach joked to his assistant, "I see they made them small this year."

Not flinching, I thought to myself, "*Screw you!*" Stomping on, pissed off, I plopped into the nearest open seat. Hearing those heckles, "You can't do it. You're too little. Hey, shorty pants," conjured up memories of Albert Kita and his shenanigans. Resenting every elementary school gym class and recalling the mumbles, "Don't pick Brown," I rode the bus without any doubts about making the team.

Football began in August, and I lived thirteen miles from school. Showing no interest in being my twice-a-day taxi service, my parents left me to my own devices to get to and from practice.

There was but one solution. Four days a week and for four weeks, I rose to my alarm at sunrise, packed a brown paper bag lunch, stuffed it in a backpack, and headed to the garage and my bicycle. With baseless confidence in the thin single-wire brakes on my twenty-year-old English racer, I flew down Mundy Street as tears streamed down my cheeks in the crisp morning air.

After receiving a bludgeoning during the two-hour practice, I devoured my sack of food and suited up for a second two-hour beating. Leaving my heart and soul on the field at the day's end, I laid over my bike's frame and pedaled thirteen miles home…uphill.

Ninth-grade football players average over five feet eight inches tall and commonly weigh over 150 pounds. That didn't deter me. Once assigned to the second-string offensive and defensive halfback positions, I thought, "*Yes, sir, I can run the ball. I'm going to outplay the bigger and faster first-string halfback. They'll see.*" I lacked girth and height, but confidence was on my side.

Physics comes into play when a 150-pound kid runs into an 80-pound kid. Spending most of my time being run over, dragged, and shrugged off by the more substantial players, I endured undeterred, always confident I would eventually get the advantage.

The coach said, "Okay, Brownie, you're in." Everyone laughed and the name stuck. From then forward, that was my nickname. I don't know if they meant Brownie like the little cake or Brownie like not yet a Girl Scout, but it didn't matter; I was "Brownie." Considering it a term of endearment, I rationalized, heck, they could have called me a whole lot worse.

As the weeks went on, each practice took its toll, and I began to lose weight. With such little mass, try as I might, I couldn't move the blocking sled. After running into the big pad, my cleats scratched at the dirt as I leaned in, pushing, grunting, and wincing with little result.

"Nice try, Brownie," the coach mumbled. "Next player!"

As part of the team, I needed to accomplish everything everyone did. I didn't want an exception because I was little. Ignoring the obvious signs, I thought I could overcome and prove myself by outperforming the starting halfback.

Repeatedly being crushed by the other players during "fumble drills," where the ball is thrown and two guys go after it, had to stop. Time after time my opponent pushed me aside, leaving me flat on my back or butt and looking a fool. Tired of losing, I could give up or do what it would take to win. As we lined up, I peered to my right where the starting halfback waited for the drill to begin.

Grinning, the coach shook his head as he watched me line up. "Take him down, Brownie," my teammates chanted. With the ball tossed high in the air, the whistle blew. Lacking in size, I made up for it with quickness, and I got the jump on him. Lurching to push me away, as everyone did before, I launched and landed on the prize with my competitor one step behind.

Not stopping, he also jumped and landed on my back, pushing the football into my chest and knocking the wind out of me. The turf shredded through my facemask, flying up my nose, mouth, and eyes. Gasping for air, I spat and wiped the field from my face. "I got it!" I won the fumble drill and finally owned that damn ball.

On the way back from practice, the coach, with a grin, leaned over to his assistant, pointed at me, and said, "We have to watch this guy; he's feisty."

Limping and sapped of energy, I climbed on my bicycle for the long trek home. Thinking about the day, I briefly relished my victory. That evening, the reality began to sink in. I beat the star halfback in one drill but wasn't any closer to the starting position. Within days, my attitude changed to despair over the impossible odds of me ever playing a single down in a single game.

That Thursday, after another grueling practice, I walked into the coach's office with my head hung low and said, "I can't do it anymore, coach; I quit." I handed in my prized gear, slithered out his door, and snuck from the locker room.

I succumbed to the fear of failing. Believing I didn't belong and couldn't compete with the bigger kids, I lost all confidence. Riding my bicycle to and from school became torturous, and with no visible upside, I searched for excuses to quit. Rationalizing I'd begin school in a few days and never be a starter anyway, I gave up on myself.

I had never quit anything before. Afterward, feeling shameful, I avoided anyone who was on the team. My nights were haunted by dreams of recovering my football uniform from the locker room and playing under the Friday night lights; only each nightmare ended with me quitting and walking away.

Decades later, as I began writing my memoir, my thoughts returned to my football experience, hoping to understand what it taught me. Researching what quitting means, I came across a *Psychology Today* article by Alex Lickerman, M.D. titled "Why We Quit."

Lickerman wrote: "From the moment we embark on any endeavor, numerous reasons immediately present themselves that push us to quit (e.g., fear of failure, fear of success, laziness, failing to believe in ourselves, etc.). One way of thinking about why we don't quit is that other, more powerful motivations to keep going command our attention (e.g., the desire to improve our level of fitness or reduce our level of fatness). The *idea* to quit remains in our minds as long as reasons exist, but the likelihood of quitting only increases when we start to pay *attention* to them."

And that's what happened to me. I made up my mind, conjuring up every reason to quit. As those reasons added up, I paid more attention to the pain and difficulty and discounted the potential rewards and satisfaction of finishing, winning. Initially, I enjoyed the miles on my bike, especially the downhill part and the exhausting practices. *I loved* to play, so I overlooked the difficulties, hard work, and dedication required. The positives outweighed the negatives, so I tucked the bad into a small box in my mind's basement and ignored them.

As my situation became more strenuous, I allowed the negatives to take over. Opening that tucked-away box, I began making excuses rather than developing a formula to overcome the difficulties. Without realizing it, I created a plan to quit.

I was a failure, a loser, short and small, all the things I'd been called to my face and behind my back, and I accepted it. My perspective went from confidence and dominance to being dominated, and worse, I let my coach and teammates down.

As Lickerman further explained: "We don't end up quitting because we find ourselves facing too many obstacles or obstacles that are too strong. We end up quitting because we're too weak. I believe, however, that the inflection point at which we can no longer avoid paying attention to the idea of quitting—that is, the point at which our strength fails us—can be changed. We can become stronger by challenging our weaknesses even if we don't succeed at first."

I never wanted to feel like that again. But I needed to experience that pain to move on, grow, and learn from it.

Being sheltered, allowed to stay, and required to do less than the other boys because of my size would have left me fully vulnerable to the possibility of quitting at a future moment when it mattered and was most justified.

Afterward, I avoided challenges, competitions, or any situations I might lose. Traumatized by my fear of failure, I did nothing to live up to my potential my entire ninth-grade year.

Going to and from school, getting mediocre grades, and living no experiences that helped mold or improve any traits, I became a sheep following every direction from my teachers, parents, and even friends, becoming nothing more than the littlest kid in school.

Needing a revelation lest my future be destined to repair televisions in the back of my father's store, I entered my sophomore year at Coughlin High School, where I got lost in the crowd. With students of all sizes walking the halls, I didn't stand out because I had no reason to.

After a "growth spurt," I was five feet tall and weighed ninety-five pounds. Sailing through life rudderless, my friend Mike talked me into trying out for the wrestling team.

"We need someone at ninety-eight pounds, and you'd be perfect," he said. "We can work out at my house; I have a weight set and bench in the basement. C'mon, it'll be fun." The opportunity sounded great, and since I'd be competing with kids in my weight class rather than 200-pound football linemen, I questioned, how tough could it be?

Weightlifting in my basement over the summer gave me confidence going into the fall season, but that damn football failure resonated in my mind. Afraid to lose and fearful I would quit, dark thoughts loomed over my decisions. Yet an undeniable need to compete, excel, and challenge myself nagged at me like a child insistently tugging at his mother.

In *Blueprint*, Plomin writes that parents and experiences matter, but your DNA ultimately leads you to become who you are. Using Plomin's reasoning, my decisions began to reflect my genetics more than my environment. With that in mind, I concluded that my unconscious move beyond my irrational fear of fear was inevitable. I couldn't keep harkening to my past, and my progress was inevitable. It was in my DNA.

Our wrestling coach, Dana Balum, was a handsome former college wrestler with a chiseled physique who led by example. We practiced in a tiny, thirty-by-thirty-foot, padded space in the gym basement. Twenty young men crammed in the room for ninety minutes executing drills. Balum, with malice, jacked the room temperature up to 95° F for each session.

Fweet!

"Single-leg takedown, go! Double leg takedown, go!"

Fweet!

"No stopping."

Fweet!

"Wrestle!"

The room got hotter and hotter: two minutes on the mat, two minutes off. Sweat collected in puddles as wrestlers repeatedly ran through the segments until our movements slowed, our reactions dulled, and our energy waned like a Christmas toy's battery about to fail. More like the walking dead than wrestling partners, our only reprieve was a giant fan at the room's end sucking the stale, putrid air from the box.

Emerging from our container an hour and a half later, limp, smelly as a dish rag, and several pounds lighter, I pushed myself farther than I ever thought possible.

As the four-times-a-week practices went by, I began gaining strength and endurance. Sadistically, Balum threw us a curve ball. He added a two-mile run after ninety minutes in the box. As a kid, I always ran around the neighborhood; a hundred-yard shortcut through the woods to get to a friend's or the quarter-mile jog to play football at the VA hospital field. But this two-mile trek exposed my weakness, and I always finished last.

As a natural ninety-six-pound person, I never needed to drop weight to make my weight class. However, my overall record revealed my mediocrity, as I lost my varsity position twice that year to another wrestler. Lacking a killer instinct and saddled with indifference to losing fueled my false sense of success. Not quitting is success in a way, right? Or, so I rationalized.

No more successful than in ninth grade, I didn't join the team to win; I joined not to lose or quit. The best wrestlers developed an edgy look in their eyes on the mat. Their body language said they intended to destroy their opponent. I didn't. Without that intensity,

I went through the competitive motions. My motivation to continue subconsciously was still my fear of quitting. I wanted to be victorious but didn't feel it would be the world's end if I lost.

Like so many people going through life who are numb to possibly living up to their potential, I remained a sheep who happened to be on the wrestling team.

In eleventh grade, I qualified for the Junior Varsity Regional Championships. In an unusual move, my parents decided to come to the tournament. Being a busy guy, my father usually dropped me off for a match and drove off. After the competition, I'd find a ride or catch the city bus home. Supporting extracurricular school activities wasn't high on my mother's or father's priority list. I'd like to say it didn't bother me, but it must have, or I wouldn't have written about it. However, the regional championship was a media event, so my father left the basement, and my mother put on a nice dress, and they came to the gym to watch.

Very different than our weekly matches, the tournament atmosphere was fair-like. The gymnasium always struck me as the Roman Colosseum—a place for competition surrounded by cheering fans waiting for the lions to appear. This colosseum's floor was covered with wrestling mats where the gladiators squared off. It appeared as if the entire county packed in on the wooden bleachers with the crowd noise a constant roar. I was seeded low with the expectation that I'd be eliminated early. Needing three victories to reach the championship, the challenge seemed a virtual impossibility as I'd never wrestled more than one match in a day. My first match neared and the roar from the stands began to quiet.

Seeing my first opponent, a guy I pinned in twenty-eight seconds earlier in the year, provided little comfort.

"*Crap,*" I thought, "*I can't lose to this loser in the first round!*"

The referee's whistle blew, and with a slap on the mat seventeen seconds later, I got my first victory with a pin. I don't know who was more surprised: me, the guy I just beat, or my coach. With that win, I earned a bye in the second round.

The progression through each bracket meant I would face better and more experienced wrestlers. My early win put me into the semifinals, where I considered my chances for victory slim.

Stepping on the mat, most wrestlers have their routine. Some stare you in the eye; others stay within themselves; I just showed up. Glancing across, my adversary was huffing and puffing, jumping up and down and side to side like a caged animal. After a quick handshake, the whistle blew, and for the first time, I recognized the cheers from the crowd. Evenly matched, we scored takedowns in the first period and no points in the second.

Chasing each other around in the third, we tired, then locked arms and banged heads in the middle. Near the period's end with the score 2-2, he attempted to take me down. Trying to escape, he grabbed my right arm and pinned it behind me, tripping me forward while grabbing my other arm. Unable to break my fall, my face was slammed into the mat with him on top and my arm wrenched.

Awarded no points for his illegal move, I still suffered the consequences. Face down and half-conscious, I lay motionless as the referee paused the match. Our thin and balding junior varsity Coach, Jackson, was hardly an imposing figure like Coach Balum. Always a positive influence, Jackson's words and tone were direct and reassuring. Helping me to my feet, Jackson stuffed smelling salts near my nose. My eyes shot open, and my head flew back. Bam! The smell got my attention like a punch right in the kisser.

"Brownie, Brownie! Wake up, Wake up!"

For a few seconds, my arm went numb; then a stabbing pain engulfed my shoulder. Grabbing my elbow, I pulled the wounded appendage to my side. "Are you okay?" Jackson asked. The crowd screamed and everyone on the bench began chanting, "Brownie! Brownie!" My heart pounded as if it would fly from my chest; I had to decide to continue or forfeit.

"You're okay, you're okay," the coach reassured me. "Listen, when they restart, you'll be in the down position with only sixteen seconds left; stand up, escape, and you win! You don't need your other arm."

With the bleachers and the ceiling still spinning around in my head, I thought, "*Ya, stand up.*"

I shook my head clear.

"I'm alright coach, I'm okay. Let's go!"

This wasn't the football field where I'd been pummeled by kids twice my size. I was in this fight.

Turning to the ref I said, "Let's go; I'm ready."

The chants from the bench continued. "Brownie, Brownie, Brownie!"

The ref signaled me to the down position, where my opponent wrapped his arm over my back, preparing to pounce on my injury, something I would do and what I expected. But instead of standing up as Jackson advised and my opposition prepared for, I brought my leg under and sat, causing him to lose control and fall over my shoulder, planting his face on the mat. Pushing him away, I stood up.

"One point," said the ref as the clock ran out. And I won.

Unlike any match before, each move instinctively happened, giving me the win in the most demanding physical event I'd ever experienced. My victory propelled me into the championship round, where I faced the tournament's predicted sure winner.

Wrapping my shoulder in an ice pack, Jackson and I sat on the bench waiting for the finals to start. Clutching my arm, I winced, and my "quit" spiral began. I found an excuse. My teammates surrounded me, their voices bombarding from every direction.

"Brownie, the wrestler from Wyoming Valley West won all the varsity matches he wrestled this year. The dude practices with the ninety-eight-pound state champ; he's gonna be tough to beat!"

Seeing me shaken, the coach took me aside. As he grabbed my face, his fingers pressed into my cheeks and looked me in the eye. "Listen, you can *crush* him...like you did the last guy."

Rubbing my shoulder, I began fearing my fear. "But my arm is killing me," I said to coach. On the mat where the finals were to take place, a spotlight was being focused. "*A spotlight!*" I thought. "*Every person in this gym will be watching. There is no way I can win.*"

Jackson stood up, pointed to my competition, and turned to me: "Forget about your damn arm! He's skinny and weak. You can take him with one arm. Now come on, get it together, Brownie. I'm telling you, you can beat him. You can win this tournament!"

Coach's belief in me stopped my quitting spiral. I forgot about my excuses and rationalization to quit.

I thought, "*Wait! Everyone's saying I can't beat this guy, but the coach says I can.*" I finally and intently sized up my opponent and thought, "*he is skinny.*" After lifting weights all summer, I was strong and confident. If I couldn't out-wrestle him, I'd out-muscle him. That's when *I* decided to crush him and finally found my killer instinct.

Meeting in the mat's center, he towered over me as we shook hands. The first-period whistle blew.

His spindly limbs continued forever, but I pulled him off his stance as we wrestled to a 0-0 tie in the first. In the second, he landed a takedown. Catching me with his long arms he picked my ankle, and bam! I hit the mat. His spider-like appendages covered me, and he led 2-0.

My shoulder was on fire with pain; I was losing and tired. Looking over at Jackson, I got no sympathy.

"Escape!" he said.

Doing what I was told, I stood up, escaped, and earned one point. The whistle blew. The third and final period came with a score of 2-1 in his favor.

We went round after round, both near exhaustion from the back and forth. With only eight seconds remaining, he shot in for what was sure to be a takedown and the championship. Sprawling my legs to prevent the attack wasn't enough. I needed points. Before he got control, I pulled his arm tight to my waist, and sensing his weakness, I ducked under and out the other side, wrapping my arm around his waist at the buzzer for a 2-point takedown. Leaping in the air Coach Jackson and the team ran onto the mat yelling.

"Brownie! You won!"

The crowd noise shook the bleachers.

Against the odds, I beat the best wrestler in the region in my weight class. Blocking out the pain and believing in myself, I decided it wasn't enough to "not give up." I had to win.

It took a thousand whistles in practice and a winning mindset to earn that victory. My perseverance and determination withstood the test.

Running from the stands, my parents came over and hugged me. My father laughed, "Wow, I didn't think you were gonna beat that guy." Maybe he didn't believe I could win because he'd never seen me wrestle.

My mother, smacking my father on the back over his comment, said, "Leo! Stop that." Coach Jackson shook my mother and father's hands.

"You got a real fighter here," he said.

My mother replied, "I taught him that!"

The victory was memorable, but sharing the moment with my parents was unforgettable.

Winning is a great feeling, especially if you're an underdog. After the tournament I stopped worrying about quitting. My focus would be on winning after learning that pain is in your head and that you don't have to give up even if you're hurting.

Prominent neuroscientists and researchers are documenting this reality.

Prof. V.S. Ramachandran, director of the Center for Brain and Cognition at the University of California, San Diego, said, "Pain is an opinion on the organism's state of health rather than a mere reflective response to an injury. There is no direct hotline from pain receptors to pain centers in the brain."

In his book, *Why Zebras Don't Get Ulcers*, Prof. Robert Sapolsky wrote: "The human body can be pushed farther and take much more punishment than your brain and nerve receptors tell you. What is surprising is how malleable pain signals are—how readily the intensity of a pain signal is changed by the sensations, feelings, and thoughts that coincide with the pain. The brain is not a mindless pain-o-meter, simply measuring units of ouchness."

When you feel pain, your mind and peripheral nerves are trying to protect your life. They work together to tell you to stop if you feel hurt, slow down if you are tired, and quit if it requires sacrifice. Your body can endure much more pain than your brain tells you it can. The brain can boss the nerves around and tell them how sensitive they will be. I proved it.

With my confidence back and as my high school days neared their end, my love of scuba and the sea led me to research colleges and possible marine science degrees.

6

UDT/SEAL IT IS

You must expect great things of yourself before you can do them.
Michael Jordan

A hopeless romantic, I've always believed in love's power and romance despite my inability to attract the opposite sex. I was susceptible to falling in love at the drop of a hat. Casual conversations led to my infatuation without reciprocation. It's understandable, as science says women prefer tall over short men. A study published in *Psychology Today* found that among 650 heterosexual college students, women generally preferred taller men and didn't want to be in a relationship with a man shorter than they were. I had my work cut out for me.

Wandering Caughlin High's halls, I searched for a girl who didn't mind if I was short and weighed ninety-five pounds. Meeting someone in the crowded hallway at school or the roller-skating rink didn't foster meaningful bonds. I was always on the hunt, however. Now, in my junior year, the incoming tenth-grade class peppered the hallways. But September and October sailed by without any romantic prospects.

On a Saturday mall excursion with my friends to drop quarters at the arcade, we ran into some neighborhood girls with an unfamiliar beauty in the group.

She had shoulder-length wavy hair, was shorter than me, and was incredibly attractive.

"Hi, you're new. I've never seen you before," I said over the Tommy pinball machine's clamor.

"Yes" was the only word I could hear in reply as Pac-Man and Space Invaders drowned out my pathetic attempt at a conversation. I didn't have the nerve to ask for her name or phone number. As quickly as she appeared, she disappeared.

Later that day, I got a crazy feeling. Would she go out with me? I had to find out who she was, so I called Debbie, one of the girls in the group.

"Who is the mystery girl at the arcade?" I asked.

"Oh, you like her, do you?" she said. Debbie loved playing matchmaker.

"She's Mary from Miners Mills. Do you want her number?"

I didn't hesitate. "Sure!"

Will she remember me, and what should I talk about? I closed the door to my room and nervously dialed. Ring, ring, ring, and a woman answered.

"Hello, ah, is Mary there?" I asked.

"Hold on," her mother replied. "Mary Kay, phone!"

"Hello. Ah…hi, this is David. We met at the mall today," I said, hoping she remembered.

She did.

"Oh, ya, Debbie phoned and said you might call." Whew! Debbie, the matchmaker, came through!

Speaking effortlessly for thirty minutes, I learned she was in tenth grade, but our paths never crossed in the crowded hallways. And true to my proclivity, she gave me her time, and I gave her my heart.

We hid in a school stairwell daily, kissing until we heard the hallway door open or someone approaching the stairs. On his usual trek to the classroom, my homeroom teacher passed with a quip, "Okay, you two can carry on." Our faces and lips, cherry red from friction, revealed our hallway romance.

Occasionally, Leo dropped me at her house, and I started assimilating into her family. What a crew they were—brothers and sisters Liz, Billy, Bonnie, and Bobby. Two parents and five kids packed into a three-bedroom, one-bath house. They ate every meal at a small wooden table, each sibling with their customary seat. Mary's mom cooked on a coal-fired stove and did the laundry in a washing machine next to the sink. Pants, shirts, and underwear dried on a backyard line in the breeze. They were a tight clan, which I became part of, notching a spot for me at the kitchen table next to Mary. Head over heels in love, I was sure I'd met my future wife.

They gathered like my family had before Melanie and Leo grew up and disappeared from our meals. Eventually, so did my parents. Sure, we had an occasional dinner together, but mostly food was prepared and left out for a fly-by meal. As necessity is the mother of invention, I learned to cook.

Steering me from the vocational-technical trades, my mother insisted I focus on college preparatory classes. My yearning to be in and under the water drew me to colleges and universities with degrees in marine science. As my senior year approached, I asked my mother about attending the University of Virginia.

She asked, "Where's that?"

Laughing, I said, "In Virginia, Mom!"

"How are *you* going to pay for that?"

Bam! I went from fantasizing about living in the dorm and spending time in a biology lab to utter disappointment. Without a word and shaking my head, I turned and walked away.

That one-sentence conversation was all we needed. After raising five kids, she didn't have time to explain why she was saying no. She didn't even have to say no; it was implied. There would be no financial aid for college for me from my parents. Like Melanie and Leo before me, I was on my own. My one hope—the military. In dire need of recruits, the services pitched tuition assistance, free accommodation, and free food. Free everything, a paycheck, and an education! Their advertising kickstarted my pragmatism.

One morning in the stairwell, I told Mary I was considering joining one of the armed forces.

"Oh, umm, okay. Where and when would you go?" she asked.

"Right after high school but I don't know where. Once I'm done training, we can get married, and you'd join me wherever that is. What'd you think?"

She backed away and said, "Well, I guess so, but that's a few years away David. Let's see what happens."

As a planner—both a flaw and a virtue—and saddled with my mother's stubbornness, changing my mind was nearly impossible.

Scientists at the Max Planck Institute for Human Cognitive and Brain Sciences in Leipzig, Germany, say a gene mutation may cause stubbornness and the tendency to refuse to accept defeat. Their study suggests that an estimated one-third of the world's population has this gene, which is nature's way of ensuring that some people keep on trying when the rest surrender.

Dr. Tilmann Klein, one of the study's authors, describes the gene's benefit this way: "Where would we be without those few individuals who refuse to accept defeat and continue to soldier onwards when common sense tells the rest of mankind that there's no use trying?"

With my college financial plans dashed, I asked my father about his time in the Army. He never talked about it or his brother Billy's service. I heard no tales of bravery. Instead, they preferred to reminisce how my Uncle George, my mother's brother, who served in Korea as an Army tank commander, was a drunk and the family's black sheep, blaming his alcoholism on battlefield trauma.

My mother's response to my interest was simple: "That sounds nice, dear." But her laissez-faire attitude didn't dampen my enthusiasm, and I marched on.

My scuba diving fascination, lust for adventure, and infatuation with spy movies pushed me toward the military, ultimately choosing the rifle bullet over the lab beaker.

Not a popular occupational choice in 1979, the armed services tempted high school students during a career day in the gym. As a senior who took part and spoke to the recruiters, I was dissed by my friends who anxiously anticipated college. The chatter in the halls was, "The only people who join the military are those not smart enough to make it as a civilian."

Brushing away the naysayers, I wanted to serve my country and have fun traveling the world. Needing more excitement from life, I couldn't see myself riding a desk or becoming a salesman like my father. He toiled in his store twelve hours a day, six days a week. His world of television vacuum tubes and chatting with customers was as far from exciting and desirable a life as I could imagine.

I discovered my ancestors were warriors and I shared their DNA. My father was a warrior in his way but not in mine. My path veered from my peer's achievement perspective, but I was never one to follow the crowd or the trend.

My first stop was the Coast Guard and its rescue swimmer program. *Who wouldn't like jumping out from helicopters to save people,* my inner Sheepdog thought. I was so interested that I persuaded two friends, Joe and Brian, to visit the recruiting office. Using talents I learned from my dad, I convinced the recruiter to give me a jacket emblazoned with a "United States Coast Guard Smokies of the Sea" insignia. Everyone put their money on me becoming a "Coastie."

But the Coast Guard refused to lock me into a rescue swimmer billet. And like Joe used to say, "If we joined the Coast Guard without a guarantee, we could be stuck painting gas cans in New Jersey." Deciding to go one door down, I stopped in to see the Navy representative and discovered UDT/SEAL teams. SEALs are well known and a big deal today, but in 1979, they were a mystery.

When I asked the recruiter about SEALs, he said, "I don't know much about it. It's top secret and I don't know anyone who made it through the training. You're wasting your time. SEALs are all muscled up, strong guys. You're way too little. I mean, be realistic; you'll never make it." He handed me a rating (job description) book and encouraged me to "Forget about the SEAL program. Pick something you can do."

I laid in bed studying each trade for weeks but always returned to UDT/SEAL. They jumped from airplanes, were scuba divers, used explosives, and carried automatic weapons. *"My God,"* I thought, *"I found my dream job!"* My imagination ran wild. SEALs were secret agents in scuba gear who swam on shore dressed in black like James Bond. My mind was made up; I would join the Navy and be like Jacques Cousteau with a machine gun!

Technical training was mandatory in the Navy before anyone went to Basic Underwater Demolition/SEAL (BUD/S) training, and I chose Operations Specialist (radarman) with little thought. Tracking stuff on the radar sounded cool, but my goal was to pass the SEAL screening test in boot camp.

In early October 1979, I signed the paperwork and was obligated to go on active duty in September 1980. Keeping my Navy Special Warfare combatant desires a secret, I never mentioned them to my parents or Mary. *"Why worry them about something that may never happen?"* I told myself. My sights were set.

About to turn seventeen years old, five feet two inches tall, and ninety-eight pounds, I was sure the next five years were planned. I wasn't cocky, I was confident.

Was I afraid? Of course.

My biggest fear? Disappointing myself.

How did I know without a doubt that enlisting in the Navy and becoming a SEAL was the right choice for me? How does anyone know what occupation will make them happy?

When American Olympic wrestler David Taylor, a.k.a. "Magic Man," stood atop the podium at the 2021 Summer Olympics in Tokyo, he said he knew from when he was ten years old that he was destined to win the gold medal.

How can someone so young know what their life will hold or what their accomplishments will be? In his book, Plomin writes: "Children actively select, modify and create environments correlated with their genetic propensities…. To a large extent, opportunities are taken, not given."

Although David Taylor seemed genetically predisposed to become an Olympic champion, his dedication and hard work made it happen. Early in his life, he created circumstances and chose the environment which enabled him to achieve his childhood dream.

Intuition kept me from enlisting in the Coast Guard and told me to continue my search. When I discovered the UDT/SEAL program, my focus became clear. My life experiences were unwittingly preparing me.

Like Taylor, I created my future based on *my* genetic predisposition. I could have chosen another occupation that was as challenging and exciting, but my life's path took me to the Navy's door, and I opened it.

I needed more scuba experience to be a SEAL and decided to get certified by the Professional Association of Diving Instructors (PADI). With November daytime temperatures in the 40s and 50s, classes were held indoors in the YMCA's comfortable swimming pool. Prior to committing to the class, my father said, "Only crazy people want to scuba dive in the winter, David." After the registration date passed, I found out only twelve people signed up for the class.

During the two-day instruction, I sat in the makeshift classroom distracted by the giant steel full-size monster scuba tank in the corner. At twenty-eight pounds, it equaled one-quarter of my body weight.

Walking into the "Y" on the third day, I went to the locker room and changed into my swimsuit. It was the moment of truth. As I stood beside my gear, the instructor padded my back and said, "We're gonna get that tank high on your back so it will be easier for you to walk. Don't worry; you can do this."

The straps carved into my shoulders as the tank's weight did its best to upend me. Grabbing my mask and fins, I inched my way to the pool, waddling like an Emperor penguin trekking the Antarctic.

Sitting on the pool's bottom, I recalled Tommy's advice. "Don't forget to breathe!" And with an immense grin, I floated like an astronaut. The heavy tank didn't matter.

We learned the basics—underwater mask clearing, controlled ascent, and emergency procedures. After two days and four hours in the water, we were ready for the open-water dive.

It was late November, and snow was in the forecast. Our sixty-foot-deep certification dive would take place at Lake Wallenpaupack, a mountain reservoir fifty miles away. Concerned, my mother stood in the kitchen as the dark clouds rolled in.

"Who's driving? Your father hates to drive in bad weather. Oh, and take a sandwich and a can of soda," she told me. "You're gonna be hungry when you're done."

Pacing back and forth, my father tried to convince me not to go.

"Why would anyone want to get in that water? Wait until the summer when it's warm! I'm not sure we can make it up the mountain with that storm."

I didn't want to get into the cold lake, but it wouldn't stop me either. The weather was an obstacle that I could overcome. If my classmates were going, so was I.

With my father navigating, I drove our Chevy Vega station wagon up Highway 84, crossing the frozen overpasses.

"Seriously, you don't have to do this today," he said, giving me an easy way out.

But I was long past any thoughts of quitting. The worse the weather, the more excited I got about the dive.

Driving by the beach area, the cabanas, picnic tables, and the sand volleyball court, we headed down a rocky dirt road to a remote shoreline where the instructor loaded equipment onto a pontoon boat. Only five other guys showed up. The other six smartly decided to wait until spring.

The flurries began as we sat in the Vega with the heater blasting.

"How cool is this!" I told my father. "How often do people get into a lake in a snowstorm?" I hopped over the station wagon's back seat and wrestled myself into the thick wetsuit. Grabbing my things, I gingerly made my way over the frozen rocks to the beached boat. As we launched, my father, bundled in his winter jacket, ran to the car, cleared the fog from the windshield, and watched.

The small two-stroke motor slowly pushed the ladened craft across the lake, finding the sixty-foot depth 200 yards from shore. My neoprene suit proved useless for providing warmth in the 32° F temperature. Snowflakes melted into water droplets that dripped from my nose and off frozen strands of hair. I shivered, crossing my arms and legs, trying to stay warm.

My swim buddy and I reviewed our pre-dive checklist: air on, fins on, mouthpiece in. In the process, I noticed my partner's angst. In his mid-20s and sporting a huge mustache, he'd never scuba-dove outside a pool. Icicles formed on his hairy upper lip. He chuckled before I jumped in, "Are we crazy or what?"

Standing by the open railing, I pressed my mask tightly against my face, and like a scene from *The Ocean World of Jacques Cousteau,* I leaned forward and stepped off the deck. Splash! Bubbles surrounded me; the 34° F water shot in like darts through my wetsuit cracks and crevices down my neck, legs, and arms. Breathless, I thought, *"shake it off, shake it off, breathe."*

Tssssss!

"Don't forget to breathe!"

After only five seconds in the frigid water, I thought, yes, we're crazy.

"Let's get moving so we can warm up," I mumbled through the mouthpiece. After the okay signal, we started our descent. Tensing every muscle and clinching down, my lips and jaw began to numb from the bitter cold.

We moved deeper along the bottom, searching for the weighted marker at sixty feet when suddenly my mask was ripped from my face. My arms flailed as the frigid water stung my bare skin, and bubbles clouded my vision. Spinning, I reached blindly and grabbed the mask before it disappeared into the depths. With no time to think, I did what was natural.

My first thought was, was I being tested?

"Be prepared," our instructor said. "Anything can happen. A strap can break, or a diver could knock your mask off. Be ready to react and stay calm."

Somehow, amid the chaos, I had the presence of mind to remember his warnings. After putting the mask on, I cleared the water and saw my dive buddy gyrating, pointing to a moss-covered metal bar sticking sideways, five feet off the bottom. So focused on finding the sixty-foot marker, I swam right into it. Shaking our heads in amazement, we continued our descent.

Thirty feet down, the light began to fade. Squinting off into the depths, I spied an orange flag atop a cement-filled coffee can in the sand—our target.

The water's chill, replaced by the wetsuit's warmth, went unnoticed in our excitement as we reached the flag. Beginning our "slower than your bubbles" return to the surface, the accomplishment started to sink in.

But a gray sky and wind-blown white caps awaited us on our return. Making our way to the pontoon ladder, I ditched my tank, handing it to my instructor, who secured it onboard. The boat, buffeted by the approaching storm, swung on its anchor.

Back on deck, I recounted my underwater bar story. Jumping up and down, I demonstrated to my classmates how my mask was ripped off and my epic struggle to retrieve and don it.

"Good job," said our instructor, with a high-five. "I told you guys anything could happen down there!" The snow began to fall steadily.

With the divers safely aboard and the anchor stowed, our instructor turned the key on the outboard.

Rrrrr…rrrrr…rrrrr.

"Oh, shit!" he said. "It won't start." The boat, now a slave to the gusty winds, strayed farther and farther from shore. One by one, each passenger gave their shade tree mechanic remedy without a solution.

In the excitement, I noticed the water draining from my wetsuit. Just as the cold lake entered the openings, the thin, warm liquid layer now followed gravity and was in my bloated booties and running onto the deck. The snowstorm advanced as the wind began to cut through the neoprene, and the motor continued to sputter, refusing to start.

Contemplating our situation, our instructor said, "Well, I was going to wait until we got back to the beach, but maybe now's a better time." Reaching into a cooler beside the helm, he pulled out beer cans. "Everybody take one."

I'd experiment with my parents' mixed drinks but never liked the taste. Oddly, my father had an endless supply of beer on tap in the living room, but it never intrigued me. Under the circumstances however, I took a can and was happy to get it, especially if it would help me get warm.

After cracking the can open, I took a big swig and discovered beer tastes better when you're freezing in the middle of a lake in a winter storm on a boat that won't start. While the brew didn't make me warmer, it did make me care less about being cold.

Rrrr…rrrr. suddenly, *vroom…putt…putt…putt.* The motor came to life.

"Yes! Hit it," everyone said as we huddled in a shivering bunch. Putting toward the beach, the snow collecting on the boat's deck and our icy black wetsuits.

Springing from the car, my father ran to meet us.

"Oh my God, you must be freezing," he shouted as he wrapped a towel around my shoulders. "I was getting ready to go for help when I heard the motor finally start. You all are crazy," he laughed.

"I have to get this cold wetsuit off!" I cried. Without suggestion, all the divers stripped, and six naked guys scrambled for our cars and heaters, laughing, whooping, and hollering.

A positive attitude in difficult situations, like being unbearably cold in a snowstorm, is a learned trait, not something passed down from grandparents.

In an *Inc.* magazine article, "Change Your Perspective, Change Your Life," author Nicolas Cole wrote, "It's never the situation that's at fault. It's the way you choose to view it. You are 'successful' when you walk your path, always learning and growing. You are doing what you love when you see every moment as an opportunity."

Failure is a state of mind. So is success. If your perspective is to learn from every situation, how can you fail? Cole continued: "If you feel like you aren't learning anything, that is nobody's fault but yours. Chances are, someone around you knows something you don't. It's on you to ask them questions. It's on you to create moments of growth and opportunity. It's on you to pay attention to the little things around you. It's on you to create your gaps, and it's on you to take your leaps of faith. Growth is rarely the result of the people in your vicinity. Growth results from utilizing the people around you and creating opportunities for yourself."

At seventeen, I didn't have the advantage of such clarity. But somehow, amid the pain and the thrill of the experience, I was building knowledge and the ability to do what Cole described.

7

YOU'RE IN THE NAVY NOW

Only those who risk going too far can possibly find out how far one can go.
T. S. Eliot

Everything I'd known was fading into the rearview mirror. My parents, fed up with Wilkes-Barre's cold gray winters, sold our house, and fled to Sarasota, FL, leaving me and my brother behind.

Living my own *Ground Hog Day*, I spent hours in the one-window basement, sweating on my weightlifting bench. Boston's eponymous first rock album shook the paneling-covered walls, and with each exercise, repetition, and set, I got that much stronger. After logging in untold miles, my running shoes were held together with super glue and duct tape. Hyperfocus and single-mindedness suited me, and by September, I tossed and turned the nights away, waiting for my Navy career to begin. I pictured the Navy as a mountain to be climbed, the next wrestler to be beaten, and a gifted horse to be grateful for.

On enlistment day, I tossed a small gym bag in the back of Leo's red Toyota 4X4, and we headed downtown to the Military Enlisted Processing Station (MEPS). Pulling to the curb, he lowered the radio and shook my hand while giving brotherly encouragement, "Don't worry bro, you got this; you'll be fine." He threw a crooked salute as I closed the door. After grabbing my bag from the truck bed, he sped off. It was the first day of the rest of my life.

My only possessions were memories and a fierce persistence to be successful.

Inside the MEPS waiting room, soon-to-be recruits attempted to wear a path pacing the linoleum floor as others sat mannequin still. Across the room, I spied Joe and Brian, my two best friends who gladly followed me from the Coast Guard recruiter to the Navy.

Scurrying over I asked, "Hahaha, you guys ready for this?"

They dissed, "*You* got us into this, you son-of-a-bitch. You owe us big time!"

The door to the room swung open, and after a crackle from the loudspeaker, an announcement came: "All males report to the examination room and line up!"

We jumped to attention.

"Here we go, boys," I said as we shuffled into the bright white room.

A doctor in a lab coat adorned with a gold oak leaf pin announced, "I'm Major Tom, and I'll be performing your entrance physicals. Do exactly as I say, I'll get this done, and you're on your way. Let's go, tall to small, move it." Jostling for position, we formed a line with me being the littlest at the end. Then our next order, "Now, strip down to your underwear and put your clothing in a pile behind you. Move it gentlemen, we have work to do."

Some would be career military men, some would become officers, and some would end up in the brig. The only certainty for me was that this was my only future. I had no place to come back to. I had no home in Pennsylvania or a room in Florida.

Turning my eyes hard left, a female nurse entered the room with a clipboard and stacked paperwork. Beginning his exams with the nurse in tow, the doctor moved down the line as we sounded off with our name, social security number, and date of birth.

Fidgeting and staring down so as not to make eye contact with the nurse, I stood in my tighty-whities as the doctor examined our eyes, ears, and mouth. Standing tall, chest out at attention, I sighed after he finished my exam: Whew!

Addressing the group, the Major ordered, "Drop your skivvies, turn around, bend over, and spread'em! Move it; we don't have all day."

OMG, really?

Naked and bent over, exposed to a stranger, and worse, a girl! I considered running like I was in second grade again. Instead, I convinced myself it wasn't happening.

But like clockwork, everyone snapped to. We dropped our skivvies, made a sharp about-face, grabbed our butt cheeks, and spread'em.

As the doctor examined butt after butt, I remained paralyzed, carefully balanced in my contorted position. Upon completing each exam, he directed the recruit to stand and get dressed. The line disappeared as he neared me.

While I am not sure what he was searching for, when he got to me, the sole naked bent-over man, he handed the nurse the clipboard, got down on his knees, and took a long gander. Staring between my legs, I could see him unblinking, gazing at my rear end like a mechanic examining a radiator's backside. The nurse giggled after he cried *oomph* as he stood up. "

Stand up and get dressed," he said. Red-faced, I spun in a flash to recover my clothing pile.

Across the room at the scale, Joe frowned. He was a big guy; we suspected he would be on a razor's thin margin of the Navy's weight standards.

Signaling to me, he shook his head from side to side, "No."

I couldn't believe it. Right off the bat, the Navy imposed its will. Joe wasn't permitted to enlist and left the MEPS building, ending his short military career before it started.

After completing our physicals, a robotic Marine dressed sharply in blue pants and a khaki shirt escorted everyone into a windowless room with dark paneling, rows of fold-out chairs, and a podium.

The waiting nurse handed out folders containing our enlistment paperwork.

"If you lose this paperwork, you will have to do it all again," she said with a grin. "You don't want that, do you?" She glared directly at me as she spoke.

Behind the podium, the US and each military service flag adorned the stage.

"Attention!"

The Marine shouted as an Air Force officer entered. Two additional Marines escorted family members to their seats.

My family, except my brother, had moved to Florida, and Leo had long since dropped me at the curb. There will be other ceremonies, I told myself, feigning indifference that I was alone.

In the months before my enlistment, my mother and I could barely tolerate each other. I remember something she said after I argued with my father during their move to Florida. "You argue with everyone; you're too damn stubborn. You have to be able to get along with people or you're never going to make anything of yourself."

She was right about one thing. I was and am now one stubborn son-of-a-bitch—perhaps from watching her my entire childhood. Yes, I was an SOB—one she helped create.

In that room, I didn't feel ceremonious. For me, the ordeal was akin to reciting the Pledge of Allegiance in grade school. Afterward, however, I stood facing the flags, realizing I was committed to serving the United States military for five years. Only then did the corners of my mouth turn up slightly, and standing at crip attention, I clinched my folder and snapped a sharp salute.

When the plane took off from Scranton/Avoca Airport to Chicago, my problems were left behind, trapped under Wilkes-Barre's gray sky. I reclined and melted into my seat, assured the Navy was now in charge.

Mary and my adopted family in Miners Mills were in my thoughts. They were my de facto support group leading up to enlistment day; I practically lived at their house, played cards at the kitchen table, and joined their weekend picnics. Bill, Mary's father, and I formed a father-son relationship. We fished, worked on his old station wagon, and drove to fill jugs with spring water from a steel pipe protruding from the mountain. Insignificant moments at the time were now my fondest memories as I ventured into the unknown.

It was in my genes to seek out my future and find success. In many ways, I was reenacting my grandfather Herman Brown's 1930s immigration journey from the Netherlands. Like Herman, I was compelled to travel to a strange territory, searching for a better life—a compulsion locked into our very being.

The sun was setting as we landed in Chicago. Two guys in black Navy uniforms met our group at the airport gate. Calling out, they got the civilian's attention as they corralled us. I'm going to serve my country, I thought, with my chin up, shoulders back, strutting through the terminal like I owned the place. Our chaperones stifled my gleeful attitude as they stuffed us into a bus like cattle.

Brian and I sat together on the ride to the Great Lakes Recruit Training Center, but I don't remember talking much. We were in our heads, wondering what would happen on this first night.

The bus stopped with a hiss and a jolt. As the door swung open, a man's face appeared.

"I'm Petty Officer Grumman," he yelled. "Grab your shit and get off this bus, NOW!"

Elbows, backpacks, and gym bags flew. A few guys fell, and the rest ran over them as we squeezed through the bus's single exit. Grabbing my bag, I barreled down the steps.

"Line up, line up. Move! Move!"

Ah…, just like home sweet home, I thought, and I went to the little end of the line.

"You're too slow. Stop talking and stop crying. You're not going home to your mamma tonight!"

The yelling came in rapid fire from every direction. Doing everything I could to suppress my laughter, Grumman's performance was as loud as it was entertaining. We recruits did push-ups under the streetlights for fifteen minutes and then walked a single file into a building for processing.

Once inside, the large room's ceiling blared wall-to-wall fluorescent lights. The Petty Officer's constant yelling was interrupted only by the chirps in front of me as each recruit shouted his shirt, pants, and shoe size to sailors behind a well-worn counter. Grabbing the clothing from huge stacks, they plopped everything down with a thud and stuffed it all in green canvas seabags. The oaky leather taste and smell of chemical-dyed canvas filled my nose and mouth as I approached.

"Shoe size?" a sailor quizzed me.

"Seven and a half," I said.

My remaining issued gear lay ready, stacked up, waiting for me. Small, small, and small/short.

"Why did you give me all smalls?" I asked.

"Because we don't have extra, extra small," he shot back, chuckling. "If these are too large, you can have them tailored on base next week." He laughed, and I didn't.

Ladened with full seabags, our gaggle lined up again under the streetlights to meet our company commander, Chief Penn. The chief was tall, handsome, and a genuinely nice guy. His job was to transform us from civilians into sailors in eight weeks, a daunting task.

After a halfhearted, stumbling, and bumbling attempt to march, we walked like a band of misfits to the barracks. Once there, an assistant recruit petty officer assigned us our racks. At 0100, Chief Penn shouted, "You are all in Flag Company 934, lights out in ten!" Throwing my seabag on the gray wooden chest at my rack's end, I stripped down to my tighty-whities, threw a sheet over the bare mattress, fluffed the stained caseless pillow, and fell asleep.

A few hours later, all hell broke loose. In the early morning darkness, four recruit assistants armed with tin garbage cans and lids positioned themselves inside our barracks. At 0500, every light snapped on, and those assholes started banging the cans like fools and shouting.

"Get up, you lazy maggots!" Confused and dazed, I kicked the sheet off and jumped onto the cold concrete floor.

"Reveille!" they continued. "Let's go. You've got fifteen minutes to get dressed and in formation. Move!"

We crashed into each other in a hilarious and failed attempt to make it out on time.

Within our first week, three recruits broke down and cried from homesickness. Quickly escorted from the barracks, the assistants gathered the recruits' gear, leaving their disposition a mystery—grown men acting like children, I thought, a curious display.

I wonder what critical life experiences they missed. What traits did they lack, or did they fail to develop? Even more shocking were their tears since I couldn't remember the last time I'd cried. Was it when I broke my thumb riding down the playground slide at ten years old or when my appendix nearly burst and had to be removed?

Long ago, I decided crying revealed weakness and wanted nothing to do with it. I no longer did it, nor frankly knew how to do it. My defense mechanism was to repress my emotions completely. It may not have been the best solution, but it seemed best for me.

Certain recruits stood out. As scientific studies predicted, Chief Penn chose the tall, handsome guy as the recruit leading petty officer, and his buddy was chosen as his assistant. The bookworm who had a few college semesters was selected as the recruit education petty officer, and I was passed over for a leadership role. The "little guy" stereotype prevailed, and I became the guidon bearer.

Holding the company flag on a pole, the guidon leads the formation as the Company Commander calls out marching orders. If the guidon makes a mistake and marches the wrong way, the drill falls into chaos, and everyone crashes into each other. Traditionally, the position is the littlest person; since that was me, the job was mine. Not an esteemed way to earn a position, but I was glad to have it.

Each recruit in 934 would learn to march and parade with a state or military flag, both for our and for the previous class's graduation ceremony. Ten standout recruits would be chosen to train as the color guard. Of those ten, the best five would be crowned and perform at our graduation. Those five would be Company 934's best. I set my sights on being in the top color guard.

The competition was open. Each team consisted of three tall recruits in the middle carrying the flags and two shorter guys at the ends who marched with and twirled rifles. Since I had no luck finding another person my height who wanted to compete, I asked Brian if he would try it.

"Dude, you're way too short for us to look good. The gun twirlers are supposed to be the same height." He laughed.

I pleaded my case. "If we're the best, they'll have to pick us regardless if you are too tall," I teased.

Brian laughed. "Fine. Shit, I got nothing else to do;" he laughed again, and we started training.

Like majorettes, we practiced twirling for hours; only we used ten-pound M-14 rifles. Our objective was to move in unison, and our finale involved spinning the gun from our shoulders to the ground while moving, kneeling, and saluting. Time after time, Brian stood up when I kneeled. He moved left, and I went right. Chaos reigned as we fumbled the weapons, bouncing them off the parade deck, but we refused to give up.

The day came for Chief Penn to select the teams; Brian and I spun and twirled those rifles perfectly. Our height difference was our flaw. The decision came in. Making the cut, Brian and I would train with three flag bearers and compete to see who would be the best and perform at our graduation ceremony.

Hour after hour into the night, we sequestered ourselves in the parade hall. Pressed against one another side by side, we counted out loud as we moved.

…1…2…3…4.

Memorizing the pace and the rifle's movements, first with our eyes open, then closed, day by day, week after week, until we moved as one.

My only exposure to a team environment had been football, something I always considered a failed experiment. Our color guard formed a bond, trying to be the best. Our dedication and commitment to duty and one another were the glue, and whatever the result, it was sure to be our best effort. There would be no excuses and no do-overs. A win or loss would belong to the group.

The company commanders gathered for the final competition. After our performance, Chief Penn came to the podium to announce the winner. We stood at attention, my eyes focused forward. I don't think I blinked or took a breath waiting for the announcement. The hall, usually with recruits practicing and chatter rising, was silent.

At the competition's start, I wanted to win. By the end, my commitment was to be perfect for my squad, whatever the outcome. I don't know why we became such a close team. We were all so different. It could have been everyone's patience when someone made a mistake or willingness to practice until we were exhausted. The dynamic was addictive and I craved the thought of winning.

After Chief Penn announced we'd won, I finally took a breath. Afterward, we celebrated as only recruits can by running around the barracks, high-fiving in our tidy whities, and sharing homemade peanut butter cookies from Brian's mom.

That celebration was cut short as my attention shifted to the BUD/S screening test. The mere thought of testing made me queasy. Had

I trained enough? Failing meant a ship and a radar scope were waiting for me.

My peers laughed, "Ha, ha, no way!" they mumbled as I dropped down to do pushups in the barracks, chow hall, and classroom. "He's the littlest guy in the company, and he doesn't have a chance of passing; he's never gonna be a SEAL."

8

BUD/S SCREENING TEST

Believe you can, and success is halfway there.
Theodore Roosevelt

It was a chilly fall in Waukegan, IL. Our 0600 march to chow got colder as the Canadian winds whipped off Lake Michigan.

Chief Penn called me into his office and said, "Brown, the test for UDT/SEAL is in two weeks. Are you ready?"

After every meal and before lights out, I found a hallway, a vacant room, or a floor to do extra push-ups, sit-ups, and pull-ups. I used my private time to run around the marching field behind the barracks in my T-shirt, rugged sole Navy boots, and blue cotton dungarees. While never outright discouraging me, the Chief gave me the exact look I got from my mother when I wanted to play football, wrestle, or scuba dive. That mom eye roll, followed by the "go ahead if you want to" expression, but you're wasting your time.

Confidently, I told Chief Penn, "You're darn right. I'm ready."

Myself and two others in the company were convinced we had what it took to be SEALs. The first was the fitness recruit petty officer. The second was a regular dude who happened to be on his high school swim team. We weren't unusually muscular and certainly did not fit the "SEAL" mold, but still signed up for the test.

The test required a 300-yard swim using breast or side stroke in 7:30 minutes, six pull-ups, thirty sit-ups, thirty push-ups in two minutes, and a mile run under 7:30. The only path to training was to crush every aspect.

After morning chow on a Thursday, we three marched to the pool, a.k.a. the training tank. Three very fit petty officers in tan shorts and blue and gold t-shirts greeted us. They managed to appear ready for inspection with their workout clothes neatly pressed. I and twenty-five other UDT/SEAL wannabes were anxiously waiting on the deck in our swimsuits.

Our lead instructor, a muscular man about five feet ten inches tall and two hundred pounds stood silently anticipating an 0800-start time. Wearing a sharp-brimmed green cotton hat with squared-off edges and a blacked-out second-class petty officer insignia, his expressionless chiseled face surveyed the men before him. He spoke slowly but firmly in a direct voice, unlike almost everyone else I'd encountered in the Navy. This guy was different; he didn't need to yell to get your attention.

With the pool's filter humming in the background, he said. "Gather around and listen; you are here to take the Underwater Demolition and SEAL Teams and Explosive Ordinance Disposal Teams (EOD) physical screening test. Both disciplines are extremely demanding, and only the best scores will be selected for UDT/SEAL Teams. If you make it through this and graduate from BUD/S, I can guarantee you will be a changed man." His words and the bite of chlorine filled the room.

Gnawing the skin from my bottom lip, I wondered how I would be transformed. I was nothing like these guys. Casing the room, there were husky men with massive muscles who I was sure would easily pass. One tapped the person next to him, pointed at me, and snickered, "Look at that guy!" He motioned with his hand like patting a dog, and they laughed. With my head down, I pretended not to hear them, just as I'd done since grade school. But bullies weren't my worry that day.

I waited for the usual line-up command, but it never came. Glancing up from his clipboard, the petty officer in charge said, "When your name is called, come forward." I was third in the first group, and to my surprise, we didn't line up by height.

A new petty officer took over and began to give directions.

"First eight hit the showers, then line up."

Scurrying under the jets, I shuttered and gasped as the water stream bounced off my face. *"Ugh…Oh my God!"* I thought. It was freezing.

The guy before me shouted, "Shit, that's cold!"

"No talking!" the instructor snapped. "Move!" We ran like scared puppies to the poolside.

He continued. "Listen up; I'm going to say this once. You don't belong in BUD/S or EOD if you can't follow orders. You will swim five laps, four starting on this side and the other four on the other. Begin on the whistle. *Do not* push off the wall at any time. If you do, you will be disqualified. Sidestroke or breaststroke only. If you do any other stroke, you will be eliminated. With the second whistle, you will have thirty seconds to finish."

Huddled together, shivering, we nodded.

"I can't hear you," he complained.

"Yes, instructor!" we yelled.

"Now get in your lanes."

The pool was comfortably warm; as I held onto the side, my feet dangled, searching for the bottom while everyone else stood.

The whistle blew, and off I went swimming breaststroke. Six minutes and thirty seconds later, I finished second in my group. Four of us completed the swim in time and moved on.

Immediately after, we received our next order, "Gentlemen, you have two minutes to complete as many proper push-ups as you can," the instructor said. "Your partner will have the official count. Your chances of getting orders to BUD/S increase the more you do."

He demonstrated.

"From the up position on the command 'begin,' go all the way down until your chest touches your partner's fist on the ground. If you do not touch his fist, it will not count. Anyone caught counting improper push-ups will be disqualified."

He looked us over to confirm we understood.

"Partner up."

"I'll go first," I said. The pool water, still draining from my bathing suit, puddled as I took the "up" position.

"Begin!"

My body flew up and down like a sewing machine; fifty, sixty, seventy, seventy-five in two minutes, exceeding my best. My chest and shoulders swelled as we switched positions. My partner managed only fifty, then fell flat on the deck, unable to do one more. We moved on to sit-ups, where I completed 110.

The months of weightlifting in my basement and grueling wrestling practices paid off, as I completed twenty pull-ups. However, coming down from the bar, I felt like collapsing. Trembling and panting, my energy, like the water from my swimsuit, finished draining onto the pool deck.

"Gents, change into your dungarees, t-shirts, and boots, and meet me outside for the run," the instructor said. My cotton pants weighed heavy, and my boots were unfamiliarly burdensome. I didn't train for this endurance level. I wasn't ready.

The instructors placed cones on the parking lot corners to identify the course. Four of us lined up for instructions.

"Gentlemen, on the whistle, you will run eight laps. If you cut inside the cones, you will be disqualified. As you pass me, I will give you your time. Any questions?"

Sure, I understood the minimum time requirement, but I never ran after so many push-ups, pull-ups, sit-ups, and swimming.

"Who's the best runner here?" I asked everyone.

The tallest guy said, "I used to run cross-country in high school; a mile should be easy."

"All right, I'm following you; I suck at running. Don't let me down, bro!" I joked.

We all laughed and approached the starting line. The whistle blew, and we were off.

Today, SEAL candidates train for months to take the screening test. Many hire former SEALs or professional athletes to prepare them. I didn't know the requirements until I made it to boot camp. Undoubtedly, I was relying on my past experiences to carry me through. But I needed more on this day.

Feeling the urgency to keep up with the fastest guy, I sprinted the first lap with the group. One fellow fell behind and dropped out. On the second lap, my legs ached as my boots clopped the pavement with laboring strides. This wasn't how I trained as I carefully paced myself around the barracks parade field. Running fresh and purposeful, I tracked each lap's time. Already behind in third place and struggling with the pace, I noticed everyone began to slow. Halfway through the run, the instructor announced the time, and we couldn't spare one second. Shit! I needed to pick it up, or I wouldn't make it. As our cross-country pacesetter faltered, he became a mental and physical obstacle to sidestep.

"One lap to go," was called out, and we were all over the maximum passing time.

I wasn't going to make it. My legs were on fire, and my lungs hurt from sucking air. Slowing even more, the excuses to quit began ringing in my head. I didn't quit but was still failing.

With the original pacesetter nowhere to be seen, I led a race with no one winning. The final dagger came as the instructor yelled, "Brown, you've got thirty seconds to cross the finish, or you're finished!" Cringing, I conceded that I wasn't going to BUD/S.

But, like my wrestling tournament finals, the decision to win or lose would be mine, with only an instant to decide. Now, or never.

Gritting my teeth, I let out an *Augh!*

I shook off my mental weight and blocked out the pain. Commanding air into my lungs, I forcefully blew it out as I sprinted the last fifty yards to make up time. With my arms pumping, I took massive strides to cover the pavement until crossing the finish line.

"Good job," said the instructor. "Now, return to the training tank and wait for everyone else." I turned around to see that no one else in my group was close to finishing.

The sweaty final ten stood in the back of the room. Neither of the two who had pointed and laughed at me earlier were there. At the podium and next to two benches, one on his left, the other on his right, the instructor said, "When I call your name, have a seat on the bench to the left." The names rolled off his tongue, and each recruit complied until I was once again at the end of the line.

Turning to me, he said, "Brown, you sit on the other bench."

Shocked, I wondered how I was the only one in the room not to quality for BUD/S. Certain I'd passed the swim and completed more push-ups, sit-ups, and pull-ups than required; I sat with my head down, hands on either side on the bench, and my boots stretched out to touch the floor; I was stunned that I didn't make it.

The instructor turned to the guys on the left. "You all qualified for EOD training. Congratulations." He paused, and he looked at me. "Brown, you're the only one qualified for BUD/S. Well done." I took a breath. He continued, "Brown, your run time was close. You ran a 7:28 and made it by only two seconds. It would be best to consider going to EOD, not BUD/S. I don't think you can make it through BUD/S with that time."

With a defiant stare, I said, "Did I qualify for BUD/S?"

He said, "Yes, but…"

I interrupted him, " I want to go to BUD/S." He smiled, wrote on his clipboard, and said, "Alright, BUD/S it is."

There was a reason I refused to quit. Research suggests that giving up is a learned response. A July 2019 article published in the medical journal *Cell* described a controlled study with mice in which specific cells in the mouse brain became very active before the animal's physical breakpoint. The cells emitted a complex molecule that suppressed dopamine, a chemical primarily associated with motivation. This suppression of dopamine caused the mice to quit seeking a reward they had been trying unsuccessfully to obtain. In mammals (in this case, the mice), the cells that underlie reward-seeking are regulated by mechanisms to maintain homeostasis – a state of equilibrium for the organism.

If you've lived in relative normalcy, you are more inclined to quit during times of stress due to your brain's attempt to maintain homeostasis. During my years of overcoming challenges, I effectively trained my brain to ignore the urge for normalcy and instead hold a chemical balance aimed toward motivation. While others' brains were trained to quit, my life experiences gave me the edge to keep going.

But it was only two seconds and barely passing. It's called a minimum standard for a reason, and although my score might get me to BUD/S, it wouldn't be enough to graduate. The instructor's words were prophetic—"Brown, I don't think you can make it through BUD/S with that time." He knew my run time, but he didn't know me.

Neither my company's physical fitness recruit petty officer nor the high school swimming star passed the test, so they returned to the barracks before me.

Chief Penn waited for me in his office.

"Brown, get in here and have a seat." The other two must have told him what happened, but he smiled and asked me anyway. "How'd it go?"

Giddy and smiling, I said, "I qualified for BUD/S! I was the only one."

Folding his hands on his desk he glanced down and without a wrinkle in his expression, said, "I underestimated you. You came here, were quiet, and found ways to contribute more than anyone else. If I had to do it all again, I would have selected you as the Recruit Petty Officer in Charge."

Collapsing into my chair, I sat stunned.

"You've done so well that I've nominated you for the Navy League Award. It's an award given to the most outstanding recruit. You will represent 934 before a panel of judges who will interview you about the Navy and current events, so be prepared."

The word got out, and one after another, guys came by my bunk, offering congratulations and a handshake. "Great job, Brownie!"

they shouted. "I always thought you could do it. Wow, we're gonna have a UDT/SEAL from our company!" The people who whispered under their breath a week earlier that I'd never pass were suddenly glad to know me.

The next day, I marched up to the headquarters buildings and waited with eight other Navy League nominees to be interviewed.

In the interview room, a single chair was placed in the middle. Two men and one woman in military uniform and three civilians sat at a long table along a wall of windows. After introductions, they asked about the Navy in WWI and WWII, who was the Chief of Naval Operations, and what I wanted to accomplish.

Finally, they asked: "What is your opinion about the Iran hostage situation?"

The headline story was Iran seizing fifty-two American diplomats as hostages on November 4, 1979, by overrunning the U.S. Embassy in Tehran. I remember Walter Cronkite began each *CBS Evening News* broadcast announcing how many days the hostages had been held captive, a daily reminder that President Carter had failed in negotiating a resolution.

My response to the judges reflected my frustration and disappointment: "We can't recognize Iran as a legitimate country if they disrespect the United States by taking our citizens hostage. Let us use whatever means necessary to return them home." It's not as if I had a rescue plan, but I am sure it was apparent that I was upset. The spittle flew from my mouth, and my arms flailed in the air as I passionately described my position to the panel. Thinking back, OMG, I was like my mother. "That is one reason I want to be a UDT/SEAL. *I* can help make a difference."

We waited for the panel's decision. The door to the interview room swung open, and a petty officer entered, scanned the room and said congratulations, Seaman Recruit Smith (or whatever his name was) won the award.

"*Damn!*" I thought. When they announced Smith's name, he jumped up and yelled, "Yes!"

But as he did, the petty officer corrected himself. Looking back at his paper, he said, "Oh! I'm sorry, I meant to say, Seaman Recruit Brown, you will receive the Navy League Award!"

As I stood up, Smith sat back down dejected. The petty officer shook my hand. "Congratulations, you did a fine job. We'll be calling over to let Chief Penn know."

I had transformed my mother's SOB attitude and used it positively, winning that award. She was wrong; I was making something of myself.

Plomin writes in *Blueprint* that "parents can make a difference for their child, but, on average, in the population, parenting differences don't determine children's outcomes beyond the *genes they share.*"

Certainly, I inherited my mother's genes, and I often mirrored her headstrong and willful personality. But I had other heritable traits that made me different. Once I discovered those traits and how to use them—first in high school and as I progressed in the Navy—I could reject her prediction that I would never amount to anything. On the contrary, I learned to believe in myself and not what the world said I should believe.

9

SUCCESSES, FAILURES, AND FOCUS

Instead of focusing on the circumstances that you cannot change —
focus strongly and powerfully on the events that you can.
Joy Page

Soon after my screening test, I began coughing and wheezing. The phlegm in my lungs gurgled with every breath, but I had to pass a diving physical to qualify for BUD/S.

The flight surgeon at the medical clinic glared at me as I walked in. She asked, "Hmm, what do we have here?" She opened my folder, paused, and asked again, "A UDT/SEAL candidate?" Giving me the once-over from head to toe, she said, "Hum...I guess so. I don't see many of you here. All right, young man, take off your shirt, and let's listen to those lungs."

I would've preferred she asked me to drop'em, turn around, and spread my cheeks. She hemmed and hawed, listening carefully, until she said, "You have bronchitis. That's a shame and a problem for your physical."

Dread took over my thoughts. *I'm not going to be a SEAL after all.*

"How'd you pass that screening test and get so sick all in one week?" she asked.

"I've been training outdoors and the cold must have got to me," I replied in a raspy voice.

She laughed. "Oh, I understand. I'm not worried, you'll get better and be good as new. So, let's find out what that chest X-ray says. If it's clean, you'll be on your way."

Sitting in the waiting room, I stared at the clock as recruits filed in and out for sick call. If I couldn't get by this exam, it wouldn't matter how many push-ups I did or how fast I ran. My future hung in the balance over a stupid chest X-ray. A hospital corpsman came through the swinging door.

"Seaman Recruit Brown?" he called out.

Jumping up like I'd won the lottery, I said, "That's me!"

"I have your physical results."

My insides were screaming, "*Tell me, you idiot!*"

"Your application package will be sent to the Naval Special Warfare Command. You should expect something from them in a few months."

"What does that mean? I asked breathlessly. "Did I pass?"

"Yes," he answered. "You passed."

Bootcamp graduation day arrived, and we performed flawlessly. With the indoor field filled with recruits, flag Company 934 lined the hall at parade rest. Flags were proudly displayed as high-ranking officers spoke of duty and potential greatness. Family members and loved ones from around the country waited in the grandstand to greet their newly minted sailors. As the ceremony neared its completion, an announcement came over the loudspeaker.

"The Navy League Award winner is…" and then Chief Penn called my name.

After handing my shouldered weapon to Brian, I marched alone, passing the formation and packed stands to the podium. With every eye in the great hall on me, I stood at attention, the littlest recruit, the symbol of excellence as judged by the most powerful people in attendance. The award read. "The Navy League Award is given to the one recruit who displays outstanding qualities of leadership and a high example to comrades-in-arms during his training period."

As perfectly as possible, without flinching or blinking, I accepted the award, saluted, and returned to my color guard position. The moment was incredible, terrifying, and sad.

My mother and father didn't travel to witness me perform, receive the award, and graduate. Leo came to the graduation in their stead. I was happy to visit with my brother, but this was my most significant achievement, and I would have loved my parents to be there to experience it, to take pride in it, and in me. There will be other ceremonies, again, I told myself.

My commendation letter, a notice of the Navy League Award, my picture, and a short newspaper article were sent to my parents. They never mentioned the award on my trips to Florida. After my father's passing, I discovered they kept the article and letter in a photo album. Success is great, but it's sweeter when shared with loved ones.

After boot camp, I returned to the Chicago airport for my flight to Virginia to attend Radarman training, also known as Operations Specialist School. Wearing my new crackerjack uniform and with no doubt in my mind why people noticed me, I marched through the terminal. I was making something of myself.

The barracks at Radarman School were a welcome change. With fewer bunks per room, private showers, and toilets rather than the hanging commode display, these were more like the free Navy accommodations the recruiter told me about and I was expecting.

On my first days in Virginia, I met Ron, an unassuming guy from Peoria, Illinois. At five feet ten inches and 180 pounds, he was sure he would be a SEAL. Many guys mused how they intended to go to BUD/S, and I laughed every time I heard their fantasy.

Whenever someone discovered I passed the screening test, after their disbelief, the conversation inevitably ended with a tale of unerring failure or supreme self-confidence, claiming, "I could be a UDT/SEAL if I wanted to." Not Ron: he was different and adamant.

Meeting for a run on our first Saturday, I bragged to Ron, "Hey, let's do five miles," supporting my illusion of badassness. Having not jogged a step since my boot camp screening test, my mouth was the only muscle in great shape. But graciously, I intended to do him a favor and show him how to prepare for the test.

He accepted my offer and said, "Ok, you set the pace."

Off we went. As we logged miles, my momentum slowed, and Ron took the lead for our return trip.

Arriving at the barracks, I stood huffing and puffing, bent over, my hands on my knees.

"So, you're a good runner, huh?" I asked.

"Not really," he laughed.

"Oh, you're saying *I'm not* a good runner," I complained.

"You'll get better," he said and assured me, putting his hand on my shoulder. "If we run a few times a week, you'll be flying in no time."

Obviously, I was unprepared for our run, but Ron softened the blow. The screening test instructor's words bubbled up in my mind.

"Brown, you'll never make it through BUD/S with that run time," and I was beginning to believe him.

Moving to Coronado for BUD/S meant another six months to a year away from Mary, and that was hard for me to accept. Catching the bus into town, I went to a local jewelry store and put a deposit on a solitaire diamond engagement ring. Tickled with myself, the only thing left to do was to ask her to marry me.

Making my way to the base telephone center on Saturday morning, I dialed her number.

Mary's sister answered.

"Hi, this is David. Is Mary there?"

"Oh, Dave, let me go and get her."

Mary got on the line.

"Oh, hi, how are you? I got all your letters." We exchanged small talk, and I said, "I have something important to ask you."

After a long pause, she said, "Um, okay, what?"

I blurted out, "Will you marry me?"

"Are you serious? I'm still in high school!" she shouted.

I whined, "But we won't see each other for another year. By then, you will have graduated. You can come with me to my new duty station to be together. I have a deposit on an engagement ring."

This time, an even longer silence. Finally, Mary demurred, "Wow, that's a lot. Let me think about it."

"Oh, okay," I said. "When can I call you back?"

"How about next Wednesday in the evening," she offered.

I tried to keep a positive tone: "Okay, I'll call you. I love you!"

"You too, bye," and she hung up.

She said she'd think about it. "*What the hell!?!*" I thought. Running from the call center in a huff, I didn't talk to anyone. With my anger bottled up, I didn't dare mention this even to Ron, now my best friend, because I thought it would make me appear weak.

Hurrying to the call center the following Wednesday, I dialed Mary again.

"Hello?"

"Is Mary there?"

"Oh, hi Dave, this is MaryAnn."

"Hi, Mrs. Bolton. Is Mary there? She asked me to call."

"Um, no, she had to work, but I'll tell her you called."

"Thanks, Mrs. Bolton." After hanging up, I had a bad feeling.

The next day, a letter from Mary arrived. It began, "Dear David." As with so many "Dear John" letters received by guys in the military, my heart was broken. My eyes welled up with tears. *"Suck it back in, boy. You don't cry,"* I reminded myself.

The personality traits that helped me succeed drove the girl I loved away. I'd lost control. My personal life spiraled down while my Navy life was soaring high. I decided one had to go, and it wasn't the Navy.

I excelled at Radarman school's academics and practical exams because I studied constantly. My waking hours were focused on being first in the class, the honor graduate. My hat, haircut, and shoes were perfect as I stood stoic, unblinking, and emotionless for each inspection.

With two weeks remaining in school, 0.5 percent separated my grade from Seaman Richards' and the top spot. I needed to ace my finals. Then, the unthinkable happened: I received a 97 on my next test. "*That can't be,*" I thought.

Radarmen work in the Combat Information Center (CIC), the ship's brain. The CIC glowed from radar, sonar displays, and computer consoles as the crew managed the warship's status and surroundings. Even minor errors could cost lives, and I got a ship's course-plotting problem wrong.

Sweat beads formed on my forehead as I recalculated the ship's direction and speed, each time coming up with the same result—my answer.

Panic turned into anger. "*I'm right!*" I thought.

"Instructor Fisher, I'm sure I got this question correct," I told him.

After a review, Fisher said, "No, Brown, you're off by one degree."

Smiling, I said, No, *you're* off by one degree. Your pencil is too thick, sir. You're using a standard yellow No. 2."

Scoffing, he curiously eyed the test paper.

I explained, "When school began, I bought a .05 mechanical pencil to be super accurate."

That shouldn't make a difference." He said.

I pulled out my mechanical masterpiece and said, "Watch!" Retracing the problem, I demonstrated why and how *his* answer was wrong due to his *fat* pencil.

Staring at the chart for a minute, his inquisitive smile turned to a frown, and he said, "Damn, Brown, you're right." My intuition was correct, and my stubbornness paid off.

You don't have to remember life's every moment for it to play a role in your decision-making. It is commonly accepted that everyone has intuition. In a *Psychology Today* article titled: *What is*

Intuition and how do we use it? Francis B. Cole defines intuition as "our innate inclination toward a particular behavior (as opposed to a learned response)." Cole further explains the difference between the conscious and unconscious mind in decision-making.

"The conscious is a logic expert and will use it relentlessly," Cole writes. "Conversely, the unconscious mind searches through the past, present, and future and connects with hunches and feelings in a nonlinear way. Its process is cryptic to the logical mind, as it defies the conventional laws of time and space…. In essence, we need instinct and reason to make the best possible decisions for ourselves, our businesses, and our families."

Not accepting failure as the outcome, I had to satisfy myself and determine who got it wrong. I wanted to be perfect, a great goal when taking tests, but an absolute necessity when an entire SEAL platoon puts their lives in your hands. I was training to be more than a radarman.

Ron took and passed the BUD/S screening test with a speedy six-minute and thirty-four-second mile. Unfortunately, he waited too long to test; he'd have to go to a ship after school and wouldn't be transferred to SEAL training for a year.

He promised, "I don't care how long it takes me. I'm going to BUD/S, and I'll see you in the Teams."

That SOB was as stubborn and determined as I was, and I was certain we would meet again after graduation.

The final weekend before graduation, the class went out to party in Virginia Beach. Celebrating by eating an entire medium pan pizza each, Ron and I waddled back to the base to work out and study. Monday came, and we gathered for our last exam. I searched the room, but my competition for honor grad was notably missing.

What the heck?

"Where's Richards?"

He was in jail. Deciding to celebrate too soon, he got drunk, jumped into a hotel fountain, and was promptly arrested.

Ha, I won! With the pressure off, I aced the written and practical exams and finished first in my class. With that, I would be meritoriously promoted from E-3 to E-4, a non-commissioned officer with less than one year in the Navy.

Things in my control went my way, some by luck, but primarily due to hard work. While always hoping to be lucky, I believe you make your luck.

As the honor graduate, I was the first to choose the ship to which I would be transferred. But I wasn't there to pick a ship. I needed my orders for BUD/S to come through. When the class was ready to choose, the instructors gave me a choice: pick a command now or step aside and let the others go-ahead of you and make their selection.

Having confidence, I stepped back. The lead instructor pulled me into the empty hallway and, speaking softly, said, "Are you certain you don't want to pick first? The chance that you will become a SEAL is almost zero. Right now, you can pick any ship in the fleet."

Shaking my head, I said, "No, my orders will be here any day; I'm sure."

Not impressed, he said, "If you don't act now and don't receive those orders, you will have to settle for whatever command is available. Or worse, if you don't make it through BUD/S, you will end up wherever the Navy sends you."

"Thanks, that's OK, I'm going to BUD/S," I said as I sat down and waited. With my entire future on the line, my decision to not take a ship was as sure as my fear that something or someone could screw up and I wouldn't get my orders. But this was my only path forward. I had to stick to my plan no matter what.

As the last student entered the selection room, a yeoman carrying a red folder entered the room and after talking for a few moments with my instructor, walked over to me.

"Seaman Brown? Hi, I'm here to give you your orders to Basic Underwater Demolition School/SEAL training in Coronado, California."

Leaping from my chair, I grabbed the red folder. Inside was my name, David William Brown, typed on orders to BUD/S. It was an unforgettable moment more precious than any award I'd ever received.

After Radarman School, I took leave for the Christmas holiday to see my family in Florida. So excited to see me for the first time in uniform, my sisters, mother, and father scurried to pose for photos by the mango tree in the yard like it was Easter Sunday. But by January, my visits' luster had worn off and I was anxious to get to California.

So naïve, I thought Coronado was a remote island where I would train for six months—conjuring up images from WWII movies where US Marines on South Pacific islands fought the Japanese. My boyhood imagination ran wild as I, the other trainees, and the instructors had to survive on the otherwise uninhabited island.

In January 1981, two months after turning eighteen, I drove my red two-seater Triumph Spitfire west on Interstate 10. A stuffed-to-the-seams seabag occupied the passenger seat while a civilian clothes-filled Adidas gym bag was plopped into the footwell.

Navigating the highways with a fold-out Rand McNally map, I slipped off my right sneaker and jammed it against the gas pedal for a makeshift cruise control. The tiny car hummed along as I passed tractor-trailers and whizzed by towns. Leaning back, using my feet to steer, I crossed the Gulf Coast, the vast west Texas openness, New Mexico's and Arizona's stunning deserts, and into southern California.

As the miles and hours flew by, I pondered how the hell this happened. By every objective measure, I wasn't supposed to be making this drive. When I picked up the Navy jobs book in the recruiter's office, no one believed I would make it this far.

No one.

My recruiter said I was too little and didn't fit the mold. He did all he could to discourage me. My boot camp peers laughed and talked behind my back. "He's the smallest one in the company; he'll never make it," they all said. Yet, I was flying down the highway with orders to my dream.

Settling in on the third night in a hotel overlooking San Diego Bay, the ships docked at the Navy base were brightly lit. I'd never seen a Navy ship before. They were enormous, even from miles away. Their gray decks tapered into the sky, and sailors moved about on the pier and along the gangway. Further in the distance, the shipless Naval Amphibious Base Coronado shined from across the water. Militarily less impressive, the amphibious base drew me in, knowing my future went through there.

Staring intently at those ships and over the bay at the amphib lights, the view was burned in my memory. If I couldn't hack it at BUD/S, I'd be "haze gray and underway" on a floating steel monster. And that became my motivation. Once on Coronado, a very inhabited island, I had no intention of crossing the bay to report to a gray Navy ship.

10

BUD/S

No one can conquer you once you have conquered yourself.
Matshona Dhliwayo

Like the thousands before me who dared to challenge their physical and mental limits, I entered the BUD/S quarterdeck. Awestruck, I approached the 111 graduating class photos lining the walls, protected by the Creature from the Black Lagoon's menacing statue. Passing the images, I sensed the faces behind the glass frames, watching and judging each would-be trainee as they desperately tried to make sense of what was to come.

It was 0800 on a Monday in January 1981, and my rank and Operations Specialist patch adorned my dress-blues' left arm as I stood waiting. Unaware, the desk watch officer sorted through his routine.

"Ah, hum...morning," I said.

Gazing over the counter and down at me. "Can I help you?" he asked.

We exchanged glances as our eyes searched for the ranks on the other's uniform. As another Seaman, I thought this would be a casual and quick check-in, like Radarman School.

"Hi, I'm Dave Brown, and I'm checking in." He scanned his roster, flipping through pages back and forth until his head snapped up, his eyes wide open with surprise.

"You're AWOL!" (Absent Without Leave), he said.

No way, I thought, then, oh shit, I'm going to the brig! How can I be AWOL?

Fumbling through my red folder, I confirmed my report-no-later-than date, pointed at his paperwork, and said, "That can't be. I'm three weeks early."

"You're David Brown?" he asked.

"Yes,"

"Right, you're checking in for the Special Boat Unit."

My lips tightened, and my eyes squinted. I said, "No! I'm here for Basic Underwater Demolition SEAL Training, BUD/S."

His laughter filled the room. "Hahaha...I don't believe it. No offense, but you are...ah...little. We get the best athletes and strongest men 'ring out.' I hate to say it, but you've got *no* chance of making it through BUD/S."

I thought, "*Who the hell is this guy?* I expected the "you're too little" comment and attitude, but what the heck did "ring out" mean? I snatched the orders from his hand and thought, "*he's just another guy with an excuse for why he didn't or couldn't make it through training.*" It didn't matter. I finally made it.

After checking in, I was assigned a third-floor room in the barracks overlooking the beach. Customarily, the space was occupied by the 'Third Phase' students but was empty after they graduated.

No sooner had I moved in than a storm developed from the north. It was Hell Week for class 113. Drenched and with little sleep, they operated twenty-four hours a day for five days. Those who remained endured night after night with pounding storms and howling winds. This was one for the record books, everyone mumbled. Even the instructors were miserable.

The enormous waves pulverized the beach and berm that sheltered the barracks from washing into the ocean. At night, I lay on my rack alone in the four-person, bare-walled, cement and brick room. Three gray-striped mattresses rested atop the metal-framed cots. The third floor was dark except for a light glimmering from the head (bathroom) down the hall and the occasional lightning flashes burst through the curtain-less windows. The thunder echoed in the empty rooms like a horror movie scene.

Thoughts as black as the room ran through my head as I stared at the ceiling. How could anyone survive in that weather for a week? This was much worse than I expected. I didn't want to endure the storm in that room, much less outside. What did I get myself into? I cringed at the thought, as not long ago, I was sleeping in my comfy childhood bed and enjoying the summer with my girlfriend. Why didn't someone tell me, and how could my recruiter fail to mention that SEAL training took place in hell!

Mustering the following day with the staff at 0800, I reported to Senior Chief Petty Officer Crescini, a forty-year-old UDT/SEAL barely taller than me. He pulled me aside as if he would whisper a secret. He said in his Filipino accent, "I'm gonna show you how to make it through this. It's not easy for us little guys, and it's not easy for the big ones, either. Remember, you take it one evolution at a time. Don't worry about tomorrow or even two hours from now. Put out 100%, or you aren't going to make it."

Those were great and encouraging words, but I had no idea what he was talking about. He assured me, "Now, *you* report to *me* and no one else until your class starts. Got it?"

"Yes," I answered, "Got it, Senior Chief."

I swept and buffed the quarter-deck floor, cleaned the classrooms, and took out the trash. Everyone thought I was support staff, except for Crescini. He and I met in the workout area daily, where he taught me exercises, and we ran in the soft sand.

"You follow in the steps of the guy in front of you," he instructed. "That's how you run in the sand. Stay close." Crescini ran out and around the obstacle course with me in chase. "Keep up, stay close! Run in my footsteps." After only two miles, I was a basket case, falling behind a man twice my age.

Soon after reporting to boot camp and at Radarman School, I was comfortable, confident, and in control. I calculated how I could rise to the top. After four weeks in Coronado and observing the punishment trainees endured, I couldn't imagine how I would survive, let alone excel. Second-guessing myself, I wondered if I should have taken a ship while in Radarman School when I had the chance.

In April 1981, Class 114 began pre-training with well over one hundred men. Some came from the fleet, and most, like me, were straight from their technical school. Having recently turned eighteen, I was the littlest and youngest, and no one seemed to notice or care. Lieutenant Mike Howard, in his late twenties and old for a BUD/S trainee, was our officer in charge. Standing about five feet seven inches and approximately 160 pounds, he was on the small side but physically fit and confident.

We mustered at 0500 at the base pool, also known as the "Combat Training Tank," wearing nothing but our UDTs, a tan, almost indestructible, button-fly short. Keeping my twenty-eight waist shorts up was a constant battle, yet essential as there was a no skivvies (underwear) rule.

The Navy-issued white cotton "Fruit of the Looms" soaked up water, trapped sand, and balled up like a diaper, inflicting rashes and chaffing in the most sensitive areas. Because of this, the requirement to go "commando" was strictly enforced. To prove it, the order, "skivvy check!" came in several times a week, and one hundred men would drop their UDTs and stand naked.

At the pool, we were introduced to our instructors. The only one I can remember specifically that day is Chief Hopkins. With light-colored hair, over six feet tall, and 200 plus pounds, he wasn't the chiseled muscle type but was the guy you wanted on your side in a fight. What he lacked in Arnold Schwarzenegger-like build he made up for in attitude, mostly bad. Not a yeller or a screamer; he played the psycho role. His shtick was that he messed with your mind. I can still hear his rapid-fire, scary, evil, staccato laugh and see his little bitty, unblinking blue eyes staring through me.

Taking center stage, Hopkins sneered and said, "Everyone, look to your left, now look to your right. Do you see those guys? Don't get too attached to them because neither will be here at the end of training."

We all passed the brutal screening test to be accepted into BUD/S, and many men had stories like mine where ten or twenty attempted and only one or two qualified. We thought we were a select group, but Hopkins ended our illusion.

On our first day and every day after, we were squirted down with 50° F water soon after arriving on the pool deck. At 0500 and temperatures in the sixties, anticipating the hose to the face was terrifying. Suffering from battered dog syndrome, we cowered seeing the water nozzle in an instructor's hand. With my muscles tensing, I pulled my arms and legs tight against my body to conserve heat. These short harassing episodes were mere precursors, tiny terrorizing bits setting us up for what was in store in Hell Week.

Pre-training started with the screening test. An event I barely passed was again ready to try to take me down. The butterflies in my stomach danced as I waited for my turn. The atmosphere was more than passing; it was survival. After two hours, all one hundred-plus men were back on the deck dressed in our cotton-green uniforms (greens). As we sat on the sun-warmed aluminum bleachers, Hopkins, pointing to his clipboard, called out a dozen names and pulled those fellows aside.

Laughing, he shook his head. "They failed." His voice grew louder. "They are *failures*; they came here unprepared and will never make it to the Teams. That test was the *minimum*." Terrified I wouldn't pass, I ran scared and improved my time by fifteen seconds, a short-lived triumph.

"Goon squad." Hopkins said, "Get wet!"

The remedial twelve jumped into the pool in their greens.

"Recover!"

Exiting the pool, they were forced to do eight-count bodybuilders, jumping jacks, sit-ups, and push-ups, while the rest sat silent, cringing on the bleachers and watching the "goons" flop around. The berated, exhausted, soggy, unorganized lot collapsed on the deck in their puddles.

Finally, Hopkins ordered, "Recover!"

Facing us, he sneered and recited the inspirational message we'd come to hear so often in BUD/S: "Pays to be a winner, gents, pays to be a winner." In an unprovoked gesture, Hopkins said, "Everybody drop! And push 'em out for letting your classmates suffer out here."

After countless push-ups, Howard was directed to run us to breakfast. "And don't be late!" Hopkins said. This was a command that became his signature warning.

By 0730, I thought we'd endured enough physical exercise for an entire day. Making our way to chow I was the last man in formation, at home at the little end of the line where I'd always been. Running and staring down at the boots of the guy in front of me, always remembering Crescini's words. Honestly, I just wanted to make it to breakfast.

Every event in BUD/S was an evolution. For instance, morning PT was from 0500 to 0630. That one-and-a-half-hour event was one evolution. The meaning seems simple, but to us, it became much more. In the days and weeks to come, everyone's survival teetered on the minutes and seconds until each one ended. You might think that you were at your limit to withstand the cold or unable to crawl another yard or paddle into the surf one last time, but you knew it would end.

"Finish the evolution, gents, don't think about what's coming up next. Just finish the evolution."

We retook the screening test in our first week, and failure to pass resulted in an immediate drop from the class. As the week came to a close, the roster lessened to one hundred. There was *no* quitting in pre-training, but you could be kicked out. Those removed did not complete a "mandatory" evolution, a test that must be passed. The other evolutions were "training" evolutions and always a competition in which the winners were rewarded, and the losers were punished.

It pays to be a winner.

We swam for miles in the first two weeks, perfecting the combat side stroke, a submerged version of the common stroke. Neither the fastest nor the slowest swimmer, I was positioned in the middle, invisible and less likely to be subjected to the random punishment instructors doled out. When not in the pool, we were running in soft sand or doing PT on the grinder, the thirty-by-forty-yard sacred blacktop area in the main compound and home to the infamous "bell." Trainees must always run when they enter the compound to cross the grinder.

The Friday before First Phase began, we were issued fiberglass helmet liners, but we called them helmets. Passed down from the prior classes, it was good luck to have one from a graduate. The hand-me-down I received was from a First Phase drop out that was soon covered in frog green paint with my last name, "Brown" stenciled on the front and back. Having a helmet meant you were in the game and surviving. Helmets abandoned on the concrete walkway next to the "ring-out" bell belonged to those who decided BUD/S and being a SEAL was not for them. They symbolically rang the brass bell three times, set their helmets on the ground, and quit.

At 0500, we formed up in the dark outside the barracks and ran onto the grinder for PT. Waiting for us, standing on a three-foot-tall podium, our instructor stared emotionless over the men gathered. The newly stenciled names on the white T-shirts' front and back gave me all the personal information I needed. I got to know very few early on. Why bother, I thought. Chances are they'll be gone in a week, a day, or even an hour.

We did push-ups, sit-ups, leg levers, and four-count flutter kicks for ninety minutes. We pushed, pulled, jumped, and twisted our bodies to a man's cadence who resembled a Greek god. PT instructors had no physical limitations, but surely, they understood ours. Their commands, issued through a bullhorn, came to us loud and clear even in the very back where I was.

As men began to falter, the pace quickened. Assistants stalked from behind, waiting for the weak to collapse. Watching from the back row, I anticipated each setup and the strike as instructors pulled victims from the formation, giving them "extra attention."

"I see you can't keep up with the rest, Smith," an instructor intoned. "Come with me so I can give you some private instruction."

Disappearing over the berm, I suspect they went into the ocean as the poor lad returned soaking wet. Exercising for nearly two months with Crescini was a blessing. I kept up the pace and did my best to hide in plain sight.

Crescini helped improve my running, but I still lagged, and now I know why. According to researchers, running on sand requires 1.6 times the energy it takes to run on a hard surface. It's almost like you are running with weights on your ankles. This happens because getting your foot up off the ground is harder while trying to stabilize in the sand. At the same time, you're also getting less forward momentum from your push-off and less stability overall. Your entire body is working more, yet you are running slower—something I couldn't afford.

Soft sand runs started in a similar fashion, in our greens, jungle boots, and white T-shirts. The instructors, certainly gazelle descendants, ran slowly for about the first hundred yards singing familiar cadence songs. As we reached the sand, everyone's freshly shaved bald heads bounced like cue balls before me. Then, without notice, the instructor broke into a sprint, and the fastest runners chased, leaving the rest, including me, behind.

BUD/S reveals weaknesses, and everyone has one. It was no secret to me that running was mine. Many classmates flew through the sand while I trudged my way. When the initial sprint started, I was left in the dust. Choosing to be in the formation's rear may have been my mistake. I surmised that it was impossible to keep up with the others' long strides with my twenty-six-inch inseam. Taking two steps to their one, I tripped them and myself, creating havoc as the faster runners were forced to swerve around.

And there, my slow-motion disaster commenced. As their pace slowed and I caught up, the instructor inevitably began another sprint. Winded, I'd fall behind repeatedly.

As far as my singing cadence was concerned, let's say that lasted until the first sprint, and after that, I mostly wheezed and gasped for air.

The long line of trainees accordioned down the Silver Strand, the narrow sand isthmus south of BUD/S, stretching for many yards and traversing hills and berms. At the halfway point, we turned to make our way back toward the barracks, with the pack circling back to pick up the slowest individuals. Nearing the obstacle course, a short distance from the compound, whoever lagged would be put into the dreaded goon squad.

Usually, me being the cutoff, I'd make my best effort to catch and pass the one instructor lagging, whom I suspected would be the one to call out the goon squad. Using all my energy, I'd stay on his heels, but inevitably, he would stop and point to me.

"Brown and everyone behind him hit the surf and come back sandy, sugar cookies, gentlemen."

Standing dejected and soaked in sweat, drool dripped from my chin as I bent over, hands on my knees and exhausted. Seconds before, I hoped to be running with the pack. Now, barely able to stand, there was nothing left in me.

Knowing our fate, some cried, and some groaned. I cursed myself under my breath on my way to jump into the ocean. With saltwater pouring from my jungle boot vents, I made my way up the berm over the crest to start my sugar cookie roll down the hill. Rolling and flailing my arms, throwing sand in the air, I called out to no one in particular.

"Hoo-Yah, goon squad!"

Back from the water, sand-covered head to toe, we were ordered into the leaning rest position, which is a misnomer. There was no resting. Often left to squirm for long periods, in the leaning rest (the up part of a push-up), we shifted our weight from side to side, back to front, and from one arm to the other, wincing in pain.

With the beach in my pants, shirt, eyes, ears, nose, and mouth, down my back and rubbing, scraping, and irritating, it was time to pay for not keeping up on the run. As much as BUD/S is a physical marathon, it is undoubtedly a mental survival game. Understand and play, and you have a chance to win. The other choice was simple. Quit.

The game included hitting the surf. Mentally, jumping into the ocean had to become like putting on your shoes or doing your laundry; it had to be done. Those who dreaded the inevitable soon left their helmets next to the bell. I didn't enjoy being soaked and cold with sand stuck in every body crevice and cavity, but it evolved into another task I expected to do each day for six months and some days multiple times. The event was akin to riding my bike to football practice. I would've loved transportation from my parents, but I had to sacrifice to play football. Hitting the surf was a necessary evil to become a SEAL.

The physical torture in the goon squad started with eight-count bodybuilders, jumping jacks, and buddy races. Choosing a partner, we'd firemen carry them up and over the berm, jump in the ocean, switch positions, and return.

Everything is a race or competition in BUD/S, and it truly "pays to be a winner." The winners returned to the barracks to join the class, and the losers went on again, most times to collapse. There was no mercy. At some point, some goons fell to the ground and gave up in agony. They were ordered to do jumping jacks while the others continued the races until the worst of the worst remained. Eventually, the last goon would be released and, if unable to walk, was retrieved by the ambulance.

Taking its toll as designed, more green helmets lined the cement walkway next to the bell after each session. It didn't take long to realize that I couldn't survive BUD/S in the goon squad.

11

SYMBOLISM AND SETBACKS

The darkest hour is just before the dawn.
Proverbs

Two hundred yards south on the Silver Strand was a conglomeration of logs, rope, metal pipe, and barbed wire obstacles known as the O-Course. The structures, though simple in their design, rose from the sand like a colossus that devours trainees at will. Its purpose was to test confidence, strength, and endurance, with reckless abandon being the sole mindset for success.

Demonstrating the nuances while negotiating the obstacles, instructor Donegan ran, slid, climbed, swung, and hurdled, making Tarzan seem pedestrian. His show was as impressive as it was useless for me. My standing tiptoe reach was less than seven feet and could no more do what Donegan did than fly with cardboard wings.

At the whistle's chirp, every trainee, little and big, received the same treatment—from the first hop onto the five-foot-high metal pipe parallel bars until jumping the final railroad tie hurdle. The obstacles gave no consideration, only resistance. There were no adjustments, only fixed distances and heights, no safety devices, only the hot, soft sand to catch the unfortunate, careening trainee after losing his grip.

I lived to climb, jump over narrow ravines, swing from trees, and fall off walls and rooftops in Wilkes-Barre, Harvey's Lake, and around the Bear Creek mountains' abandoned mines. Playing like a kid prepared me to conquer every O-Course obstacle but one.

Sixteen obstacles lay between the start and finish. From the two-stage, triceps-burning parallel bars to scaling an eight-foot wooden plank vertical wall, the course increased in complexity and difficulty. Some obstacles stood out more than others, like the three-tier platform tower that had to be scaled from the outside one floor at a time. Dangling from each floor, I swung and pulled myself up until the final level, twenty feet in the air. Reversing the process, I jumped, tucked, and rolled into the sand from the second story.

Further on, the "slide for life" required a telephone pole climb to a height of thirty-five feet. Once atop, I leaned off a small deck and reached high to grab a three-inch thick, eighty-foot-long, horizontal, callus-tearing hemp rope. Hanging with no safety net or harness, the goal was to shimmy down the line to where it was safe to drop into the sand. By this time, my upper chest and shoulders burned from exhaustion, and my forearms cramped. Maintaining a grip was a constant mind-over-physical-pain battle.

The most feared obstacle was the rope cargo net, demanding a fifty-foot ascent straight up to a dizzying height that offered a miles-long view. Waiting at the crest was a four-inch-thick steel bar. Traversing the bar with weakened and shoulder fatigue was precarious, but I had to be sure-handed, or I'd be on a deadly quick trip down.

Pulling and swinging on some obstacles, I hopped, balanced, and weaved on others, contorting to overcome each dilemma until I reached the "dirty name."

More than any, the dirty name, or obstacle No. 9, was my life's metaphor. The structure was made of three horizontal logs, each about sixteen inches in diameter, placed on a tiered frame. The first log rested on the sand, the second was five feet higher and four feet away from the first, and the third was four feet higher than the second and another four feet away. It was the first two logs that gave it its reputation.

The objective was to use the first log on the ground as a jumping platform to launch into the air and onto the second, hopefully propelling you high enough to grab on and pull yourself up. Imagine a gymnast running at the pommel horse without a springboard and padding, and once on the first horse, another pommel above had to be conquered. The many and varied curse words uttered by countless trainees gave birth to the obstacle's name as men lamented as they slid off and fell helpless to the ground.

In my first attempts, I careened and slammed my chest into the second log. Wrapping my arms around the smooth wooden pole, I'd slip under, falling to the sand. Frustrated, I considered my options. It was not possible to shimmy up or long jump onto it. Unlike the other obstacles, I could navigate over the dirty name in only one way—jumping as high and as far as everyone before me, which was surely impossible.

Exhausted by the time I reached the damn thing, I needed to summon energy I didn't have and nail a performance I had never achieved. Peak output at the most challenging time is the BUD/S' algorithm. Every failed attempt hurt like hell and made me weaker. Like the tackle sled in high school football, this obstacle beat me black and blue. And like my wrestling coach, the instructors cheered me on as I ran right into the log as fast as possible. Repeatedly.

Crescini always waited, yelling: "Come on, Brown, run like hell! You can do it!"

After sliding off the second log, he encouraged me.

"Relax, breathe, take another shot."

For those few minutes, Crescini was my friend like he was before training began. He knew that my failure on obstacle No. 9 wasn't due to a lack of effort but rather to my stature—little like his. I received encouragement but got no consideration. They'd drop me in a heartbeat if I couldn't figure out how to conquer the beast. He understood I wouldn't quit, but he couldn't tell me how to be successful.

Too many people who failed the O-Course gave up on themselves. The course exemplified the higher point: SEALs must be analytical and problem solvers, but unlike a math test with only one correct answer in BUD/S, the solutions were individual.

After numerous attempts at the dirty name and with the clock ticking, I turned my back and walked away. Ten yards later, I reversed, and with hands on my knees, I stared at the logs that seemed to mock me as I rested. Panting to catch my breath, I stood still as my classmates attacked the obstacles behind and after me; I, with intention, did nothing. My breathing slowed as I sensed Crescini standing patiently beside No. 9, waiting for me to do something.

Regaining my strength and composure, I inhaled deeply, grit my teeth, and ran yelling at that son-of-a-bitch with all my energy. Launching into the air, I sailed onto the second log for the first time and then to the third.

I had to conquer my inner Goliath before taking on the obstacle. *I* had to control the situation, understand my limits, and find a solution. Did I sail over the dirty name on my subsequent attempts? Hell no. Usually, it took me several tries to beat the damn thing. And I cursed it with each attempt.

By the first Friday's end, I'd endured PT and soft sand runs for ninety days. My jungle boots' rugged black plastic soles slapped the pavement for miles. Not designed as a running shoe, my ill-fitted footwear caused massive water blisters, and the laces put pressure on my lower shin and ankles, causing chestnut size welts.

Historically, the Vietnam-era green boots were a menace for trainees. With no sympathy from the training staff, everyone had to grin and bear the pain or concoct solutions. Medical rollbacks and men quitting from boot injuries happened regularly, so backroom remedies for the inevitable ailments trickled down from trainee to trainee and from class to class.

It was too late when I began to fix my boot problem; I tended to the symptoms. Waking up every morning in agony, I diagnosed my dilemma as shin splints. Pounding the blacktop almost fifty miles a week, running to and from chow, and the soft sand and timed beach runs took their toll. Like a daily ball peen hammer beating on my shins, the running caused my tibias to crack. Not accepting my severe condition, I self-medicated, swallowing Motrin to kill the pain. And like an obedient sailor, I reported to muster at 0500.

On the second Saturday of First Phase, I woke early and was unable to get out of my rack as my groin muscle tightened from injury. Rolling over in a fetal position, I reached for and downed the Motrin in my locker drawer. In addition to my shin and ankle pain, my right leg was now immobile from a pulled muscle during log PT the day before. With less than forty-eight hours to heal, at 0500 Monday, I made formation and limped my way through the day.

Training continued, and the next day, Tuesday, at 0500, we readied on the beach for a four-mile timed run. Keeping silent about my injuries, I popped more anti-inflammatories and prayed for the best.

Pain is a funny thing. One minute, you think something hurts until you have another that hurts even more. My shin pain and the stabbing sensation in my inner thigh and hip battled it out to see which was the most debilitating. With Class 114 clustered in the dark at low tide, the whistle blew, and off we went, a shaven-headed gaggle in white T-shirts and green pants running like hell toward the North Island Naval Air Station. Limping the first two miles, I managed the pain, but on my return, my muscles began to tighten, and my ability to run ceased.

Hitting the three-mile mark, I resembled Igor from Young Frankenstein, hobbling and dragging my right boot through the sand. With the entire class now long finished, I limped over the line. I had only one thought.

"*Complete the evolution. Don't think about tomorrow or even an hour from now.*"

Crescini's words rang in my head. Waiting and watching, Instructor Hall checked his clipboard as I dragged my leg over the finish four minutes behind the maximum time.

"Brown, sick call, now!" he said.

Gimping across the grinder, I encountered Chief Hubbard, an instructor and hospital corpsman, at his desk. He made a quick examination and seeing that I was favoring my left side, said, "Follow me."

As I stood under the pull-up bar, he ordered, "Jump up on the bar and hang."

"*You've got to be kidding me,*" I thought. "*I can barely walk, and you want me to jump up?*"

But this was BUD/S, so I miraculously leaped and grabbed the bar. As I hung, he circled and returned to his office.

To my surprise, he reappeared with a yardstick. "*What the heck is he planning to do?*" I thought. Putting the stick under my boots, he mumbled, "Hmm, wait there."

Hanging on the bar, the minutes ticked by until he appeared again, this time with another instructor. Leveling the stick under my boot soles, Hubbard said, "Shit, one leg is shorter than the other. Okay, Brown, get down."

"*One leg is shorter than the other! What, is he nuts?*"

With all the poking and prodding in the Navy physicals, I was sure they would have found that long ago. I hoped he was wrong; he thought he was right. Hubbard handed me a written order to go to the medical clinic for an evaluation.

That afternoon I had an appointment with a real doctor. After a thorough exam and eventual bone scan, my diagnosis was multiple stress fractures in both legs and a pulled groin muscle. If Hubbard's "field opinion" had been accurate, I would have surely been dropped from training. The true diagnosis, however, allowed me the chance to start over with a new class.

My fate rested with the Trainee Review Board's decision.

The week before Hell Week, I and other classmates who failed a mandatory evolution or were injured faced the board to determine if we would be rolled out or back to Class 115. Ten yards from the ring-out bell, I stood at attention in my greens with my First Phase helmet under my arm. My eyes fixated on the steel door where behind it, the board waited. This situation differed from my Navy

League Award experience as I was not there to impress anyone with my current events knowledge or to be graded on the shine of my boots. I was nervous and certain my failure to perform a mandatory evolution would surely result in my transfer to a big gray ship across San Diego Bay.

Warned that I was too little and had *no* chance, I awaited my fate.

Three classmates before me went in and came out one by one without saying a word. They shook their heads and left after placing their helmets in the protracted line beside the bell. With my heart in my throat, I limped into the review room, where four instructors sat with my file on the desk. The meeting was quick.

Addressing me, Instructor Hall said, "Brown, we had to let the other guys go; we rolled them out. They are returning to the fleet and will have another chance if they want to be a SEAL badly enough."

"That's it; I'm done."

My run times sucked, I was constantly in the goon squad, and I failed my last timed run by four minutes. There's no reason for them to keep me. I wasn't in competition for honor graduate as I'd been in Radarman school. I was ready to accept my defeat.

Hall continued, "You've been a good trainee with excellent academic test scores, and except for your run times, you are doing well with the physical part." Very intently, he said, "Anyone who can finish a four-mile run on two broken legs and a pulled groin deserves another shot. You'll be rolled back to Class 115. Retrieve your gear from the barracks and report to the Amphibious Base, where they will assign you for two months until your new class forms up."

I gasped. *"My God!"* I wasn't going haze gray and underway. I've got another shot.

Not a failure, yet not a success. My meteoric rise in the Navy stopped, and I needed to deal with it. I realized I had options. I could relax for the next eight weeks and enjoy my time off from the daily pounding that brought me to my knees, or I could develop a plan to win.

I was a planner, not from being taught but from my sheer desire to achieve. But now, I had no control over my environment. Unable to depend on others for comfort, I took solace in knowing I'd made it this far and had pride in my ability to attempt the impossible. They said I was too small and slow to be a UDT/SEAL. I intended to prove them wrong.

The Navy was a much more imposing adversary than I imagined. It would be so easy and understandable to give up, to join the eighty percent who quit. Happy sailors walked around the base daily, fulfilled with their accomplishments. Why couldn't I? Why was I so compelled to keep chasing an improbable dream?

12

HAZE GRAY AND UNDERWAY

I am determined to be cheerful and happy in whatever situation I may find myself in. For I have learned that the greater part of our misery or unhappiness is determined not by our circumstance but by our disposition.
Martha Washington

On my first evening in San Diego, in what seemed like ages ago, I promised never to leave BUD/S for the ships across the bay. But I never considered the possibility of crossing the street to the small gray boats at the Coronado Naval Base.

Like my body, my confidence was damaged as I walked gingerly into the Bachelor Enlisted Quarters (BEQ) at the Amphibious Base.

Returning to the regular Navy felt ugly after spending the past four months in an utterly different world. The color at BUD/S was combat green rather than Navy blue, and the men were hardened. Our routine was crisp and purposeful, and we lived in a daily inspection atmosphere. Any mistake, however slight, was punished, and occasionally punishment came without error. The blue Navy simmered slowly in common activities, people, and effort. Or was SEAL training so extreme, uncommon, and precise?

Comparatively, my new temporary quarters were luxurious, and I shared a room with only one other sailor, Alphonse Siciliano. His New York accent and demeanor are unforgettable.

Enlisting to escape his home less than a year earlier, he couldn't wait for his active duty to come to an end and go back to his familiar places, friends, and family. Sporting jet-black hair with a medium build, his crooked yellow front teeth were always on display. He never lacked for an offensive comment, yelling, "I'm getting old waitin' in this fuckin chow line," as I cringed over my association with him.

Constantly badgering and berating people, he used the F-word in every sentence and context. Still funny and, at times, a likable guy, he possessed no fighting skills to back up his abrasiveness.

"Someone's going to make you eat your words one day," I said.

"You're going to be a SEAL; you can protect me, right Brownie!"

"This was going to be a long eight weeks," I thought.

With no other BUD/S rollbacks in the building, I was an odd duck with two months to kill. Would I spend my time picking up garbage or doing laundry? I envisioned schlepping in the chow hall, peeling potatoes, or a menial assignment from the Master at Arms, the senior enlisted guy responsible for every dirty job on base. From the high of the Navy League Award recipient to Radarman School honor graduate and SEAL trainee, I was sure to descend to be the mopping and waxing floor trainee. Boredom set in within hours as I stared at the bare BEQ walls wondering what the next day would bring.

The School Command assigned me to the Amphibious Landing Craft School the following Monday morning. Searching my seabag, I resurrected my blue dungarees, ironed them, and readied for inspection.

My new assignment was in a small Quonset hut, with a pristine military jeep parked out front next to a hand-painted "Navy Assault Boat Coxswain School" sign. Accepting my fate, I conceded it was time to rest, heal, and ride on the cool assault boats.

Checking in with the chief, a salty old boatswain's mate—barely taller than me, but twice my weight, with a round red face, a smile, and a contagious laugh—he immediately made me feel at home. "You're gonna be an extra hand to support and help manage the students, and we'll let you scrub the landing craft too." He laughed.

"Sounds great, Chief," I said, "but I'm only here for eight weeks and must stay in shape to return to BUD/S."

He assured me, "Don't worry; scrubbing the boats will keep you in excellent physical condition."

As the unofficial caretaker, I cleaned and secured the building every afternoon. Unbeknownst to me, there is an unwritten Navy training command rule that you go home when the students are gone, no matter what time that is. The entire staff, except me disappeared the second the trainees left.

The first to go, the Chief surveyed the area. "Well, fellas, everything is ship shape. See you tomorrow bright and early," as he scurried out the front door. Following him and only after ensuring I stowed and locked up the equipment, the Leading Petty Officer would slip out the back door with the other four instructors behind him. The staff leaving me alone, didn't bother me; I had nowhere to go. After cleaning, I'd prepare the classrooms for the next day and headed to the gym. It was a meager existence and a lesson in patience.

After working in and around the building for weeks—making training material copies and washing and waxing the jeep—the Chief wanted to speak with me.

His quaint office only had space for a file cabinet, a standard-issue gray metal desk, and one other chair.

"Have a seat," he said. "Take a load off, son. We can't have you mopping floors and taking out the garbage the entire time you're here, so how'd you like to go through the school and earn your Assault Boat Coxswain certification?"

"I would!" I replied without hesitation. Now, we were both smiling.

"Excellent, you'll be in the next class," the chief explained. "Of course, you'll still have to do all the other duties you were assigned. Got it, partner?"

"Absolutely, Chief," I replied with a grin. I was excited to learn how to ram assault boats onto the beach.

Discovering my dilemma, my parents and little sister Wendy piled into the family sedan for the long drive to visit. Playing tour guide, I chauffeured them through the base and BUD/S. Seeing Class 114 run by on their way to chow, my father asked, "Is that what you're gonna have to do?"

"Yeah," I joked, "and that's the easy part."

My mother couldn't comprehend what a SEAL was beyond scuba diving.

My father said. "I never thought you'd go from scuba diving in Harvey's Lake to being a Navy diver…and watch out for dead bodies when you're in the ocean!"

Growing up in Wilkes-Barre, my family stayed close to home as my mother was terrified of flying, and my father was afraid to drive over bridges. My career path left no leeway for such problems. Lucky for me, research suggests not everyone with parents who have anxiety develops the disorder, and not all of those predisposed develop it either. Even if anxiety is genetic, you can still "train" your way out of it, according to experts.

I'd accomplished more than my mother ever expected, and my father told me he was proud. His words were comforting, and as we stood on the BUD/S quarterdeck, I believe he began to understand the enormity of my challenge. His cheeks red from smiling, he beamed admiration and love. He didn't have to say it. I felt it.

I realized that they had done all they could do for me. Any disappointment I conjured up about their lack of support was on me. My parents, neither of who finished high school, were successful, and they lived up to their potential.

Yet, in my mind, success was miles away. I was rolled back but hadn't quit or failed; I learned. My time away from training allowed me to mentally and physically reset how I would approach my second

BUD/S attempt. I planned to take every advantage once I was back in my greens.

Strategically, I committed to devour the Navy and BUD/S like an elephant, one bite at a time. Crescini's advice to "take one evolution at a time" began to have meaning. His words were as profound as any from Socrates or Aristotle.

Older by only two months yet years wiser, I was calm rather than anxious. My experiences provided opportunities to be successful, and I welcomed that. Familiarity will do all that if you permit yourself the luxury.

13

FIRST PHASE REDO

Believe you can, and you're halfway there.
Theodore Roosevelt

Being strong, fast, intelligent, and determined to become a SEAL is not enough. Every man on my review board desired a trainee they could trust with their life, someone who would never quit when facing adversity or danger, even if that meant self-sacrifice. Demonstrating those qualities in my first attempt, I know it was not luck giving me another shot. I created opportunities using traits developed in elementary school and high school sports. But I wasn't finished—far from it.

In mid-June 1981, when I checked in at the BUD/S quarterdeck for the second time, no one questioned why I was there or if I would be successful. I looked different because I was. No longer was I the five-foot-three-inch, 110-pound little boy trying; I became the person who would be a SEAL.

After receiving my greens, I folded and jammed my blue dungarees into my seabag's very bottom, never to be seen again. Motivational experts say clothes make the man, and my psychological shift from blue to green was transformative. My persona was sharp, strong, and confident again.

Within days, our barracks were filled. One, two, then four roommates stuffed into the small cement-brick rectangular berths. At ease with the accommodations, I realized there would be empty beds soon as men rang out, were injured, and rolled back.

Watching eager classmates enthusiastically go out for "good time runs," I rested, knowing how to gain the advantage. Soon, we would endure the ten-mile-a-day, bone-cracking, pavement-slapping chow hall runs, so I avoided any extra physical stress. Training would provide all the punishment; I didn't need to help.

On Sunday, June 28, we gathered to our north in the picnic area for the customary head-shaving and helmet-painting party, eating pizza and laughing it up. With over 110 trainees, forming any bonds would be pointless. Mingling amongst the sea of smiles, chiseled bodies, and freshly shaved heads, I knew what they didn't—a freight train was heading our way, packed with incredible pain and suffering, and we volunteered for it.

These would be our last fun moments for relaxation. Monday would bring the water hose to the face, the PT for hours, and constant harassment. I convinced myself I was ready.

At 0400 Monday, I awoke thirty minutes before everyone to retrieve and shine the sacred bell, a duty I happily raised my hand for.

A gift from Class 58, the brass ornament symbolized both victory and failure. Polishing it meant I didn't have to report as the watch on the quarter deck during the week. Training may have ended at 1600, but we were in the Navy, and the two-hour quarter deck watch regimen continued into the night and early morning. By far, I preferred waking early to polish the bell rather than being startled to stand watch in the middle of the night.

Shining the brass symbol was therapeutic. Some trainees avoided going anywhere near it, but I used it to my advantage with my usual deference to no one and nothing. Alone in the dark, I ran across the grinder in the wee hours. The normally trainee-filled bustling compound was eerily silent, except for the ocean waves battering the beach. I'd casually unscrew the large nut holding the tarnished hunk of brass in place and carry it to my room. I rubbed and buffed the bell for twenty minutes until it glimmered like new. Wrapping it in a towel like a newborn, I returned it to guard the portal that my failed peers would pass through on their way out.

There was something about seeing the men's fingerprints who quit on its side that made it easier for me not to. Every day, I polished off some poor guy's hopes and dreams of becoming a UDT/SEAL, and the bell stood shiny and irreverent with no regrets, ready for the next quitter.

Instructor Donegan ordered us to "line up" by height in the first week to assign boat crews. Scurrying to the little end, I waited as everyone scrambled to determine if they were a half-inch taller or shorter. In no time, from across the grinder, Crescini commanded....

"Drop!"

As fast as lightning, his voice clapped across the black pavement.

"What the hell is going on here? This evolution should have been completed long ago!"

After our punishment push-ups, I had a new crew: Ensign George Coleman, Parachute Rigger Second Class Ken Rice, Torpedoman Second Class Ken Emihl, Seaman Quartermaster Chris Cobb, Seaman Radioman Steve Cooley, Machinery Repairman Second Class Clay Barnes, and me. The taller, Cobb and Rice, were in the bow, followed by Emihl and Barnes. Finally, in the aft was Cooley and me. Poor Coleman, the coxswain, took the brunt of the stern's weight as he stood five foot seven inches tall next to Cooley's five foot five inches and me at five foot three inches.

Coleman was our crew's leader, as well as the class officer. A handsome Asbury Park, New Jersey native, he and his friend, Ensign Tom Schibler, had recently graduated from the University of Rochester. They both wanted one thing from the Navy: to be a

SEAL. But there was much between their fresh commissions and earning a Trident.

Schibler was over six feet and muscular, completely my opposite. Anything easy for me was hard for him, and vice versa. He paid the price for being an officer and big; he couldn't hide amongst the men. We spent hours commiserating over who had it worse. I think he did.

Coleman, Schibler, and eight newly minted officers started in Class 115, but only one could be the class leader. The story goes that they drew straws to determine who would be responsible for accounting for everybody and everything. Coleman lost.

The officers maintained two rooms, one in the officer's quarters and one in the BUD/S barracks, subject to inspections. They arrived early and were the last to leave. And regardless of fault, the Class Officer always paid the price in push-ups. Of the ten officers who began, three graduated.

An IBS is a twelve-foot-long, 200-plus-pound rubber inflatable boat, and IBS drills dominated First Phase. Nicknamed the "Smurfs" because my crew was the shortest, we failed miserably in landraces as the long-legged men flew by our pattering little boots. Whoever said that short guys had the advantage never witnessed trainees five feet seven inches and under try to win a four-mile race with an IBS on their heads.

Issued the worst ratty, rotten, and leaky little boat that took on water like a sieve, caused us to lose every waterborne competition. A fully inflated IBS is easier to carry and paddle, and we may have started with an air-filled boat that lasted only minutes.

We Smurfs didn't know each other before training or how long we'd stay together as a crew. Melding after week one, we carried anyone in need, kept each other warm, and were patient when some got frustrated. Winning and losing as a team, we got better daily.

I didn't know their family history experiences or how they prepared for BUD/S, but we all brought similar character traits. We were in outstanding physical condition, and no one dared to whisper the word quit; our only strategy was to win, like my boot camp color guard.

By week two, we could read each other's mind. Operating like one in, under, and on the IBS, we went from surviving to excelling. Our bond was organic, which was rare. Put together by chance; the boat crew selection was not an exercise in matching personalities for compatibility. On our own, we searched for and found ways to cohere.

On Friday of our second week, between 1300-1600, Rock Portage glared at us from the schedule. Trying to laugh it off, we realized our lives were at risk when landing our IBS on the jagged rocks.

Hopkins, the menace instructor from my previous class, was lurking. Carrying our black, flatulent raft on our heads over the sand berm, we elephant walked in formation up the Silver Strand towards the historic Hotel Del Coronado and the rock jetty.

"Elephant walking" meant Hopkins moved out at a trot, with boat crews struggling to keep up in a single file line, "nut to butt." The resulting run/walk/run caused boats to collide, jarring our necks and shoulders. With each shove and push, crews devolved into disarray, men yelled and complained, falling behind and out, tripping over one another, and dropping their IBS, a mortal sin. Those who failed became victims as the shark instructors pulled them aside for "extra attention" to detail.

Hopkins yelled through his megaphone, "Keep up, gentlemen; more than one boat length between boats shows your lack of attention to detail. Failure to maintain a proper distance will result in the entire class suffering."

After the one-mile jaunt, we arrived at the jetty—"late," according to Hopkins.

"Too slow and unorganized," he said, and our punishment was extended arm push-ups, holding the IBS over our heads, and push-ups with feet on the boat's main tube.

Exhausted, we readied ourselves for surf passage. The IBSs lined the beach with paddles stowed perfectly, ready to attack. We planned by counting the waves as they crashed on the twisted shore. The crews navigated into the Pacific one by one and waited for the "paddle" command.

Seeing our signal, Coleman said, "Let's go! Stroke... stroke... stroke...stroke."

And like a college crew team, our tiny, leaky boat moved toward the rocks. The swells lifted the aft as the cadence grew.

"Stroke...Stroke...Stroke! We need speed," Coleman growled.

The waves' energy catapulted us forward, pitching up the aft and giving us a vantage point looking down on our unwelcoming landing zone. Timing the swell perfectly, Coleman pulled a heavy starboard rudder, steering to the rock mass as the main tube slammed into the jetty. Chris, the bowman, sprang out, securing our position as he perched himself on the rocks above. Scrambling to avoid being crushed, we heaved the shrinking craft out of the ocean.

The evolution continued as boats careened sideways, capsizing. Trainees were tossed onto the boulders, temporarily trapping, and crushing them. A few made the journey unscathed, as others failed spectacularly. Overseeing the event, Hopkins stood tall on the highest stone, his voice echoing through his electric megaphone.

"Move, gentlemen! You're late!"

Surviving the afternoon was delightful, but the emotion was fleeting as *night* rock portage was on schedule. As we planned for our night onslaught of the jetty, the ring-out bell was busy.

Ding, ding, ding.

More green helmets joined the line on the compound's sidewalk.

We flanked our IBSs at dusk and watched as instructors handed out ChemLights to tie to our kapok life jackets.

"We need a way to find the corpses of trainees dumped into the ocean or stuck between the rocks," Hopkins said as he passed out the glowing sticks.

Our fear was confirmed; men quit over it. They'd seen the catastrophes from miscalculating the approach. Anxiety increased with each evolution, and the Smurfs fed off it. We were energized when crews balked at the waves' size, the evolution's difficulty, or the impending danger. It was a twisted enthusiasm originated by Steve Cooley as he laughed at peril and scoffed at insurmountable odds.

From the barracks, we paddled towards the famous hotel. The moonlight framed our green-glowing ChemLight silhouettes. Always drawing a crowd on the beach, night rock portage was live reality entertainment.

Staged outside the surf zone, the rubber boat flotilla dotted the horizon. Flashlights from the instructors signaled each crew to begin. Waiting our turn, we listened to the pounding ocean and the muffled yelling as crews smashed against the rocks.

Our IBS softened, then the distant flashlight signal came, and Coleman commanded, "Paddle to the light!" Up and down, the swells passed under.

"Faster!" he ordered. In the distance, white water surged into the jetty as the swell's spray flew high into the air with a boom.

"Stroke! Stroke!" Coleman yelled.

Caught by a large swell, the stern flexed up, and our ride into the darkness was underway. With only the jetty's black outline visible, he aimed for our final approach. At full speed, we crashed head-on into the jagged granite. *Kapow!*

The IBS' front main tube blew apart from the impact. Cobb, the bowman, leaped onto the rocks, pulling on the line with all his might. The mortally damaged boat flopped against the stone as its deflated bow sank deep into the boulder's crevasses. Jumping from the hulk, we began to heave the flooded rubber mass up the steep incline. Intently scanning for incoming breakers, Cobb screamed, "Water!" as another wave pounded, crushing us from behind.

Bam!

Smurfs disappeared under the surf and into the darkness. Trapped under the rubber mass, I squeezed between the rocks and gasped for air as the water receded.

"Is everyone okay?" Coleman called out. "Sound off!"

As ChemLights popped to the surface, voices rang out.

"Rice…here!"

"Cooley!"

"Brown!"

"Barnes!"

"Emihl!"

Scrambling from the impact zone, we heaved the floppy mess over the boulders, dragging it to the shoreline.

Dripping and relieved, we stood laughing on the beach at the gaping two-foot hole torn in the front main tube. "Well, that's it for us tonight!" we joked. The other crews had at least one more attempt.

A very unhappy Hopkins approached.

"Coleman, what have you and your men done?" he said. "Drop! You damaged government property. What are you going to do, Mr. Coleman?"

"I guess we'll have to secure since our IBS is destroyed, Chief."

That meant ending our evolution. Hopkins, in his rapid-fire laugh, spat back: "I don't think so, Mr. Coleman. There's nothing wrong with your craft's stern. You must complete your mission. Tie the bowline to the ass-end, and it will become your bow. Rally your crew onto that boat and make your way out to sea for another attempt. Move it. You're already late."

We stood perplexed. Seven men on half a flooded IBS paddling through the surf appeared impossible. *This was suicide,* I thought. But it didn't matter what you thought or how hard or wild it sounded; whatever an instructor commanded, we screamed "Hoo-Yah!" and did it.

"Hoo-Yah, Chief Hopkins!"

We rolled up the front main tube, tied the bow line to the stern, and dragged the floppy, half-sunken derelict into the ocean. With Coleman sitting in the water on the rolled section, we began our new mission and started to paddle.

Sitting nut to butt on half a main tube, we progressed through the waves at a snail's pace slamming and banging our paddles as the other crew members laughed.

"Holy shit, check out the Smurfs; they only have half a boat!"

With the flashlight signal to come in, we again attacked. Turning and twisting, the waves thrust our misshapen rubber tube until we bailed out and crashed uncontrolled onto the jetty with a thud. The instructors and the crowd stood laughing and cheering. As we made our way to the beach, a bellowing Hopkins met us.

"Drop! Push'em out. Mr. Coleman, your boat crew is secured."

"Hoo-Yah, night rock portage!" we cheered, dragging our deflated beast down the beach.

The following Monday, after 0500 PT, Master Chief Ray summoned the Smurfs. Waiting for us on the grinder was a *new* IBS. More push-ups for destroying government property and a final, "Hoo-Yah, old IBS."

The new IBS would change everything for the Smurfs.

14

BEYOND IMPOSSIBLE

The only way to discover the limits of the possible
is to go beyond them into the impossible.
Arthur C. Clarke

In 1997, Tim Noakes, an emeritus professor in the Division of Exercise Science and Sports Medicine at the University of Cape Town, South Africa, proposed the "central governor" theory. Noakes suggested that "fatigue is a protective emotion rather than a physiological state." He deduced that the central governor limits exercise by reducing the neural recruitment of muscle fibers. The brain requires a steady flow of nutrients and oxygen and demands a reliable mechanism for transport (your body). Anything that might jeopardize these things will be tightly regulated. Otherwise, athletes could run themselves to death by destroying skeletal or cardiac muscle or starving the nerve tissue of nutrients and oxygen. This reduced neural recruitment of muscle fibers causes the sensation of fatigue.

Some people are born runners. Others learn to love running and experience a short-lasting euphoria or bliss known as a "runner's high." Fatigue is what I experienced when running. I needed to overcome my central governor and become faster.

Running over fifty miles per week—to chow, on the beach, and during conditioning runs—chances were I'd become faster or eventually break… again. Narrowly, I could pass the mandatory four-mile timed run on the hard-packed beach, but I paid the goon squad price for falling behind on the soft sand conditioning runs.

Joining me in the demeaning and demoralizing goon squad were other losers who, like me, had a mental or physical running challenge. Running was our albatross, an unbearable burden sure to do us in. We were not quitting, but we weren't succeeding, and daily moving closer to being a statistic.

Schibler and Tony Gumataotao usually joined me. I shuttered at the thought of throwing either man over my shoulders (fireman's carry) and transporting them a great distance in the sand.

One fateful day in our second week, we set out on a conditioning run, heading south on the Silver Strand past the demo pit and up and over the dunes. The circumstance was unfortunately familiar, with most of the class sprinting ahead, leaving me and the slowest runners to catch up only to have them dash away. Tagged again as the first person in the goon squad, those behind me were also condemned to its ranks.

Concerned about our ability to keep up, instructors warned us that our days were numbered unless we figured out how to run as if our life depended on it. But now it was time to pay the price for our failure. The upcoming severe lesson was supposed to help us with our attention to detail, sharpen our focus, and strengthen our resolve. Designed to be worse than any condition we experienced in a successful evolution, the goon squad was intentionally made unbearable. Near exhaustion, I struggled to regain my breath as I hunched over with my hands on my knees.

The torture began with an instructor's command.

"Eight-count bodybuilders, gents. Mr. Schibler lead the count. Go! If you had put out the effort like your classmates, you'd be taking a shower now." The instructor lamented, "I don't want to do this, gentleman, but you forced me to. You are all making me be the bad guy, and I don't like it!"

Each remedial activity was more brutal than the last. We paired for our races as the order came in: "Brown and Gumataotao pair up for the fireman's carry."

Weighing in at 114 pounds and five foot three inches tall, I stood next to the 230-pound, five foot ten inches tall Gumataotao. The other goons stared, and some mouthed, "Oh shit, Brownie."

Schibler walked up to me and with sweat pouring down his sand-covered beet-red face, said, "It's okay, Brownie, you got this."

I didn't have time to be afraid or consider whether I could haul him to the ocean; I only thought, "*We had to win this race.*" Every trainee faced overwhelming odds, and at one time, a decision to continue or quit. Most chose to ring out, while others narrowly hung on.

"Up and over the berm, hit the surf, and back," the instructor bellowed. The whistle blew, and the race was on. Throwing me over his back like a rag doll, Tony sprinted up and over the massive sand hill, leaving the other pairs far behind. Flying down the other side, we made it to the shoreline, and I jumped off as we dove into the Pacific.

"Move, move, move. Let's go!" I said. Soaked, we ran to the berm's base and stopped. Leaning over, I prepared myself.

Covering me like a giant spider over its prey, Tony begged for forgiveness, "I'm so sorry, Brownie, I'm so sorry." As if someone had put a Volkswagen on my back, I sank into the sand, forcing the water to jet from my boots.

Holding my breath, I bore down to stop from collapsing.

Go, go, go!

Slow, methodical steps up, I began my ascent. Grunting, grinding my teeth, and spitting,

Go, go, go!

Tony's arms and legs hung motionless, dragging along as he encouraged me, "Come on, Brownie, you can do it. You're almost there!"

Shaking under his weight, my shoulders and back cramped, and my heart readied to explode when we reached the peak. After sucking air and with a loud groan, I started down the other side. In the distance, instructors stood in amazement as I opened my stride, taking longer steps and letting gravity pull us down. Tony's weight was more than I could control, and I tumbled face first, with his 230 pounds burying me in the sand.

Cresting the berm, the other teams closed in as the instructors called out, "Get up; you're going to lose!" Jumping up with sand blurring my eyes, caked up my nose, and crunching in my mouth, Tony halfheartedly fell across my back. We collapsed over the finish line, moving more like a three-legged race than a fireman's carry.

"You did it, Brownie! We won!" yelped a happy Gumataotao.

Spitting the crystals lining my tongue, I glanced up at the laughing instructors.

"Good job. That was one of the funniest goddamn things I've ever seen," one said. "It pays to be a winner, gents. It pays to be a winner! Brown and Gumataotao, you're secured."

How did I make the impossible possible?

According to Jeff Wise, writer for *Scientific American*: "Hysterical strength, also known as adrenaline rushes, are displays of extreme strength by humans beyond what is believed to be normal, usually occurring when people are in life-and-death situations. When our hypothalamus senses danger, it sends signals to the adrenal glands to release adrenaline and noradrenaline. These chemicals together cause a rise in heart rate and blood pressure, an increase in respiration, dilated pupils, slowing of digestion, and contraction of muscles. A reserve of power is triggered and used in a high-stress situation. You get an adrenaline rush when you do something frightening or in a fight-or-flight situation as the chemicals flood the body. You have extreme reactions and superhuman abilities."

In this second week, we had three runs. On Monday and Wednesday, I fell victim to the goon squad. Now Friday, as we prepared for the week's last conditioning run, terror set in. I hit the running wall. My journey, my dream, was in jeopardy.

Beginning our first sprint soon after leaving the training area on our way past the O-course, my mind pleaded with my body to keep up. Why can't I run faster? We headed south down the Silver Strand, zigzagging for miles up and over the berms, with the group circling back to pick up the usual stragglers and me.

With the class caught up, it was time to return to the compound. Running down the access road near the demo pit, I fell behind again. My breathing was labored, and my legs were fatigued as my class pulled away.

Overwhelmed, I slowed and started making excuses. The weight of my quagmire lay heavy across my shoulders as the sand gripped every step. I became the person everyone told me I was—an unimaginable fear set in that I wouldn't survive another goon squad.

I started crying, yelling, and cursing as my classmates pulled farther away. My sobbing was not from my physical pain but from the fear I was about to fail. Even with no intention of quitting, I was not good enough and didn't know how I would ever be. I swore off crying as useless, but crying was all I had left. Sweat and tears poured down my face; there was nothing more I could physically do.

Lurking close behind, the ambulance taunted me.

Get in, get in.

You're not going to make it, Brownie.

You're not going to be a SEAL.

It is a cliché, but my life flashed before me, all the barriers, hurdles, and mountains. Time compressed as I relived every traumatic event.

In that moment, my life changed forever.

My mind disconnected from what my pain sensors were screaming, and with an altered perspective, I watched hovering above as the situation unfolded. While that sounds crazy, neuroscientists are beginning to understand these Out-of-Body (OBE) experiences, which occur in up to 10% of the population. OBEs happen, according to science, when there is a transition between different states of consciousness and can be caused by disease, extreme stress, or near-death situations. These experiences occur when the brain works in overdrive to integrate sensory information that places a person's sense of self somewhere in space.

Seeing the ambulance only paces behind me and the distance to the pack in front of me, my vision became clear. My body would race and catch up, or it wouldn't, and if I couldn't, I would die right there on the Silver Strand, trying.

This was not physical; my physical-self failed me. This revelation came from the core of my being.

I surged with improbable strength and speed as my stride stretched like never before, catching the class in seconds. As expected, the instructor sprinted, and as the accordion effect reached me, I also dashed. Staring at the man's boots in front of me, I ran in his footsteps. Almost as soon as the sprint started, it slowed, and cheering erupted from my classmates. "All right, Brownie!" they shouted. "Way to go. Keep up."

"Run in the footsteps of the man in front of you."

Crescini's words finally made sense.

My goon squad days were over. I unlocked my limitless potential by releasing my mind's central governor control of my physical ability, catapulting me forward to overcome my most difficult obstacle—myself—and destroy the slow progression to failure.

Everyone's path to success travels through soft sand, trying to catch up and staying with the pack. Overcoming obstacles like the dirty name and carrying Gumataotao reminded me that despite my shortcomings, I could be equal to those around me. Enabling my body to ignore its self-preservation protections was transformative.

BUD/S was the catalyst, not the reason. Without my developed inherent traits and my boyhood experiences, I would not have had the capacity to search inside myself to find the key.

Now, I could pursue my potential without any visual and conceptual perception constraints. I buried the stereotype. My odyssey wasn't over, but from then on, *I* set the bar to measure my progress, and only *I* judged my success.

Only some people who want to be a UDT/SEAL can be, but everyone can be successful. Being a Team guy goes far beyond the title, the job description, and a gold pin. It's not a transformation; it's a revelation. Every person can achieve greatness; it's genetically programmed.

Potential and success are a journey defined by you. Some happily run with the pack, and some find their own direction. My revelation birthed a lifelong philosophy for overcoming obstacles and a never-ending quest to reach my potential.

My classmates either hardened themselves or unraveled. PT, swimming, and running led us to one unimaginable five-day endurance test—Hell Week, a mandatory evolution that sets the gold standard for special forces training worldwide.

The king and his warriors warned David not to fight Goliath, the same as I'd been warned I would never be a SEAL. I was sure my weapons of persistence and determination would bring me victory in this weeklong battle from hell.

15

HELL WEEK: UP TO THE BREAKING POINT

If you are going through hell, keep going.
Winston S. Churchill

Hell Week Goals for Students (an excerpt from BUD/S training material, circa 1981): "Hell Week is termed such because it is the ultimate test of the student's mental and physical capabilities. It is designed to instill in the BUD/S student the qualities and personal characteristics important in becoming a professional in the Special Warfare community: determination, courage, level-headedness, self-sacrifice, and a strong team spirit."

That Sunday, relaxing or sleeping was impossible. The hot iron hissed as I pressed the spray-on starch across the pockets and folds of my inspection greens. Emptying every item from my locker, I squeezed a toothpick, scratching the dirt from its corners and seams, and then sat tepidly waiting on my rack.

Pacing the hallways, counting the cement blocks, and having small talk were all we could do to pass the time as the seconds ticked. Walking by Cooley, I said, "Steve, they can kill us…" and he'd finish with, "…but they can't eat us, and if they do, they won't like it!"

A nervous laugh and a Hoo-Yah! followed. Our trepidation was hidden behind a thinly veiled gladiator persona anticipating the coliseum gates opening.

As the sun set, I went to the berm protecting the barracks. After counting waves, I watched the large sets turn into little ones and back again. The sandpipers darted from the ocean ripples as the surf receded. If we were about to do a timed beach run, the low tide was a beautiful sight, but this tide meant we'd have an incoming tide for the first night of Hell Week.

At 2100 hours, my head sunk into my pillow. I stared at the ceiling after lacing and tying my jungle boots for the fifth time. Noticing my roommate Emihl fast asleep, I thought, "*You lucky bastard.*"

"Break Out," the official beginning of Hell Week, started in the barracks on the first floor. At 2200, I heard rustling outside our windows and men talking in faint low tones, an M-16 rifle bolt smacked forward, and finally, an M-60 belt-fed machine gun cocking handle chambered its first blank round.

Turning to my other roommate Steve Heinze I said, "Shit dude, they're…" The lights went out.

Blam! Blam! Blam!

A bright light flashed, and smoke filled the hallways.

"Steve, smoke, let's get the hell out!"

Instructors in camouflage and gas masks ran into our room. The M-16 bullet casings flew as the intruders commanded, "Get out, get out, and muster up on the grinder, now!" As suddenly as they stormed the barracks, they disappeared into the darkness.

In the blackness, I crashed into the walls, making my way to the front exit, but the door was sealed shut. We stacked up in the main hallway like cordwood.

"Whoever finds a way out, yell," a voice from the dark pleaded amid the chaos.

"The backdoor is blocked. We have to go through this way," another said.

Then the flash and concussion of yet another smoke grenade filled the hallway as the front entrance flung open. And like moths, we flew to the flame. A water jet greeted us at the threshold, catching me in the chest and tossing me back into the building. No tiny garden hose like at the pool; this was a firefighter hose that piled up bodies in the doorway. Toppled like bowling pins, we were pushed into the bushes and covered with sand and mud. On and off, the water blasts went, giving only instants to clear the impact zone until we all made it onto the dark, smoke-filled grinder.

Machine gun fire enveloped the compound as spotlights flashed through the haze while boat crew leaders crisscrossed, searching to find their men. Ken Rice, the class-leading petty officer and senior enlisted man in our crew ran about grabbing Smurfs by our t-shirts and dragging us to our IBS.

"Brownie, stay here. Grab'em if you see any other Smurfs, but don't leave this boat!"

Hearing a piercing whistle, we dove onto the ground, covered our ears, opened our mouths, and crossed our legs—within seconds, bam! and a bright flash only feet away. The concussion grenade blast smacked at my chest like falling on the football during fumble drills.

The sunglass-wearing Master Chief Ray stood over me, his M-60 machine gun ejecting a fountain of searing brass bullet casings. Finding its way between my crossed thighs, a red-hot casing landed like a hornet's sting. I grabbed scorching brass and cried, "Shit!"

Expecting sympathy, I showed the casing to the Master Chief, who sneered and said, "Down!" as he continued firing.

Bam! With another flash and explosion, the second whistle signaled to belly crawl toward the instructor. My thighs burned as I scrapped across the pavement, tearing my bare skin like sixty-grit sandpaper. The third came, the whistle to recover. Jumping to our feet, Rice and the other crew leaders futilely attempted a head count.

We endured the firehose, smoke, concussion grenades, whistles, push-ups, and gunfire for another half hour. Standing at attention beside our IBSs, soaked, bleeding at the knees and elbows—and some, like me, burned—we managed to survive our first trip into the Colosseum.

"Mr. Coleman and Rice drop!" Master Chief Ray barked. "Where's my headcount, gentlemen? You have people missing; where are your men? Drop and push'em out until every man is accounted for." The game went on.

"You have two minutes to change into your greens. Move," the master chief commanded.

Quite the impossible task as everyone reversed their efforts and ran into the barracks while being harassed by the on-again, off-again fire hose.

Upon our return, Hopkins said through his bullhorn, "You're all late. Drop!" More push-ups, whistle drills, smoke grenades, and flash bangs.

After more push-ups, I looked to my side.

"I don't know how many more I can do," I told Emihl, whose feet were perched on the IBS main tube and his chest flat on the grinder.

Laughing, he said, "Shit, Brownie, I quit doing 'em ten minutes ago."

Our push-ups began to resemble anything but. Some preferred to stick their butts in the air; I sagged in the middle. Our arms shook, and our heads and necks bobbed up and down like a chicken pecking feed.

Marching over the berm to the beach at midnight, the incoming tide greeted us. On that cloudless night, the moon shined like a spotlight. The large breakers ended on shore in white froth as we started our "conditioning."

Locking arms, Hopkins gave the command, and we marched into the surf's knee-deep foam.

"Halt, Class 115, take a seat!"

We sat interlinked in 60° F water. Waves pounded my chest and face, pushing me around like seaweed as the swells ran up and down the disappearing shore. With Barnes on one side and Emihl on the other, I pleaded, "Guys, I'm not on the bottom. I'm floating. If you let go, I'm heading to sea with the next wave."

"Don't worry, Brownie; we got ya. If you go, we all go," they assured me.

As the ocean surge pushed our crooked line onto the beach, Hopkins shouted again.

"On your backs, gentlemen! Someone, lead the flutter kick cadence."

Schibler sang out, 1,2,3,1,2,3, ...as the froth crashed over our heads.

Donegan goaded us, "If one person quits, just one, the class can recover and head to the nice warm showers." But no one quit; why would they after only three hours?

"Recover, everyone out of the surf, move! Pair up with a swim buddy. It's time for some hot showers, gents. Line up!"

Hopkins laughed. Men ran, tripped, and fell over each other trying to form the two-man column.

"Too slow! he said. "You almost made it. About face, lock arms." Our heads were toward the ocean this time, and our feet faced the berm.

The first guy quit the second or third time Hopkins sent us back into the waves, precisely what the staff and those who began their quitting spiral were waiting for. And the floodgates opened. Classmates broke from their locked arms one by one, moaning, "I'm done! I can't do this anymore; there's no way I can do this for five days."

Each must have decided they wouldn't make it even before the night started. Having made excuses and justifications, they gave up. The option to ring out and go to the regular Navy seemed more attractive than enduring that night, much less the entire week and the next five and a half months. My resolve may have hardened, but I still prayed, hoped, and counted the seconds for the evolutions to end. As Crescini said, "Don't think about tomorrow or even an hour from now; finish the evolution."

"Which days are the strongest?" Emihl cracked, spitting salt water, his chin quivering. "Sa-Sa-Saturday and S-Sunday...the rest are *weekdays*! Why don't squirrels swim in cold water? Because their nuts shrink!" He laughed. The jokes never stopped as we feigned confidence by telling each other that so many others made it before us, and we would, too. We all would.

Already exhausted and only hours into Hell Week, my weakness proved superficial, like running too fast on my first lap for the BUD/S screening test—a tiredness regular people experience daily. We hadn't begun to scratch the surface of exhaustion.

The instructors pushed us physically in the beginning hours and days, for as the week progressed, our bodies would begin to fail, leaving our minds to command our feeble movements.

Later that night, blessed with our new IBS, we navigated a picture-perfect night rock portage landing and extraction. Not every classmate was so lucky. Waiting for our second attempt, an ambulance with lights flashing raced down the beach from the jetty loaded with an unfortunate classmate. Not wearing protective helmets as they do today, I heard he smashed his head on the rocks after being thrown from his rubber boat.

I didn't know who he was and can't recall asking. He was from another boat crew, and we were losing men daily. The effort to care was exhausting and impossible, and instructors led by example, casting off quitters like toenails needing to be clipped. Like a simmering pot on the stove, someone quitting didn't weaken the broth; it made it stronger, more concentrated, and better.

Wet and cold for over a day and a half, our body temperatures plummeted. Bordering on hypothermia, our next evolution, treading water at the steel piers, would be the endurance test to defeat our mind's self-preservation control mechanism. Consciously and subconsciously, our brains would command us to swim to shore, get out, and survive. It was easy to listen, swim in, walk up to an instructor, and quit. But then the bell was waiting.

In the dead of night on Tuesday, we stowed our IBSs on the ramp along the pier.

Coleman asked me, "How are you holding up?"

"I'm freezing and haven't even got in yet, sir." I said.

"I hear ya, me too, but this is only one hour. When we're done, we hit the chow hall for some hot coffee and food. Hang in there, Brownie."

The corner warehouse security lights reflected like stars on the bay's flat surface. At 2300, we walked down the ramp and into the still-black water. Entering, the bay slowly crept into my jungle boots, filling any void and saturating my thick woolen socks.

"Hey Barnsie, you got any chocolate bars tucked in your pants?" I asked. "I can sure use a Snickers right now."

Clay said, "I got a couple stashed nearby. Let's finish this, and I'll give you both of them Brownie."

With our boots tied at their laces and slung over our necks, we began treading for our fifteen-minute test. With less than six percent body fat, I didn't float, so I created a scheme to cheat—I grabbed two zip-lock bags and put them in my shirt pocket. Staying afloat in the darkness, I inflated one at a time, putting it under each armpit. With the bootlaces digging into my neck, pulling me down, I swam in circles wincing from the cold but staying afloat.

Nearing the fifteen-minute mark, I slipped underwater. Coming up for a breath, instructor Hall said, "Brown, I need to see your face, or I'll pull you, and you'll fail." In a panic, I pushed off the pier with my foot to stay on the surface, a failing offense. I waited for my punishment…but nothing came. Or perhaps Hall choose not to see.

When the whistle blew, I discovered my armpit bags had disappeared. Their usefulness was more mindfulness than buoyancy. Treading was over, but we had another forty-five minutes in the bay. Permitted to float using our training, we all removed our pants, tied the legs' ends, and inflated them.

Bare butts broke the surface as we removed and filled our trousers like balloons, but the joking stopped. Trembling, with lips pale blue, we reached our end. After forty-five minutes, the cold penetrated so deeply from the 60° F water that I could feel nothing. I merely existed.

From under the pier, Hall called out, "Recover, gents! Everyone out."

Swimming to the ramp, I emerged from the bay on my hands and knees, boots slung around my neck, and dragging my pants. Our waxy skin and sloth-like movements revealed our deteriorated state. My bones were cold.

"Class 115, head carry, Mr. Coleman, take your men to midrats." This was a midnight meal in the chow hall.

As we marched, I cringed as my skin touched the wet cotton surrounding me. The cool night air turned our wet uniforms into ice felt coverings, compounding the misery and deepening the agony.

We occupied only a few tables next to the food line in the large, brightly lit, warm building. Struggling to direct my hand to grasp and hold the hot coffee cup, my first gulp scalded yet had little effect, diminishing the shivering tremors. *How in the hell can I go for another three days?* I asked myself. It was unfathomable that anyone could continue at this pace and in these conditions. I was sure they were killing us, but I should have realized we were winning. We were still alive.

Staring at each other, the saltwater puddles formed under our tables as we hunched over our piled-high trays. Suddenly, Loo and Ross, Strom, and Kelz started laughing. As others joined in, pancakes and bacon shot from our mouths as we laughed.

"What the fuck else can they do to us?" Schibler said, shaking his head.

"Yea, fuck them! Hoo-Yah! Hell Week!"

Then everyone, in unison, "Hoo-Yah! Hell Week!"

With our arms in the air, we chanted.

"Hoo-Yah! Hoo-Yah! Hoo-Yah!"

And there, across the table, my dischuffed, stubble-faced classmates were smiling. They were smiling because we had won a decisive battle—the battle within us and the one being waged by everyone and everything else. We were led to believe it was us against the world, and in those moments it was.

I was honored to be in that nearly empty building that night. The sailors and civilians who ran the base, the clinics, the support boats, and the chow hall were all there for us, and they were in awe that we had survived so far.

Dwindling to thirty-ish men from over 100, we refused to quit, but that's not enough to win. There were three more days of Hell to endure.

Thinking back on my final goon squad experience and the epiphany on my soft sand run, I realized everything was possible except failure.

16

HELL WEEK: TIJUANA MUD FLATS

Men are not prisoners of fate but of their minds.
Franklin D. Roosevelt

Prussian general and military theorist Carl von Clausewitz said, "Every plan is a good one—until the first shot is fired." Imagining and planning how you will react is helpful; discovering what you will do is enlightening.

Our class was dwindling, leaving us to realize who could not cope with the ever-changing battle plan. The cold, wet, sleepless nights revealed our inner discipline or lack of fortitude. The Smurfs held together by taking every advantage and capitalizing on our individual strengths.

Wearing women's pantyhose became my second attempt to cheat. After putting on the nylons, I ripped out the feet and pulled the leg part of the nylon up under my UDT shorts to be undetected. The stockings kept my thighs from chaffing and added a warm layer, although warm is an exaggeration. Thankfully, they stopped the sand from tearing the skin off my crotch.

For weeks, Master Chief Ray chimed, "Cheat if you must, but don't get caught, 'cause if you do, shame on you." His words remained in my thoughts as I slid the nylon legs down to my calves each time I changed from my shorts into my green trousers. Like my magic buoyancy zip lock bag's uselessness, the "cheat if you must" pantyhose disintegrated into a twisted waistband after succumbing to the elements.

When you think you have it bad, it sometimes helps to understand what others are going through. My machine gun casing burns from break-out on the first night became bright red welt patches on my inner thighs, and my swollen, pasty feet were wrinkled and blistered, yet my spirits remained high. My injuries were minor compared to some. The unfortunate agonized as the skin around their groin was slowly worn off from the sand and wet clothing wear. Sun blisters formed on noses, lips, and ears. One guy's head swelled, and puss oozed from his welts.

Following a pre-dawn hour-long paddle stowing competition, our IBSs lined the berm's crest. With three days and two more nights remaining, our mouths hung open from exhaustion, and our jaws trembled from the cold as the morning sun hit our backs, causing steam to rise from our shoulders and wilted cotton hats.

"Listen up," Hopkins said through his bullhorn. "On the whistle, you will conduct a surf passage, dump boat drill, then paddle to the Tijuana River on the Mexican border. Are there any questions?"

As tired as we were, the Smurfs scooted over the sea towards Mexico, arriving first at the Tijuana Slough National Wildlife Refuge. Our first-place prize was a nap. We propped up our IBS with paddles into a lean-to on the beach and cuddled up like a newborn kitten litter.

Some argued that waking up after a short nap was more challenging than relaxing. Sleep became a precious commodity. I slept if I got a chance, even if it was only for minutes. Sleeping at a moment's notice, at any time or place, became a learned skill. After the last crew arrived on the border, the braces of our IBS were kicked out, and the inflatable crashed down, jarring us from our rest and jolting us back to reality.

Setting up camp in the wooded area past the high-water mark, we used a single rain poncho as a two-man "A" frame tent. "Camp Swampy by the Sea" would be our home for the next sixteen hours.

With the tide going out, we moved inland to begin our games in the river mud. As we sat in the mud, we formed a human chain by wrapping our legs around the next man's waist. Like a centipede, each seven-man chain moved using only our arms. The winners rested while the losers carried each other into the swamp again and again. The stench of river bottom mud caused some to gag and everyone to hope the slime was nothing more than a biodegrading marsh. The untold truth was we wallowed in cesspool muck from Mexico.

Back and forth in the sludge, we raced until our green uniforms, bright orange kopak life preservers, and skin color were chocolate brown. As the sun began to set and with only the whites of our eyes visible, our instructor's attitude and the tide shifted. The playful afternoon with fanciful games was soon transformed by their Cheshire Cat grins.

Rushing toward us like a biblical plague, the 60° F ocean tide overcame the sewage warmth, filling the trenches we'd worn into the river bottom.

How quickly our own mindset and attitude changed. The leisurely competitions became an all-out race for survival from the frigid ocean tide taking over our pit. The losers were repeatedly cast back into the freezing bog as the sun set and until the final competition whistle. But no one escaped the final order to hit the surf to rid ourselves of the Tijuana sewage.

After the Pacific rinsed what it could from our shivering bodies, the instructors announced "chow time" as they sat around their fire pit. I couldn't wait to devour whatever was in the small white box in the truck's bed.

"No, gentlemen," Hopkins said. "No eating without protection. You must guard your six. Mr. Coleman, organize your men and dig a safe place for everyone to eat."

We dug a two-foot-deep hole with our paddles big enough for the entire class to squeeze in. Finally, Hopkins said, "Gentleman, come get your boxes, but no one eats until the last man is in the hole. Now go, you're already late!"

Tearing through the cardboard and plastic as if I hadn't eaten in weeks, I intended to devour every crumb. But from the darkness came a screech, "incoming," as instructors threw sand, covering us. Sheltering my cold bologna sandwich between bombs, I stuffed the remaining bread triangle into my mouth, crunching through sand nuggets and washing the wad down with warm canteen water.

Sitting under the stars, we became one damp, quaking pile of hungry men in a ditch on the Mexican border. Depending on your perspective, we were either pathetic or brave. Huddling like chain-gang prisoners, we waited, not knowing what would come at us next from the dark.

Instructors continued to sniff out weak trainees, testing their commitment to their classmates and mission.

Trainee Lydee was a target. With a marijuana leaf tattoo on his arm and an instructor's bullseye on his back, he moaned and groaned, causing him and everyone else extra push-ups. He may have been a liability, but he was our classmate. "You're only as fast as your slowest man," instructors would say, so in solidarity, we encouraged him not to ring out but to shut up.

Sitting in our giant meal hole, instructors focused on him. As the night grew colder Lydee huddled in the middle of the man pile and mumbled, "I'm freezing!"

From out of the dark came, "Lydee hit the surf!" from instructor Donegan.

Lydee stood up and said, "No! I'm not hitting the surf."

Donegan replied, "Fine, you don't have to; all you have to do is *quit*. A hot shower and comfortable bed await you back at the barracks."

"Okay, I quit!" he said. "You win. Ya'll been trying to get me to quit since I started, and you win, I quit."

"That's what they want, don't give in!" we said. But he left the hole, got in the ambulance, and drove off.

The reasons to quit overwhelmed Lydee. He didn't succumb because they told him to hit the surf; we'd all done that a thousand times. He gave up because he lost his battle within. A prisoner of his mind, the negatives won.

His excuse, "I'm quitting because you want me to," was his scapegoat.

If removed from training, you packed your seabag, and you were gone. I know because that's what happened to me. Once medically rolled back, I emptied my locker, and by the time I returned to the quarterdeck, my temporary orders were waiting.

Removal, no matter where we were, was instantaneous because BUD/S was about winning. No second-place trophies, no consolation prizes, and no hard feelings. You disappeared from everyone's sight and thoughts. Again, the broth got better.

In the truck on his way back to the compound, Lydee became just another guy who quit. Hell Week, however, continued. The night hours slowly ticked by, filled with torment and competition. The winners sat by the fire while the losers hit the surf and became sugar cookies.

At midnight, we paired up to share a single poncho tent. For the next sixty minutes, one person got out from under their tiny cover and ran the camp's perimeter, yelling the time (0001, for instance) and, "All is well at beautiful Camp Swampy by the Sea." Upon return, he tapped his mate, who advanced the time by one minute while running. If you dozed off with a guy screaming, you might be able to rack up a few minutes of sleep. But, if the sentry failed to execute, everyone would find themselves sitting in the ocean. Every man in their tent sensed the urgency to be on time to run. Camp Swampy was a test to see who would value themselves over their classmates' safety and security, a challenge we passed convincingly.

The night's final evolution was a hide-and-seek game called Escape and Evade. For three hours before sun-up, we disappeared into the dunes. If found by an instructor, you'd be in the surf until sunrise. Emihl and I bolted, hiding behind a dwarf palmetto.

Thinking we were being hunted, we dodged the silhouettes bobbing over the mounds.

As a helicopter flew over, we dove under the scrub brush. Distant flashlights shined in search, so we ran, circling back and moving toward camp. At first light, the whistle blew, ending the game. Upon our return, we discovered the instructors sitting around the fire. No one had been searching for us after all.

"What about the helicopter and the flashlights?" we asked.

"That was Border Patrol chasing illegals. No one got caught!" laughed Hopkins, "and we didn't have to chase you, so we're all winners."

Once again, assembled nut to butt in our dinner pit, Hopkins asked, "Who wants McDonald's?"

It was Thursday morning, and we were weak, exhausted, cold, and hungry when someone said, "I want The Big Breakfast!"

Hopkins took out a pen and a yellow legal pad and, like a waitress, began taking orders for McMuffins, pancakes, and coffee. After carefully documenting each hopeful request, he jumped into the gray Navy 4x4 pickup and disappeared on a mission to retrieve our piping-hot meals.

"Do you think he's going to McDonalds?" Emhil asked.

"Sure, why would he take all that time to write everything down?" I said.

Returning only minutes later, he backed the truck and dropped the tailgate, revealing the stacks of cold box lunches. Laughing, Hopkins said, "I wanted to give everyone a delicious meal, but you all were late coming in from your last evolution, so box lunches it is." As we did the night before, we sat in the hole and ate sandy bologna sandwiches between the "incoming" sand bombs.

Leading up to Hell Week, my crew created a plan to hide candy at strategic locations around the barracks, on base, and particularly in our IBS. On our paddle back from Mexico, as we pulled away from our competitors, Coleman gave us the incentive that if we had a large enough lead after the next fifty strokes, we would stop paddling, and everyone would be rewarded with a stashed treat. The closest boat but a speck on the ocean behind us, we approached our goal, yet a different order came.

"Let's do fifty more before we rest."

Clay Barnes, a most mature and calm man, turned to our leader, put down his paddle, and said, "No! You said we would have a break and have a candy bar, and that's fifty. I want my chocolate!" It was Clay's breaking point.

"All right, gents, Barnsie says it's time for a Snickers," Coleman said. So, we stopped, pulled the crushed, melted, and salty wet confection from under the IBS inflatable floor, and sat floating in the still Pacific on a sunny day, enjoying our treat.

I attended many team-building exercises during my twenty-eight years as a federal special agent. The efforts, while sincere, had short-lived effects. Why? Because for a group to bind, everyone must be invested in more than a superficial way and have complementary personalities.

In a *Harvard Business Review* article, "Great Teams Are About Personalities, Not Just Skills," Dave Winsboroug and Tomas Chamorro-Premuzic wrote, "A study of 133 factory teams found that higher levels of interpersonal sensitivity, curiosity, and emotional stability resulted in more cohesive teams and increased prosocial behavior among team members. More effective teams were composed of a higher number of cool-headed, inquisitive, and altruistic people. Along the same lines, a large meta-analysis showed that team members' personalities influence cooperation, shared cognition, information sharing, and overall team performance. In other words, who you are affects how you behave and how you interact with other people, so team members' personalities operate like the different functions of a single organism."

While it is commonly accepted that, in general, personality is inherited, the most effective teams are those whose members understand their personality traits as well as those of their team members.

Taking turns accommodating each other's highs and lows, we never let the worst moments bring us down. We Smurfs were determined not only to finish but also to win Hell Week as we relished another victory and napped under our lean-to IBS.

After our Thursday midrats, we set off on the "Around the World Paddle," trudging south to the end of Silver Strand State Beach, coming ashore, crossing Highway 75 and into San Diego Bay to begin a long predawn trip back, guided by the brightly lit base in the distance. As dawn broke, the hallucinations began.

Cobb pulled his paddle from the water and yelled, "Stop, don't you see the wall?" His face was white with fear, and his shoulders sank, realizing what he'd said and done. "Oh my God, I swear it was there," he said.

Barnes called out "sharks," but no one else saw them.

Cooley flinched from paratroopers falling from the sky and phantom ships bearing down on us. I fell asleep mid-paddle, slumped, and began to slide overboard.

Coleman, grabbing my shirt, yanked me back onto the main tube, where I continued stroking like a wind-up toy with an eternal spring.

As exhausted as I felt only hours into Hell Week, now, five days later, I couldn't comprehend my limit. The week's rhythm of moving and eating became an endless cycle that, in my mind, could be endured as long as commanded. My delirious and improbable sense of invincibility obscured my absolute vulnerability.

The welcome morning sun dried our damp, musty greens as they hung off our tattered bodies. Easily mistaken for a homeless lot, we managed a crisp pre-Hell Week inspection-ready "ATTENTION," standing tall next to our inflatable brother.

By noon, I convinced myself we would soon secure from Hell Week.

"This is it, gents; I think we're done," I said as we elephant-walked north from a Hopkin's three-mile tour of the base.

"I hope you're right, Brownie," Emihl whispered, but Coleman scoffed as he knew better. Instead, we went to the chow hall.

After lunch and in the parking lot, we heard, "Line up, head carry. You are nowhere close to being finished! Mr. Coleman, this class hasn't completed enough Hell Week hours, so another elephant walk is now on the agenda." Hopkins chastised us and said, "You men have been late all week, and we need to make up that time."

"*Shit!*" I thought. We faced another three or four-mile run-walk.

"That's bullshit," someone from the back cried. As we'd done the past five days, we heaved our 200-plus pound IBS onto our heads and began our next evolution.

We once again shuffled around Turner Field and by the steel piers. The base became an endless maze of streets and turns. At 1500, we passed headquarters, and Hopkins abruptly commanded, "Stop, down boat. I'm trying to help this class graduate from Hell Week, but you keep screwing up. Again, you all are too slow. You blocked traffic. You made officers late for meetings, and now the commanding officer, wants to reprimand you all. You may have to go another twenty-four hours to compensate for being late."

Shaking our heads, I whispered to Cooley, "He's full of shit, right?"

An apparently unhappy CO emerged from the large double doors. My head drooped as I thought, "*Damn, I can't believe it; maybe this time Hopkins is spot on.*" Standing atop the stairs, eyeing the battered, stinky lot, he smiled. "I've watched every one of you go through hell, and while I've seen several classes finish Hell Week, I am always deeply moved by the dedication and perseverance of our Navy's finest. Congratulations, Class 115, your Hell Week is secured!"

From the tallest point on my saggy green hat to my torn leather boot tips, I was truly happy. Arms to my side, I leaned to my left against the IBS with a blank stare. "*It's over!*" The class cheered with the loudest Hoo-Yah we'd ever produced. We hugged, shook hands, and congratulated each other. Then we Hoo-Yah'd the instructors, especially Hopkins.

But it wasn't over in my mind. Only moments went by before I fretted about returning the IBS back to the training area, washing it, and securing our gear so we could *complete the mission.*

The Smurfs won Hell Week, but I can't recall our prize. Its significance was fleeting. Like those before us, we'd exceeded what common sense would accept and the common man could take.

Bad never lasts forever, and every person will surely endure their form of Hell Week. Not everyone can become a SEAL, but everyone will experience difficult times and either emerge stronger or succumb to the pressures. A failure only exists if you accept it. Failure's definition is a lack of success. The definition of success is an accomplishment. With the belief that every attempt is an accomplishment and a progression to be better, failure can't exist. Never accept failure, never give up, control your perspective, and live up to your potential.

Some who quit came back and graduated in later classes. They didn't see quitting as a failure but a temporary setback, a lesson learned. A setback can lead to a step forward by changing your mindset.

No, not everyone is successful the first time or even the second. Even those who never graduated from BUD/S went away successful because they left better people for having tried.

Failure and success are what you perceive them to be. We are not prisoners of fate.

17

JUST UDT

History is written by the victors.
Winston Churchill

Naked guys were scattered in and outside the barracks, propped up with oozing wounds covered in Neosporin. We protected our modesty with only a towel draped over our privates, as being naked was the least of our problems.

Lying in the sun and the shade, we were doing everything possible to heal the missing skin from our backs, fronts, heads, and groins. Our water-logged, swollen, pasty feet regained their original size, and we prepared for Monday.

I slept only ten hours after Hell Week secured and woke antsy to do something, anything. The experience imprinted me, and I would now always anticipate my next evolution.

At 0500 Monday morning, my rested class mustered for PT. The gracious instructors treated us to a light exercise regimen, with our only run that week, a Friday morning "good time" jog through Coronado's residential district.

Crazy with excitement, we were ready to fly through the streets by the week's end. Running as if we had wings on our sneakers and in civilian nylon shorts, we glided by the beautiful homes, drawing crowds as we ran by.

Singing cadence songs like choirboys, we laughed and joked. But like any other evolution, this one would last only so long, and we'd soon be back in our greens and jungle boots, remembering we'd only completed five of twenty-three weeks of training toward becoming frogmen, the Navy's most elite warriors.

The idea of Navy frogmen started with the Underwater Demolition Teams. From the first concepts in Hawaii and Fort Pierce, Florida, during World War II, UDT cleared the way for amphibious landings in the Pacific. Their missions continued into the Korean War, and in the 1950s, UDT first operated beyond the beach, executing night raids against the enemy and employing guerrilla tactics.

The successful experimental programs in Korea were adopted for regular use by the late 1950s. Aqua-Lung development, locking in and out from submerged submarines, parachuting, and testing miniature submersibles were incorporated into UDT training.

With the collapse of French Indochina in 1954 and communist influence in the region from the Soviet Union and the People's Republic of China, the US recognized the need for and the benefit of unconventional warfare. In 1961, the Navy moved to organize such an e:ort by pulling men from UDT teams and, in early 1962, created SEALs. The SEALs—the letters of which stand for Sea, Air, and Land Teams—involved counter-guerilla warfare missions and clandestine maritime operations. SEALs trained South Vietnamese forces, infiltrated behind enemy lines and ambushed and raided to capture highly prized prisoners.

From the 1960s until UDT and SEALs merged in 1983, the question of who was "better" swirled among the Teams. While I don't know if there is a correct answer, it is commonly accepted that without UDT, there wouldn't be SEALs.

We were all BUD/S graduates and always tried to best the other by competing at every opportunity, including intra-base sports competitions. No matter who won, we'd end up at the local bar drinking beer and talking up the "frog hogs," which is what we called the women who frequented the bar. As I started my frogman journey, I admired old-school UDT or, as SEALs called them, "Just UDT."

Frogmen operated in the water, conducting hydrographic reconnaissance ("Hydro Recon"). Simply put, we surveyed and mapped from the shoreline to a depth of 21 feet *before* any other troops were deployed. This depth allowed the largest beach landing craft to safely land and offload.

We boarded patrol boats with an IBS tied alongside and were transported to the beach. As the boat sped parallel to the shore, one by one, unarmed swimmers got the "go" command and slid off the rubber boat into the water.

While treading, we formed a straight line, lowered a lead weight on a string to determine the depth, and then recorded that information. After the recon, the speeding boat retrieved us using a sling to pluck us from the ocean. The cartographer collected the data on the ship and drew a chart for the amphibious craft to follow.

We were also cast and recovered by CH-46 helicopter. The chopper flew at an altitude of fifteen feet and, moving forward, dropped swimmers into the water. As my classmates exited the helo on our first attempt, I sat on the helo's floor, my legs dangling from the 3x3 opening called the "Hell Hole."

As the bay scooted underneath, I leaned over, grabbing the thick steel bar that spanned the hole. With a tap on my shoulder by the crew chief and a "go," I swung through, and stretched out from my fingers to my toes under the aircraft. Once in position, I looked up through the hole and let go. There was only silence and stomach butterflies while falling, and then *impact*. Toes pointed and legs together, I knifed into the water at thirty mph.

The extraction was next. As in a James Bond movie, the helo swooped in and dropped a rope ladder, dragging the first rung across the surface. The man before me reached for the highest rung and scurried up as fast as possible as the chopper got to me. With a tight grip and my feet on a ladder high in the air, the bird dipped, and I crashed back into the bay.

Damn! I held my breath as the turbulence began to peel my hands from the rung. Within seconds after being dunked, I was yanked out and launched into the air, clinging to the ladder with a death grip as the helo regained altitude. "*Climb! Go! Go!*" I thought as we approached the next swimmer. The crew chief waved at me to climb. Once in the chopper, he slapped my back.

"Hell, son, I thought we lost you!"

"No way Chief. I was too afraid to let go. You said, hold on no matter what, and that's what I did."

So young and impressionable, I did everything the instructors told me to do. We all did; it's how we survived.

What was the common thread for those who finished First Phase? We didn't resemble each other or sound alike, but undoubtedly, we shared character traits. Humans are 99.9 percent genetically identical; the 0.1 percent difference makes us individuals.

Plomin writes in *Blueprint* that genetic influences are probabilistic propensities, not predetermined programming. Collectively, we took different paths yet developed our 0.1 percent differences enough to bring us together and succeed when most couldn't. Was there a single reason *why* we were successful?

The easy answer is that we didn't quit. Not quitting was the minimum to stay in training and guaranteed you nothing. The true but complicated answer is that we all found ways to succeed.

We progressed and became a family. No one cared about my size or rank; we were all equal going forward, and I was happy with that. Our hair grew, and our presence evolved. That weekend, we received our brown t-shirts, and our helmets were painted blue for dive phase.

Surprisingly, our class continued to shrink.

18

I WANT TO BE UNDER THE SEA II

Be careful what you wish for, lest it come true!
Aesop's Fables

After a year in the Navy, I was finally going to scuba dive, but not in the places nor for the same reasons I did before. "Leisure" and "recreational" weren't used in BUD/S. Scuba was a tool to complete a mission, something to master as we pushed our limits.

We mustered on the grinder for PT. Sporting our UDTs rather than our heavy, long, green cotton pants, my attitude was light and upbeat. I'd made it to Second Phase.

All weekend, I fantasized about the night sneak attacks we would execute on enemy ships—swimming into harbors undetected, planting explosives, and escaping as our target was destroyed. Hell Week was behind us, so surely, we'd earned some respect from the instructors.

Our phase officer, Lt. Calland, and our leading petty officer, Senior Chief Hubbard, met us on the grinder. I remembered Hubbard. While hanging from the pull-up bar during Class 114, he opined that one of my legs was shorter than the other when, in fact, I'd pulled my groin muscle. The other instructors didn't recognize me. It was as if I hadn't existed until that day.

"Training is *not* over, and it's only going to get harder," Hubbard said. "If you do not pay attention to detail, you and your swim buddy will die. The pressure in those tanks can cause your lungs to explode," he said as he paced among our ranks. Oh, but that was the common theme; everyone would die if you made a mistake or lacked attention to detail. And while that was true, I became desensitized after hearing it for many months.

As a "certified" open-water scuba diver, I was finally in an enviable position, comfortable in and under the water and familiar with diving physics. Not an officer or a senior enlisted person, I was okay at PT and swimming and no longer the slowest runner; I was invisible. Later, classes would call it being the gray man and a gift.

"One two three, one. One two three, two." I counted the flutter kicks as Master Chief Huey walked over.

Standing over me, he looked down. With his jungle boots touching each ear, he said, "Brown, who the hell are you? I've never seen you before. Did you sneak into this class?"

I tried not to look up because there was a no skivee rule in BUD/S, and since I had his boots on either side of my head, a glance would give me a view I didn't want. He said again, "Brown, did you sneak into this class?"

Chin to my chest, as my feet went up and down, I said, "No, Master Chief, I've been with 115 since the beginning."

"Well," he said, "you've been getting away with murder because no one realized you were here, so *hit the surf!* You've got some catching up to do."

So much for being the gray man or Mr. Invisible. I got up, ran over the berm, and dove into the ocean. Running back to the grinder, I thought, "*Boy, I hope I don't become THAT GUY!*" You know, the one whom instructors focused on to try to weed out—another Lydee. Upon returning, I said, "Hoo-Yah, Master Chief Huey!" and continued the exercise. He walked away laughing and mumbling, "You can't hide anymore, Brown."

For weeks, when Huey came by, I'd hide—scurrying behind the biggest guys like Schibler or Ross. They'd laugh but play along. He must have realized I was hiding, but he never picked on me again. Maybe his brief attention wasn't harassment but an acknowledgment—a thumbs up for making it that far.

The cadre didn't compliment trainees, but they could find ways to make you feel accomplished and good about being there. Soon, I was invisible again, in the middle of the pack, focusing on one evolution at a time.

Early that week, I received the news that I would be meritoriously promoted from Seaman to Third Class Petty Officer because of my first-place finish in Radarman School. The benefit came in time, as my bell-shining duties were left behind in First Phase. As a non-commissioned officer, I'd supervise the watch rather than standing it, making training easier. It paid to be a winner.

The classroom dominated our first week, learning diving physics and safety procedures. We trained with not one but two tanks, called twin 72s, weighing thirty pounds each, over half my body weight. Thankfully, they were lighter than Gumataotao, but I would have to carry these beasts long and far. To don them on my back, Emihl heaved up and held them in position as I worked my way into the harness.

After saying, "I got the weight," he slowly lowered the cylinders.

The first time I gasped, "Oh shit," as the straps dug in.

"You, ok?" Emihl asked.

"Yeah, I'm got'em." They were heavy, but they were now mine. It was just another obstacle like the dirty name.

With the tanks on my back, the thought of being underwater soon gave me relief. All we needed to do was get to the pool as we left the dive locker onto the grinder. Wrong! We were going to PT. Shaking my head in disbelief, I walked out the dive locker door, staring at the feet of the man in front of me. BUD/S would try to make me hate the thing I loved: scuba.

Hubbard took to the podium and said. "This will be a modified PT session. Listen to my instructions and do exactly as I say. Now drop and give me ten push-ups." Squatting to my knees, I got in position and surprisingly rattled off ten push-ups. Hubbard got creative, and we did pull-ups and dips. The exercises' quality and quantity were meaningless. Everyone had to do at least one of everything, and miraculously, I did.

We were tough and in shape, but he made us "earn the right" to slip underwater for our first dive, not something that he gained popularity for. Seeing he'd beaten the class into the grinder, Hubbard ended the evolution. In the long run, the torture had value. The twin 72s never felt as heavy or uncomfortable again.

A far cry from Tommy O'Brien's simple instructions: "Don't hold your breath and breathe through the regulator," our Navy instruction lasted three days, giving us the privilege to walk a quarter mile, tanks on our backs, to sit on the bottom in a damn swimming pool.

I could have been Jacques Cousteau himself and still been required to attend every minute of training. The protocol was strict because the risks were significant. We were about to undergo the most intense underwater test ever designed.

Some had little or no scuba experience, and you could see the terror in their eyes as we made our way to the training tank. The procedures we practiced led to one thing—the final pool competency test. Before it was called "pool competency," the mandatory evolution was known as "pool harassment." The name changed, but the details remained the same. Instructors sent students to the bottom in scuba gear and harassed them to measure confidence, problem-solving, and proficiency.

What frightened me most was the thought of my mouthpiece being yanked out as I exhaled, leaving me without a breath. Using old-style dual hose regulators like on *Sea Hunt* and *Voyage to the Bottom of the Sea*, instructors kinked and tied them in knots to restrict the airflow, sending divers shooting to the surface and failing.

As my test began, I swam along at a depth of 10 feet, waiting. Presented as an oddity, I imagined the instructor chuckling as he glanced down from above at the two steel tanks with arms and legs scurrying across. In the first attack, he pulled off my right fin. Then, my mask was plucked from my face. This was no dilemma for me. I'd had my mask ripped from my face in a nearly frozen lake. Finding it,

I put the mask on, pressing against the top and blowing air through my nose, forcing the water out.

The second assault came. My mask was the first to go, and my air supply was shut off. With only half a breath, my hands flailed to find and open the valve behind my head. After one breath, my mouthpiece was yanked and tied around the tank's manifold beyond my reach. Reaching behind and over my head, there was nothing I could do. I was in trouble.

Pulling the harness quick release, I shed my tanks. Resting on the bottom, I cradled the cylinders like a baby while I figured out the problem. My lungs screamed for air, but I had to stay or fail.

Panic and shoot to the surface or decide to push my limits as I'd done before? I cranked the valve on my tank, and bubbles exploded in a stream from the mouthpiece. Stuffing it back in my mouth, I cleared the water and inhaled deeply. *"Whew...that was close!"* I thought. With my tanks cinched next to my chest, I continued swimming, bouncing with one fin and no mask.

Coming down to finish the job, the instructor pulled the 72's from my grasp, and my mouthpiece ripped out, tearing one hose from the manifold. The torn piece flailed, spewing air; I was out of options. Dropping my weight belt, I made the slow ascent to the surface, my tormentor in tow.

"You're lucky you didn't ditch the tanks the first time I took your mouthpiece, Brown; you would've failed," he said. "Well done. Now recover your gear and get out."

SEALs don't dive for fun, well, not in training. Scuba got us to a target and back; now it was time to learn how to navigate underwater. Using a compass and estimating how fast we could swim got us where we needed to go. Swim partners were connected with a (rope) buddy line. Attached to the buddy line was another line with a three-foot round inflatable orange buoy so the instructors could see if we were going in some wayward direction, like to Mexico by accident. (It happened.)

We moved on to night courses because that is when SEALs operate—in the darkest, wettest, nastiest weather. Why? Because we want the people at the target to be preoccupied with anything besides us sneaking up on them.

With zero visibility, our night dives tested our focus. Swimming in the blackness was a mind control game, knowing our senses could only detect objects within inches. The only light was the bay's phosphorescence (algae) glow. With it, I could see Emihl's outline as he pushed through the dark like an apparition while we swam full speed ahead.

As the designated driver on our first night course, I led our team with a compass and depth gauge. After setting a bearing using the lights of the naval base across the bay to backlight the target ship in the distance, we pulled our buoy into the bay.

This night was the very thing I fantasized about as a kid. For us, the stakes were high; it was us vs. them, the scenario from which action films are made.

Marking our time, we slipped underwater, following the contour and leveling at ten feet. The ship, only one-half mile away, seemed easy pickings. We planned to plant our limpet mine, an explosive device we attached magnetically to the ship's hull and return to the beach in under an hour.

Only a few minutes into the dive and swimming our fastest, I hugged the bottom intently, watching the compass while Emihl hovered above in zero visibility. Then, there was a hard pull on our buddy line. Yanked backward, I smashed into Emihl's face like a Keystone cop. Pushed sideways, my mask flooded. Something had a hold on us, and we couldn't move.

Repositioning and clearing my mask, I discovered he and I were nose-to-nose, saying, "What the hell?" Reaching down, I found a thick cable between us. As we untangled, our buoy line was pulled, so we surfaced. A flashlight glared in our eyes.

"What in God's name is going on down there, Brown? Are you two fighting a sea monster?" Mask up, regulator out of my mouth, I pleaded our case. The instructor said, "Quit screwing around and get moving! We don't have all night to finish this evolution."

Our days were extended into the night. We did PT, soft sand and timed runs, timed ocean swims, and conducted underwater navigation courses two nights a week. The pace didn't slow; it hastened like a bass drum, faster and faster. Our only solace was ridding ourselves of the twin 72s and transitioning to the much lighter closed-circuit rigs.

But first, we had to earn the right to shed our sixty-pound tanks.

19

HE'S NO DIFFERENT THAN THE REST OF YOU

Treat a man as he is, and he will remain as he is. Treat a man as he can and should be, and he will become as he can and should be.
Stephen R. Covey

The evolutions came and went, but the one that I failed stayed in my mind. As much as I wanted to forget about Mary, she became a recurring dream. It was a dream that she said yes to my proposal, and we were engaged. Why did the break-up haunt me? Girls were plentiful in Coronado and San Diego, and I should find one, I tried to convince myself. Or was Mary the one, my soulmate?

In a February 2022 BBC article, *The allure of The One stretches across time and cultures,* author Katie Bishop wrote: "The concept of a soulmate might have existed for thousands of years. On a planet of nearly eight billion people, it's quite a coincidence that so many people's soulmates are just in the next classroom. Yet the idea of a soulmate has persisted across numerous societies and time periods – what is it about the concept of *The One* that people find so irresistible?"

Brad Wilcox, a professor of sociology and director of the National Marriage Project at the University of Virginia, notes a rise in the appeal of soulmates since the 1970s with the advent of what he calls the "me decade" and a culture of individualism shifted our approach to relationships.

Whatever the science behind it, I couldn't shake the desire to rekindle our relationship and correct a failure. A failure I could not accept. But I still had a lot of training in front of me, and I couldn't afford the distraction of a serious relationship.

Diving with twin 72s would soon end, and our spirits were high as we entered our final underwater evolution with the steel monsters. Our transportation to and from the beach was an old cattle semi-trailer. The rickety wheeled metal box was fitted with spartan welded seats, providing a welcome albeit uncomfortable ride.

Standing on the bay side of the Silver Strand at midnight, swim booties filled with water and fins in hand, we waited to board the lighted car. Having completed our last mile-long navigation course, we were all smiles.

To our surprise, the transport pulled away without us.

"Gentlemen, it's time to earn your new rigs," Hubbard said. "Empty your booties. We're running back to the compound."

I gasped. *"Run with twin 72s?"*

After removing our regulators and weight belts, we loaded them into a truck, and with tanks strapped high on our backs, the order came—"Class 115...forward!" Lighting the way with a spotlight, our instructor-guide ran in front as we sang cadence songs.

Our footwear was never intended for running, and the slippery neoprene slid from side to side, collecting sand and sawing away at my ankles and feet as we inched our way. Except for our guiding light, we crossed Silver Strand Blvd in complete darkness. My hands reached behind, propping up the weight that dug a groove into my wetsuit top. Heading north, we stopped at the O-course next to the last horizontal ladder, where I prayed we would rest.

"Gentlemen, file in," Hubbard ordered, "cross the ladder, the hurdles, and fall back in. "Move! The longer it takes, the less sleep you will have."

"Oh my God, there's no way!" I'd done pull-ups and push-ups with twin 72s, but this was a fourteen-rung ladder.

Watching from the back as my classmates swung from rung to rung with little effort, I cheered. There would be no monkey swings or skipping rungs like on my regular O-course runs. One mistake, one hand or finger slip, and I would be on my back in the sand.

As I reached out to begin, the others from the class completed the evolution. The tanks pulled like Albert Kita wrapping his meat hooks around my neck.

"One, two, three," I said. Pulling upward with every muscle in my fingers, hands, and shoulders, my head cocked back as I stared at the ladder and into the starry night sky.

"Eight, nine, ten, eleven," I continued. With only a few more to go, I stopped—a huge mistake. Water dripped from my sandy booties as I hung motionless, wincing.

If I dropped, I would be the only one who didn't make it. I sensed Hubbard staring and waiting.

"Brown, are you gonna finish this?" He said in an encouraging tone. "We don't have all night. Get it done!"

Gathering strength I didn't have, I started swinging. Back and forth, back and forth.

"Twelve, thirteen," and "fourteen." I finished.

"Okay, get off there, Brown, move." Hubbard scoffed. Dropping to the ground, I collapsed under the weight.

"Are you hurt?" he asked.

"No, Chief." In the distance, my classmates cheered as I stood. Covered in sand, booties sideways on my feet, I reached the first hurdle.

Two years earlier, at the YMCA, simply walking to the pool with the steel tank seemed a miraculous feat. That night, I had to leap over six four-foot-high obstacles—each wooden beam dug into my torso, followed by a long drop into the sand. By the sixth, my wet suit was shredded, and my chest bled as I ended the course on my hands and knees.

Emihl and Barnes ran over to help but were admonished by the instructor.

"Stay where you are," he said. "He's no different than the rest of you. Let him finish."

Hubbard turned to me and ordered, "Brown, recover and return to formation."

After standing, I shuffled to the back of the line, my safe place. After straightening my tanks and adjusting my booties, the class gave a loud "Hoo-Yah, twin 72, O-course!"

Convinced or brainwashed, after fifteen weeks, I believed I was unstoppable. In a funny way, like Monty Python's Black Knight. No matter the situation, "It was just a scratch," and the fight continued.

We dove three closed-circuit rigs: the Emerson, the Drager LAR V, and the MK 15. Each was more complicated and modern than the last. Closed-circuit means the inhaled air and the exhaled breath is recirculated in the system. With only oxygen being replenished in the closed system, a small tank of O2 was all that was needed, resulting in the rigs being light and compact. With no gas released into the water, there were no bubbles, making the underwater experience silent except for the sound of our lungs sucking in and pushing out. With that, the water's blackness became more intense. On night dives, I often wondered what was in front, atop, or below, lurking beyond our senses.

Our days went from twelve to sixteen, sometimes twenty hours. Hell Week taught us that we could operate for extended periods with no sleep. This phase revealed we could complete repetitive operations for weeks with little rest and still maintain attention to detail. One slip-up—a strap misplaced or a missing O-ring— meant First Phase-level punishment. Every day was harder than the last, but so were we.

My classmates were alike in many ways but also different. Some loved chewing tobacco, some ran, and others, like me, searched for girls on our brief weekends.

I had a cool red sports car, and Bill, a classmate, and I set off for the movies one Saturday night. Standing in line at a cinema, we noticed two attractive gals.

"Hey Dave, let's see if they're here alone. Maybe they'd be interested in two future SEALs," said Bill.

"Okay, But you have to do the talking; pretty girls usually run when I open my mouth."

Bill ducked under the zig-zagged ropes separating us from the girls and said, "Hi ladies, how'd you like to go to the movie with two future Navy SEALs?" He sure looked the part—tall, handsome, and strappy. At best, I was a little version.

They giggled, "Oh really? Are you two sure you want to see this movie? Because we don't. We didn't have anything better to do," the blond said with excitement. "Maybe we do now." I couldn't believe it; he got the girls with one line. One thing led to another, and we skipped the movie and cruised the streets of San Diego.

Like a romantic comedy scene, we squeezed into my two-seater convertible, cranked up the radio, and sang songs from America and The Eagles. The blond gravitated to Bill while the petite, curly-haired brunette hung on my arm the entire evening. So, this is how it works after high school? I was giddy. I had an evening companion.

Not old enough to drink alcohol, we spent hours driving around, eating, talking, and laughing. I'm unsure if others in the class had done it, but we snuck our guests back to the barracks late that night for a make-out session on the vacant third floor.

Out of my element, the petite, curly-haired cutie took charge. Always the guy that girls said no to, I'd never experienced being pursued, yet there I was with the young lady taking off all her clothes. What do I do? Be careful what you ask for! For me, "girlfriend" was two words: a friend and a girl. This situation turned it into one word—girlfriend.

Oh no, what the heck did I do? I hardly knew her and still had feelings for my Pennsylvania sweetheart, Mary. But that didn't stop me. Bill didn't see the blond after that first encounter, but he asked me later if I was going to see my "Cinema Girlfriend," and the nickname stuck.

I'd given the Navy 100% of my attention, effort, blood, sweat, and tears. My Cinema girlfriend became a welcome weekend distraction, a slice of life I hadn't experienced in a long time. I was a different person, and for the first time, I didn't see my new companion as "the one," but certainly the one for now. Unbeknownst to me, she thought differently than I did, and the results would be dramatic. In *Night Moves*, Bob Seger sings, "I used her, and she used me, but neither one cared." In my mind, Seger's lyrics artfully summed up our relationship.

20

FORGING THE INDESTRUCTIBLE

Do not follow where the path may lead.
Go instead where there is no path and leave a trail.
Ralph Waldo Emerson

I measured success one evolution at a time. The feeling of completing each became the source of a dopamine rush and fueled my addiction.

So ingrained was the compulsion to complete each mission that I became anxious for the next and the next. The pursuit morphed into the objective. I wanted to be a SEAL, but I was taken over by the process of becoming one even more. BUD/S enveloped my emotional being, or it's better described as deadening it.

I permitted—no, I welcomed—the thought of suppressing my emotions. Deciding long ago not to cry for any reason allowed me to turn down the road where I closed myself off. And training was the perfect facilitator.

The divorce rate among SEALs is high for many reasons. I won't say the training caused me to be emotionally callous; it was something I was open to. The environment permitted it. I was a willing subject to play the physical and mental tough guy role.

Warm, loving relationships seemed an ill fit for the job. The curriculum didn't address how to manage your family life or how to be a great husband and dad, along with sentry stalking, killing a man with a K-bar knife and a garrote. The two are not mutually exclusive; however, I was a nineteen-year-old boy from Wilkes-Barre, PA, who lacked the maturity to understand that there needed to be a balance between military and civilian life.

The class officers and senior enlisted had a leg up in the emotional intelligence category. They were educated and had life experiences beyond high school. Some had wives, kids, and mortgages. Except for Cinema Girl, I'd had one other girlfriend and parents who left me for Florida.

The Navy never promised, nor did I expect, that it would make me a better person. It helped encourage and reveal the individual I was and unleashed the possibilities within me. That's a double-edged sword. A famous comedian once joked about personalities: "I told a guy, 'Tell me, what is it about cocaine that makes it so wonderful,' and he said, 'Because it intensifies your personality.' I said, yes, but what if you're an asshole?"

It was up to me to become the person I would be. With the military being the dominant force in my life, I molded my personality to fit what made me successful in its structure: a warrior persona with the capability for extreme violence.

Our last phase taught me to kill in multiple ways without remorse. A knife across the throat or plunged through the clavicle or from behind into the kidneys, all designed to eliminate a sentry, the enemy. On the way home, don't forget to pick up some milk and a birthday card for the wife. We lived in a wicked dichotomy.

To embrace the former, the latter suffered. I engaged in each evolution as if my life and my teammates' lives depended upon everything I did. As the saying goes, if the Navy wanted you to have a wife, you would have been issued one in your seabag. Relationships outside the Teams often became collateral damage, and in my case, it was compounded by stubbornness.

In October 1981, we moved to the barracks top floor. This was the intimidating space I first reported to in my initial days as a terrified eighteen-year-old doubting his decisions and ability. Now, the seniors, my classmates, and I strutted around the compound like peacocks. Chiseled-bodied specimens, we resembled the best instructors rather than students. We eyed the new class and made bets on how many would quit in their first week. For obvious reasons, I cheered for the little guys and shared Crescini's advice and inspiration.

As in the First and Second Phases, a time that seemed eons ago, we painted our helmets, this time red and mustered on the grinder. The worst was behind us and gone were the days of endless PT and eighteen-hour diving operations. It was time to shoot machine guns and blow things up. At least, that's the way I envisioned it.

Now hardened, only some instructors could match our conditioning. Our exercises focused on endurance as we trained for extended missions, with our ultimate test being the fourteen-mile beach run and a five-and-a-half-mile open ocean swim.

After enduring the tedious classroom process and before we touched a single bullet, we had to earn the right to load our first magazine. Our small-arms and light weapons training covered the M16 rifle, the M-60 machine gun, the MAC-10 machine pistol, the M203 and M79 40 mm grenade launchers, and the Model 39, 9mm semi-automatic handgun. Our final was a one-on-one exam with an instructor who asked questions as we disassembled and reassembled the arms.

The weapons morphed into a physical extension. At first, the individual stocks, pins, and springs were nothing more than pieces from a forged metal puzzle. The more I handled them, the more personal it became.

Similarly, as you can walk through your own home at night with the lights off because you know the placement of every corner, chair, and ottoman, I broke down and reassembled the weapons with my eyes open and closed while talking about current events, the weather, and the cyclic rate of fire.

Unlike previous tests, the weapons familiarization final didn't involve writing answers, nor did it challenge us physically. This was the ultimate cognitive, finesse, and dexterity assessment. With only one way each weapon would come apart and go back together, the wildcards were the instructor's questions. The left and right brains had to work perfectly in the allotted time.

Walking into the armory, I knew the consequences if I failed, but I'd already decided that wouldn't happen. I aced the test, and the ordeal took only fifteen minutes. Was it stressful? Absolutely. But that's what we trained for. I waited intently for the next evolution. Like an addiction, the pursuit, challenge, and conquest became habitual.

We studied land navigation, patrolling, fire, and maneuvering for three weeks. On a trip to Camp Pendleton, we tested our compass skills on a long-range course. Covering over twelve miles in full gear with weighted rucksacks, we hiked on a beautiful sunny day, making our way without instructors hovering or yelling. That glorious day would be the closest to an "easy day." I was even glad to see our box lunches waiting for us at the halfway point, and this time, we all ate them sand-free.

Three of our final four weeks would be on San Clemente Island. Before leaving for my island getaway, I was happy to learn that after graduation, I would be assigned to UDT-21 in Little Creek, VA. However, that meant I had some unfinished business with Cinema Girl.

Wanting to tell her about my transfer in person, I thought a carnival would be a perfect place to break bad news. As we sat in the parking lot, the music from the festival played, and the Ferris Wheel spun.

I turned to her and said, "I'm being transferred to UDT-21 in Virginia, so I'll be leaving for the East Coast soon." I was sure she would be disappointed.

Instead, her face lit up; she smiled and said, "That's wonderful! I'm coming with you!"

My mind raced, and I thought, "*Oh shit! I wasn't expecting that.*" And like the Grinch who stole Christmas having been caught by little Cindy Lou Who, I had to think up a lie and think one up quick.

"Umm, no, you can't," I told her. "We're not married, and I'll be deploying on a ship. You'll have nowhere to live. You can't come with me."

Her smile evaporated, and her eyes turned down; she opened the door, got out, and walked off towards the carnival. After a few moments, I went after her to explain. I searched in and around the game booths, rides, funnel cake, and hotdog vendors for over an hour, but she had disappeared.

With one more disastrous relationship under my belt, I couldn't wait to be on an isolated island for a while.

Seventy-five miles northwest of San Diego, San Clemente is the southernmost of the Channel Islands of California and is owned and operated by the United States Navy. With only *one* tree mockingly nicknamed the San Clemente National Forest, this big rock off the coast was barren except for a short airstrip long enough to land a passenger jet. On the opposite side, located in a cove, was the BUD/S training area.

The barracks were a well-worn shotgun-style building with old steel Vietnam-era bunk beds, a few mice, and cockroaches. The November winds whipped up a daily ocean chop on the windward side, the nasty side.

As always, we spent our first days in the classroom, this time learning about explosives – terminology, demolition tools, blasting caps, time fuse, detonating cord, etc. Sitting still in a warm room triggered our Hell Week ingrained survival tactic to sleep at a moment's notice in any place or situation. One after the other, as the instructors droned on, we'd take turns doing the rubber neck tango. An ice water dunk tank outside the ramshackle schoolhouse was positioned to accommodate anyone not keeping their eyes open. The instructors could have been dancing girls; still, we would have fallen asleep. I sucked on orange peels to stay awake while the others chewed tobacco and nasty Copenhagen snuff.

One morning, after breakfast, Strom put in a "chew," meaning he jammed snuff in his bottom lip.

Loo wisecracked, "Is that all the chew you can take?" He jammed a quarter can wad of Copenhagen in his mouth, resembling a colossal marble between his gum and lower lip. And with that, the challenge was on.

In a "Hey, watch me do this" redneck moment, more went into Strom's mouth, then into Loo's. This went back and forth as they plowed through the whole can. Their cheeks puffed like two squirrels hoarding nuts.

Instructor Wood, who had been watching the antics, interrupted the duel.

"Ok, gents, time to move into the classroom," he said. Pointing to Strom and Loo, he ordered, "You two first. And no spitting!"

No spitting?

You have to spit; that's the whole point of snuff. The tobacco made you salivate, and you either expelled or swallowed the nasty liquid that built up like a clogged drainpipe.

Filing in the unpainted plywood room, we all sat down. The two tobacco-chewing contestants began squirming in their folding metal chairs, mumbling incoherently as dark, snuff-filled saliva bubbled from their bottom lips. Finally, Strom darted outside, pulling the dark brown mush out, coughing as his stomach pushed his breakfast through his mouth and onto the dirt. Loo, the snuff jam winner, followed close behind.

Despite being hot, cold, wet, tired, and hungry every day for six months, the shenanigans lifted our spirits and brought us closer. For me, we were more than a team; they became my family. Our training experiences led to off-color comments and sometimes crude behavior, but no one took offense. We all understood we were trying to be more human in our inhuman existence.

Receiving the obligatory "you need to pay attention to detail, or the upcoming evolutions could kill you" speech, I realized more in this phase than in the others that the warning was valid. When handling an electric blasting cap, static electricity on you could result in a *Boom*! Fingers or a hand gone in an instant.

Demolition was the most mysterious and dangerous tool of our trade. These little TNT boxes or the C-4, canvas-covered white clay socks seemed so innocuous. Long tubes filled with plastic explosives were treated like Tiffany crystal, and we played with explosive rope powerful enough to remove a limb.

I won't lie; the first time I squeezed the non-sparking crimping pliers, pressing my first blasting cap onto a time fuse frightened me. Squeezing a device designed to explode, I closed my eyes and squinted as I pressed down. It wasn't exactly another day at the office or television store. Our attention to detail kept us alive, and we were aware of that, but it was as if I couldn't be killed, a dangerous distinction for me.

Just because I felt that way doesn't mean everyone did. This is called genotype-environment interaction, or the effect of the environment depends on an individual genotype. The genotype of an organism is its complete set of genetic material. Plomin describes the interactions simply as "different strokes for different folks." In other words, people react differently based on their genes. I doubt others in my class thought they were indestructible, but I did.

We prepared and detonated dozens of demolitions on land and in the ocean. Heaving fragmentation and white phosphorus grenades into a pit and shooting what seemed to be a million rounds of ammunition, our days were intended to breed familiarity and confidence. We were fast becoming the very warriors in body, mind, and heart that our training was meant to create.

Our luck ran out. Planning and the perfect attention to detail are no match for Murphy's Law. Our last water demolition shot went bad. We placed 500 pounds of MK-8 hose in a checkered pattern at a cliff's base. We all wanted to be the person to shout, "fire in the hole!" and turn the handle on the blasting machine to set off the charge. Classmate Bob Ross, who had the highest academic scores, was honored to be the man. Tony Gumataotao, range instructor Rick Wood, and Lt. Yarborough were inside the bunker with Bob. The rest of us either fell back half a mile or were in the nearby bunkers.

The open side of the bunker faced the ocean and was high above where the explosives were located. We and the instructors assumed any rubble from the explosion would go straight up the cliff face and fall harmlessly back down. With the "all clear," Bob cranked the blast handle.

With a thunderous clap, the detonation sent rocks flying, darkening the sky and showering the area with water and shattered rocks. Somehow, some debris defied physics and flew into the bunker. Gumataotao and Wood received minor injuries, but a piece of molten metal the size of an orange struck Bob in the lower leg, vaporizing his right fibula and damaging his upper ankle. And just like that, we were down to twenty-three men.

Taken out by Medevac, Bob spent months recovering. Amazingly, contrary to all predictions, he returned to BUD/S and graduated with Class 116. This was a feat not possible for a mortal man.

Grouped into four six-man boat crews, we conducted fire and maneuver drills, giving us a taste of realistic patrol and ambush exercises. We trained in hand-to-hand combat and knife fighting. It's almost comical to think about it now, as we did stuff right out of the action movies I watched growing up.

One night after lights out, it all hit home: why we suffered doing the torturous physical training for hours, days, and months. Our ability to physically endure an operation could never be in question. We did a million pushups to stay alive, but successful missions involved more than muscle. We had to transform during stress. Our survival teetered on split-second decisions.

Ten months earlier, I checked into BUD/S at five foot three inches tall and weighing 110 pounds. Now, with my graduation at hand, not any taller, I was conditioned to believe, and I was confident that

I was unstoppable, unbreakable, and could complete any mission at any time. Compared to what had transpired over nearly a year, I had just a few *easy* days ahead.

But as the saying goes, the only easy day was yesterday.

21

FINAL NIGHT SURF PASSAGE

Everyone's immortal until they're not.
Victoria Schwab

Our boat crew, nearly identical to the Smurfs in the First Phase, prepared for a night surf passage as evening fell. Me, George Coleman, Ken Rice, Ken Emihl, Clay Barnes, Dan Fozzard (a new addition), and Steve Cooley had all survived six months together, and this would be our last tussle with the waves. We were confident and a bit cocky. And why not? We were about to graduate.

The night's evolution would have a twist as we were scheduled to carry live ammunition and demolition in the IBS. Coleman gave us our operations briefing.

"Here is our gear list for the operation: H-gear (a harness that held equipment), magazines, ammo pouches, M-16s, K-bar knives, flairs, canteens, flashlights, jungle boots, greens, UDT life vests, and 300 pounds of C-4 plastic explosives in haversacks (canvas bags)."

"Holy shit," I thought, *"300 pounds of C-4. That's like adding two more Smurfs."* Our leader flashed a nervous grin when he signed for the demo and a can full of 5.56 rounds for our M-16s. Burdened with getting the munitions back to the bunker and keeping us alive, I'm sure I saw tiny beads of sweat on Coleman's brow.

After loading the IBSs into 6X military trucks, we traveled to the island's other side, the windward side. The legend is that King Neptune always mustered up giant waves for night surf passage. The all-mighty sovereign of the sea decided we were in for a treat.

The mood was upbeat in the truck. We talked and laughed about our soon-to-be graduation and our new commands. As we crossed San Clemente, the sun set, and the sky turned bright red. For a sailor, that's a welcome sign for the next day's evolution. The saying, "Red at night sailors delight, red in the morning sailors take warning," came to mind. I was glad for the omen, and as we approached the beach, the last sliver of light dipped below the horizon. The 6Xs, with their headlights beaming into the frothy water, abruptly stopped in the sand as the airbrakes hissed.

In the distance, the crash of thundering waves pounded into our ears like cannon fire. Our voices went silent as we looked at each other and listened. Some call it a game face, but it was a transformation for us. Our senses were heightened, every movement and response calculated, and what little emotions we had were suppressed. We were operational.

It was time to move. Coleman kept chirping at us to be sure the demo and guns were tied tight so nothing the ocean threw at us would dislodge them. Losing one bullet would cost him and us dearly.

The cloudy night ruined any hope that we'd benefit from the moon and starlight, but the conditions presented perfect operating weather: complete blackness. The launch beach was small, fifty yards wide, and large rock formations flanked the sand.

With our IBS ready, Master Chief Ray called out, "Mr. Coleman, you're up!"

Being burdened with the extra weight on myself and in the IBS made me nervous, and I didn't want to be the first to see what was beyond the foam washing ashore.

The key to a successful passage is to count the waves and time your assault into the ocean, ensuring you progress into the *small* breakers. If Coleman was on, we'd do as we always did: paddle like hell at the perfect time to enter the surf zone as little rollers came in; then we'd be in the clear, smooth ocean in no time.

Standing at the water's edge, waiting, and listening, the minutes ticked by as the breakers got louder. Biding our time, we counted until, after clearing his throat, Master Chief Ray commanded, "We don't have all night, Mr. Coleman!"

Coleman paused only momentarily as if there was more than one option. No one flinched. Snapping out of his trance, he said. "Well, are you all ready? "

It was go-time.

Rice called out, "Hoo-Yah, Mr. Coleman. Let's go!"

The hair on my arms was on end as we shouted back, "Hoo-Yah!" and grabbed and lifted the IBS handles.

Ladened with weapons and demolition, the IBS didn't budge.

"Lift!" Coleman said.

With all our strength, we yanked up with both hands, but it wouldn't move. With no time for talk or debate, Coleman ordered, "Drag the son-of-a-bitch," and we did, across the beach and into the ocean. The instructors stood tall and silent above the lapping incoming tide, staring us down with arms crossed. Like Samaritans, we entered the waves, pulling and tugging our beached whale back into the sea.

Usually, we'd be dry from the waist up as we paddled, but that was not to be. The water flowed over our main tube and splashed in our faces forcing our lanyard green hats from our heads. Yet the unwavering cadence continued.

"Stroke! Stroke! Stroke!"

Slowly, timidly, we progressed toward the thunder in the distance.

Coleman stopped evaluating the surf's condition. It was time to get acquainted with whatever was in front of us. Like a beating drum, our movements got faster.

"Stroke! Stroke! Stroke!"

The extra weight gripped the boat like a dragging anchor.

"Paddle harder! Dig, Dig, Dig!"

Over the bow, whitewater crashed, nearly tossing Rice and Fozzard into the sea. Cooley and Emihl, seated behind them, grabbed their H-harnesses and pushed them back onto the bow.

"Holy Shit, we got some biggins," I said.

"Stop talking and keep paddling!" Coleman scoffed.

The pounding from the last wave halted our progress, and that was only the fluffy stuff from the still-unseen waves.

"Let's Go!" Coleman yelled. "Stroke! Stroke! Stroke! Do...not... let up! Dig, dig, dig, pull, pull, pull!"

Angry at the ocean for screwing with us days before graduation, I forgot about the wet and the cold and that the odds were against us. I was invincible.

Together, we shouted like one voice with all our breath.

"STROKE! STROKE! STROKE!"

Perfectly synced, we smashed through the froth. Coleman continued louder and faster.

"STROKE! STROKE! STROKE!"

Suddenly, everything changed.

The IBS picked up forward speed and raced through the water, but not from our paddling. We were being sucked into the wave's trough, pulling us in head-first. No strangers to large surf, we'd dug deep and plowed through giant waves before, and I was sure this would be no different.

As we slid down its gullet, it came to be this tsunami dwarfed our twelve-foot boat. My vision was pinpointed, and my breath was gone. Surrounded by the blackness, our only weapons were confidence, determination, and paddles.

Our frantic paddling became inconsequential as the IBS turned onto the surging wall.

Rice cried out, "We got it, we got it!"

Then it came into view. The immeasurable mass appeared as the crest curled several feet above our bow.

Time passed slowly, like a movie, one frame at a time. As we neared the top, Rice and Fozzard were ejected—tossed out as if by a massive explosion. The bow bent backward, and Emihl and Cooley toppled past, disappearing into the depths. Coleman and I followed as the IBS was ripped from under us, shooting straight into the air and flipping.

Tons of seawater crashed on our heads, sending us tumbling below the surface.

A cardinal rule: don't lose your paddle or the boat; you are useless without them. As we flipped, I squeezed the tube with my thighs and tossed my paddle as I desperately tried to hold on. The torrent of water peeled me off as if King Neptune himself reached up from the depths. Somersaulting in blackness, my equipment's weight sent me deeper into the depths.

We were not wearing the bright orange kapok life jackets from First Phase. The bulky, heavy floatation devices saved our lives each time we were dumped into the ocean while doing dozens of IBS drills. Instead, we were combat-loaded and had no active flotation.

Spinning uncontrolled like an insignificant speck of sand, without intention, the sea was about to kill me. "*This is how people drown,*" I had the clarity of thought. But I was trained to be drown-proof. The instructors warned us many times over the months, and now their prophetic words rang true. The seconds ticked by as I was churned in the ocean's violence. Understanding the sea, I waited for a pause in the wave's movement where I would have only moments to act. As the turbulence slowed, I fought my way up and gulped a life-saving breath.

On the surface, accompanying the air was trouble. I was dead in the middle of the surf impact zone, trying to keep my head above water, and it wasn't working. The next wave grabbed me, heaved me up its face, and slammed me headfirst again. My H-harness constricted around my torso, and the only mouthful of air I had ran out. Convinced I couldn't survive another ride, I pulled the CO_2 cartridge actuator on my life vest.

Issued to me six months ago, I cleaned the life vest daily. Sitting on my rack with a scribe and sandpaper, I scrubbed and picked at its parts until it was presented as new for my locker inspection. Now, it had to work.

Bam! It inflated like a punch to the jaw, and I shot to the surface. Ready for the next pounding as I gasped and held my new best inflatable friend with a vice grip. Slam! Cartwheeling in the whitewater, I was carried forward, away from the waves. The ordeal lasted only minutes. In my struggle to survive, I lost my crew.

Disoriented, I started swimming toward what I thought was the beach when large rock formations appeared only a few yards away. The ocean yanked back, pulling me into another wave. "*Shit*," one more set of breakers, and they were crashing on the rocks.

I was going to be thrown onto those boulders. "*If I keep my eye on them, I can land on top. A broken leg is better than a busted skull.*" Up the face I went. With the crest turning over, I led with the soles of my jungle boots as the surge launched me into the air. Traveling with the force of the water, I touched down on the massive rock feet first and stood up. Not a scratch!

Jumping from boulder to boulder as the wave receded, I climbed away from the impact zone, exhausted and shaking. Pausing for a minute as the saltwater dribbled from my mouth, I faced the Pacific. As the sea emptied from my ammo pouches and H-gear, my green hat, still securely tied to its orange lanyard, dangled at my side. An eerie calm enveloped me. Starring at the waves crashing on the boulders below, I listened to my breath, realizing the razor-thin line I walked between life and death. Like Biblical David's weapons, the sling and the stone that saved him, my weapons of confidence, persistence, and determination saved me.

The sea could have taken me, but it wasn't her decision to make. My training and persistence rescued me from the most likely result, as it should have. Instructors weeded out trainees who would not survive such a situation and, by doing so, gifted them the opportunity to reach their potential.

I spied for anyone who might have made it in from the waves, but no one was there. Down the shoreline, a quarter mile, the lights from the trucks were cast into the night. Making my way over the rock-covered shore, I ran back to the launching area.

Lining the beach, the cadre searched for signs of life in the water with worry on their sea-mist-covered faces. Sure, we had mishaps. Trainees got injured, logs crushed men, guys were pulled from the pool an instant before they drowned, and some tumbled off high obstacles and broke bones as they bounced off the sand. This night stole people.

Already ashore, our IBS rested upside down, everything safely tied in, with our paddles crossed on its bow. Running closer, I was met by an unhappy Master Chief Ray.

"Brown, why the hell didn't you pop your flare?"

"Sorry, Master Chief, I was busy trying not to drown."

"Where's the rest of your boat crew?"

Sheepishly, I said, "I don't know, Master Chief. We got wiped out by a giant wave, and I haven't seen anyone since."

Scanning into the darkness, the other crews searched for their lost classmates. The surf continued thundering. A light appeared in the distance, past the breakers, down the beach, and far offshore. It was my missing Smurfs. Ray signaled the floating men with his flashlight, directing them in. All five made it back to dry land with only one injured, Fozzard, who took a paddle hit to the eye.

The five stood before everyone, vests still inflated, dripping, and shedding the ocean. The evolution was cancelled.

We were shaken, but I would have flipped the IBS over and had another attempt if ordered to. We always succeeded and always found a way, and I believed it was possible, but we were not afforded the chance. The situation was enlightening. We were not invincible, and this mission would not be completed.

We returned to the 6Xs and the training area. That night, I came to grips with the reality that I wasn't Superman, and the instructor's warnings to pay attention to detail or I would die were true. We didn't fail at night surf passage. We learned.

Overconfidence can kill as fast as a lack of attention to detail. With that knowledge, I added a new trait to my skill set: pragmatism. No less confident; however, my near-death experience was life-changing. The unexpected had to be considered; an escape route must be developed; always have a plan B.

The following day, we moved on and, without incident, completed our five-and-a-half-mile open ocean swim as if it were a daily event. For some, it was the achievement of a lifetime; to us, it was just another long morning skimming through the waves. Afterward, we conducted field training exercises, which lasted into the early morning hours.

On our last day, we readied for the flight up Frog Hill. This traditional run up a steep dirt trail came with a twist. Master Chief Huey gathered us 100 yards from the hill's base and said. "We are going to honor Navy aviation with today's evolution; here are your wings," he laughed as instructors handed out wooden pallets for us to carry.

Unlike the cardboard wings from my youth, the awkward oak boxes were an unexpected burden. It was a blessing to be small because my larger classmates received metal pallets for their "cargo flight." And the worst was a galvanized steel turnbuckle for a helo flight given to Schibler.

To play the game, we had to make airplane noises and ask permission to take off at the start. But Schibler was a helicopter forced to spin in circles and make a whoop...whoop...whoop sound. As I said before, he had it worse than me.

Requesting clearance from the tower, a.k.a. Master Chief Huey, to take off, we flew with pallets and a turnbuckle towards Frog Hill. Shuffling my feet up the narrow path, my movements devolved into what resembled a hunchback stroll. The cadre along the way began yelling.

"Straighten up and pick up the pace! Move, move, move! We're gonna miss our flight back to Coronado!"

Even in the waning hours on the island, instructors doled out First Phase harassment. And with that, we ran faster with our temporary wings down the hill to complete the evolution. Schibler came in last to the class cheers as he spun in circles shouting "whoop, whoop, whoop," crossing the finish line.

It was a perfect 50° F December morning back in Coronado. After breakfast, we lined up behind the barracks for our fourteen-mile run. With the tide going out, we would soon have a large hard-pack beach to glide across. Running south, in formation towards the Mexican border, we sang UDT and SEAL cadence songs.

The unexpectedly slow pace picked up after five miles, and at BUD/S beach, the ten-mile-mark instructor Hall said, "Four-mile timed run, up and back. You're on your own!"

With that, the fastest runners took off, and the mass began to thin, but I didn't fall behind, I ran with those who had outrun me over the past six months. Instead of slogging boots, I strode at full speed like a graceful animal, a gazelle, or a cheetah. At its peak, my thoughts were dreamlike, as if my feet had left the ground, and I flew like a bird in my boyhood dreams. My entire physical body and conscious mind felt connected; every muscle cooperated and worked together to move forward down the beach. This holistic sense of my body moving was my first runner's high.

Suddenly, I understood why people loved to run. As much as the feeling was euphoric, it was liberating. Considering my hate relationship with running to rediscover it as desirable was welcomed. I'd earned the right to feel free and give myself the only break I would receive in BUD/S. Crossing the finish line, I was greeted by my faster, smiling classmates.

Ken Rice, a prolific runner, walked up to me, shook my hand.

"You've come a long way from the goon squad Brownie!"

And that I had, but my journey wasn't about skimming across the sand like the wind. Physically, I could have run as fast months ago. I didn't because I didn't believe I could.

After the last man finished, we celebrated, "Hoo-Yah, fourteen-mile run!"

On 4 December 1981, Class 115 graduated from Basic Underwater Demolition/SEAL Training. Captain Cathal L. Flynn spoke and handed out our certificates. The simple folding metal chairs were staged in perfect rows on the grinder, and friends and family filled every seat.

In attendance was Class 116, which, as we did for 114, sang traditional cadence songs for us and our guests. *Anchors Away* played as the ceremony began. In a single file, we *walked* across the grinder for the first time and the last time as trainees. I entered the courtyard behind three commissioned officers, Coleman, Schibler, and Slyfield, and two enlisted men, Barnes and Boswell. I wasn't at the end of the line and would never be again.

No one came to see me graduate. It was my achievement alone. I accepted that fact and understood that success did not occur on that one day but was intertwined in all the days leading up to the ceremony. When it ended, a certificate in hand, I thought I'd reached the pinnacle of my existence…..for about an hour.

The Smurfs gathered one last time to celebrate our Hell Week win and comaraderie. We said our goodbyes, and the crowd dispersed. The instructors returned the sacred grinder to the trainees, who ran across it in respect and fear.

Packing my few possessions, I loaded them in my Spitfire. I was different from when I began. But was this success the measure I would forever compare all future successes to? The answer shouldn't be surprising. No. I continued to strive for my elusive success, only now moving forward with greater clarity and intensity, one life evolution at a time. BUD/S was not the goal but was a critical step in seeking success.

It was time to press on. For all that I had accomplished, I realized something was missing—someone. I'd dedicated myself to finishing training, and every personal matter had taken a back seat, but now I wanted a life partner.

My thoughts always returned to my high school love, Mary. Rejected once, I had to try again to determine if our failure was due to youth or our circumstances. Was it over between us?

Army Airborne training at Fort Benning, Georgia, was scheduled for January, nearly a month away. I decided to drive the 3,000-plus miles to Wilkes-Barre and ask her myself.

I received a Christmas card from Cinema Girl's mother in my final mail call. Having made several inquiries at her home about her well-being, her mother appreciated my concern. In the card, she wrote, "Dear David, Kalie called last week. She said she was fine and having the time of her life touring the United States with the carnival. She has always been a free spirit much like me, and I am glad she met you. Good luck in the Navy, and I hope our paths will cross." My instincts served me well as I put the card in my seabag and headed east to my future.

How does anyone survive BUD/S? Is it nature or nurture or some combination?

As the fourth of five kids, I had a "normal" upbringing. I was fed, clothed, and cared for enough until I could fend for myself. Far from having helicopter parents, I wasn't encouraged to play sports, do well in school, or focus on one occupation or another. But my mother was there when I needed her. I guess my rearing was a lot like most animals. We are born with instincts; our parents show us skills, but it's up to us to thrive.

In *Blueprint*, Plomin examines nature vs. nurture and writes that parents can make a difference for their children, but, on average, across the population, they don't make a difference beyond the genes they share. He doesn't say they can't make a difference. Only in general, they don't.

For all that I'd achieved, success was always a day away. Each accomplishment only led to the beginning of greater challenges without me feeling complete or satisfied, like a book missing its final chapter. At nineteen years old, there were still holes in who I was and what I wanted to accomplish. BUD/S, the impossible task, disappeared in my rearview mirror, becoming a memory like my boyhood as I flew away from Wilkes-Barre to join the Navy.

My next evolution began. With lessons learned and drawing from my training experiences, I left Crescini's advice to the students. I was done walking in the footsteps of the man in front of me. My future wasn't destined by fate. Plomin's theories were proving true. Heritability is what you are, not what you could be. As the only person in control of my future, my days of solace in the back of the line were over.

22

MY TRIDENT

Not everything is as it seems, and not everything that seems is.
José Saramago

Every BUD/S trainee dreams of earning his Trident, the gold medal pin on the left breast of the uniform that identifies him as a SEAL. The insignia depicts an eagle perched on a horizontal three-pronged spear, an upright anchor, and a flintlock pistol. The eagle represents the United States of America, the anchor is the Navy, the spear symbolizes the warrior's connection to the sea, and the pistol signifies that the person possesses the highest warfare capabilities. He is ready to fight, fire, and complete the mission at any cost.

As newly minted weapons in the Navy's arsenal, our next stop was Army Airborne School, a necessary and brief requirement, albeit an annoyance in our quest to gain our enlisted classification—5326 Combat Swimmer/SEAL. However, the airborne training had to wait until after the Christmas break, allowing me to visit Mary.

My cross-country crusade to see if our emotional connection that went cold could reignite took priority. Heading east in my tiny convertible, I was alone with my thoughts and the open road. Now confident in my career, I was drawn to fix my personal life—a silly, contrived notion for a nineteen-year-old. Yet there I was, humming toward the Mississippi through the Midwest on an imaginary mission that needed to be completed.

The three-day trip seemed to be a few "easy days," the first I'd experienced in a year. Like a wild animal, I anticipated my perspective would be to burst from the cage in excitement to be free, to go as I pleased. There was no 0500 muster or concern that the slightest lack of detail would be deadly. I should have relaxed and enjoyed the moment.

However, and intentionally, the Navy sharpened my persona, and I woke early to PT in my hotel room and ate each meal as if it were my last. I flinched at a whistle's blast as I did during Hell Week and avoided garden hoses. Alone in the wild, I contemplated how to position myself to gain every advantage and kill the men who walked through the door as I sat with my back to the restaurant wall. Taught that "surprise and violence of action" are paramount to overcoming an enemy, I surveyed my situation, assessing who had superior numbers and firepower.

My directives ran through my head constantly. My mind refused to go on "leave" and relax. As I continued my aggressive march forward, there was no reprieve from the Navy or my dream of becoming a SEAL.

Driving along Interstate 80 into Wyoming Valley, Pennsylvania, my childhood memories flashed back. Teacher conflicts, outdoor adventures, scuba diving at Harvey's Lake, wrestling matches, and relationships were all the experiences that enabled my success, at least so far.

The Spitfire stopped unannounced at a white two-story duplex in Miners Mills. Because no happenings on Chandler St. escaped Mary Ann, Mary's mother, the window curtains fluttered at the unfamiliar sound as I parked across the street. The single-lane road was as I remembered. The worn concrete sidewalks and stone curbs bordered the coveted parking spaces in front of the 1940s and 50s, well-lived-in houses. When I reached the steps, Mary Ann swung the door open to greet me with a smile.

"I knew you'd be back," she said as we hugged. From the porch, she shouted for Mary using her nickname. "Kay, Dave's here."

Running from the kitchen, Mary stopped in the living room. "You're here! You came back!"

"I drove from California to see if you'd like to get some pizza," I said.

She laughed. "I'd like that."

What a time we had that weekend as if the prodigal son had returned. We sat, ate, and talked for hours. Bill gave me the biggest bear hug, nicknamed me Irving and occasionally called me Vern. We played the card game Uno at the kitchen table and gorged on scrapple and eggs for breakfast.

As much as we wanted to be together romantically, our options were few. In a house with three bedrooms and five kids, privacy was nonexistent. A high school stairwell wouldn't satisfy our needs and desires, so I made up a story that she and I planned to travel to my sister Melanie's house in New Jersey overnight. We were both over eighteen and adults, but we had to keep up appearances. Mary hastily gathered her things, and we headed out.

Sixty miles into our drive, I pulled into a Marriott. I approached the clerk and said, "I need a room for two, please."

"Are your parents with you? the clerk sneered, "You must be eighteen and have a credit card to rent a room here."

"You've got to be kidding me," I thought. Punching him in the nose was the first thing I thought to do. "Here's my driver's license and Visa," I snapped. "I'm in the Navy, for Christ's sake. Check me in!" It didn't matter about my training; I still resembled a fifteen-year-old. With a key in hand, we retired to our room.

On our way back to Wilkes-Barre the next day, Mary and I got our story straight about our visit, and until now, no one has been the wiser. She and I planned for a permanent relationship, but I never mentioned marriage, not wanting to make the same mistake twice. We were boyfriend and girlfriend again, and with this evolution complete, I shifted my focus to earning my jump wings at Fort Benning.

Thinking back, I wonder if my compulsion to pursue my relationship with her was for love or my hatred of failure. Our failed puppy love affair stayed with me and haunted my dreams.

According to *Psychology Today*, dreaming of failure may be a good sign, predictive of success and not failure. However, recurring dreams can also reflect everyday internal conflicts. Maybe you're struggling with an important decision or feel uncertain about a recent choice you made. Until you make your choice and come to terms with it, you might experience recurring dreams of being lost, failing a test, or otherwise making a mistake.

After I visited Pennsylvania, my relationship nightmares stopped. I'd resolved a meaningful internal conflict and freed my subconscious fear of failure. On to the next mission.

On an unexpected 32° F morning in Georgia, BUD/S class 115, less our officers, began Army Airborne training. Our combined service (Army and Navy) class huddled near 55-gallon burn barrels to stay warm as the sun rose, melting the frost covering the parachute tower.

Jeeps, boats, and trucks parachute. It's a brainless activity. Besides having the guts to jump out of a perfect airplane, the only requirement is to walk out the door and allow gravity to take over. Using a parachute stuffed in a bag with a long cord attached called a static line, we prepared our first fall from the sky.

The military doesn't make small, medium, or large parachute harnesses; one size fits all, and this one hung off me like a pair of twin-72s. The reserve chute clipped onto the front straps, adding weight and bulk, but it was comforting knowing there was a plan B. With the straps tight around our legs and chest, we walked to the aircraft, looking like crotchety old men crossing the street.

Anyone who says they're not nervous on their first jump is a liar. With over 100 paratroopers crammed into the large C-141 jet aircraft, the side door was closed and locked. No one said a word as we collapsed into our webbed seats with the engines spooling up. Inside the brightly lit fuselage, row upon row of green helmets bounced as the aircraft jerked and moved onto the runway. Without hesitation, the pilot went full throttle. I scanned the crowd trying to detect fear but was surprised by the smiles and air of excitement. Holding my static-line clip in one hand and web seat in the other, the jet radically pulled nose up.

"Stand-up, hook-up!" the jumpmaster barked.

Being in the first "stick" meant we would go first. I shot from my seat, hooking the clip to a steel cable suspended from the ceiling. The aircraft door slid open, and the 140-mile-per-hour wind burst into the cabin. Standing in the door, the jumpmaster threw streamers to determine wind direction and speed, and the green light above the door flashed.

"Go, go, go!" the jumpmaster shouted.

The solid line of men moved toward the door. We were packed in so tight I could have picked up my feet and still been carried out the door with the momentum from the line. Like dominoes, we fell out, disappearing into the white sky.

Closing my eyes and tucking my chin to my chest, I squeezed my arms tight and grasped my reserve as I bounced through the air. The seconds ticked by as I waited for a sign that the chute was out of its bag and doing its job. The chaos stopped, and a beautiful round green canopy filled the sky above me.

Floating under the thin nylon, I watched as my stick hit the drop zone (ground). Some jumpers left dust clouds, while others were dragged by the wind across the open field. Leading up to our first jump we endured two weeks of classroom instruction and repeated practicing our PLF, or "parachute landing fall." Right before touching the ground, we were to put our knees and feet together and bend slightly at the knees. The position was mandatory for every jump, but the problem was the instruction assumed every paratrooper would hit the ground with such force they'd have to tuck and roll to prevent injury as they landed. And most did. Not me; at 115 pounds, I landed light as a feather, standing up, a failing grade. I found it ridiculous to fall on the ground when I didn't need to. But, to graduate, I'd dramatically fall to the ground after touching down, feigning my PLF and passing the course.

After five more jumps, some of which I opened my eyes, we received our Army winged pin. As a slight to the Army, we called their gray pin "lead wings." I wore the Army's wings only once, not because I had anything against the pin but because of the events of the next sixty days.

In February 1982, I walked into a WWII-era white, one-story building on the Little Creek, Virginia Naval Amphibious Base. A round marquee over the door read "Underwater Demolition," and under that, "Team 21." A barbed wire fence protected the compound, and the potholed pavement in the foreground gave way to a dirt field back forty where run-down support buildings and Quonset huts were scattered about.

Despite its dilapidated appearance, I felt as if I'd reached the Promised Land.

"Hi, I'm Petty Officer David Brown checking in," I said with a monster smile.

A small gray metal desk, with a black rotary dial phone atop and the US and Navy flags posted in a corner, made up the wood-paneled room. The watch, shuffling through his paperwork, looked up and paused. Oh, no, I thought, here it comes, expecting to hear "*You're too little to be a frogman.*"

"Brownie!" he exclaimed, "Ensign Coleman said you'd check in this week. Welcome aboard." Without anyone questioning my size or why I was there, the Teams quickly revealed what everyone said they would be.

When I met with the command executive officer (XO) on my third indoctrination day, he asked, "Petty Officer Brown, are you settled in yet?"

"I don't have much to settle," I said, "it's only me and my seabag."

He laughed, "Perfect, you can travel with me to the Special Warfare Detachment at Roosevelt Roads Naval Station, Puerto Rico, to do RDT&E. He explained that meant "research, development, training, and evaluation." I eventually discovered it always involved risking my life trying new equipment or attempting extreme operational methods.

My seabag wasn't fully unpacked since arriving from Georgia a week earlier, but I stuffed what I needed into a kit bag, and the XO and I boarded a Navy transport plane to Puerto Rico. The Special Warfare compound we nicknamed "Rosie Roads" sat on a stunning spit overlooking the Caribbean. The old wooden building was a converted hotel with peeling paint that felt like an oasis from the Navy base. Our mission was to test an experimental underwater mapping device.

I sensed the XO was excited to travel away from the Team area. A "regular guy," he treated me not as if he were an officer and I enlisted, but as two operators with an evolution to complete.

After leaving Coronado, keeping up the savage pace didn't cross my mind, and it should have. We woke at sunrise for a vigorous PT and ran four miles. I thought I'd left the muscle-burning PTs behind, but we worked out as hard as any day in BUD/S. The only easy day, indeed, was yesterday. It was no longer only a saying; it was a lifestyle.

With multiple scuba tanks ready, we entered the Caribbean shallows and swam mapping grids on the ocean floor for three days. As we sucked our twin 72s dry, we surfaced and got new ones all day, day after day. The XO moved through the water so fast I couldn't keep up, and he often dragged me along.

"Didn't they teach you how to swim in BUD/S?" he joked.

How could I have difficulty keeping up with this old guy? I needed to become stronger and faster in the Teams. The same as passing the BUD/S screening test didn't guarantee I would make it through training, graduating didn't assure me I'd earn my Trident.

Surprisedly, on our final day at Rosie Roads, I received orders to ship out and join the 3rd platoon already deployed in the Mediterranean

Sea. One of their members was removed after being arrested by the Spanish police for public intoxication. I would replace him.

Once back in Virginia Beach from Puerto Rico, I was given forty-eight hours to arrange to pay my bills and store what little I had and was whisked onto a Military Airlift Command flight to Rota, Spain. From there, I flew by helicopter to a ship to meet my new teammates.

Having only three weeks of experience, I was joining a fully operational UDT platoon as an FNG, or "Fucking New Guy," a fact they didn't let me forget.

SEAL Qualification Training (SQT), lasting twenty-six weeks, prepares recent BUD/S graduates to operate in the field. I hadn't begun SQT and was an unknown and untested asset for my new platoon.

The friends I'd made in BUD/S were scattered to different commands, and the few people I met in the Team area I left behind. I found myself on my way to a foreign land to try and live up to a reputation with real operators who were strangers and hopefully pass tests I wasn't prepared for.

The helo set down on the fantail of the *USS Trenton*, a Gator freighter. Considered ship's company meant we berthed below in non-airconditioned decks in spartan and cramped quarters. With one 12"x12"x12" locker and racks (beds) three high with no partitions, we lived out of our sea bags and shaving kits. Sleeping inches from each other on rope-stretched canvas supporting a single four-inch mattress, we were stacked up, down, and side to side. Sharing open galley heads and a few water-rationed showers with the regular crew, privacy didn't exist. Turns out, the conditions on the ship were much worse than boot camp.

A tight-knit bunch of odd gents, the 3rd platoon included a Texas cowboy, a Black Hispanic Puerto Rican, a cornfed midwestern redhead, a Chicagoan, a Boston intellect, and everything in between. I was the FNG replacing a teammate they trusted and spent the last five months with preparing to deploy.

They teased, "Brownie, you're so new you're still shittin' BUD/S chow and wearing those stupid issued woolen socks." No stranger to being the lowest on the totem pole, I was given berthing space cleaning duty, and every job no one wanted.

As I'd done in Assault Boat Coxswain school, I sucked it up and did what I was told to do. The leading petty officer assigned me as the platoon's second intelligence gatherer, and I immediately began learning to collect and report information. I was also the cartographer trainee, overseeing the hydro recons, and drawing charts for the ship's captain and the Marines before the amphibious landings. At the same time, I got a crash course in every other UDT operation.

Was it fate that put me on that ship, or did I create my opportunity, my own luck?

Checking into the Teams in Virginia, I was animated as I explained to the XO that I hoped to deploy and was free to travel. Unencumbered by a wife or kids, I can only assume I received the RDT&E mission and joined the 3rd because of my assertiveness.

After leaving the XO's office, I overheard him tell the CO, "He volunteered for everything!" They laughed. But in my mind, I wanted every benefit of schooling and mission.

Things may happen for a reason, but I have no doubt I influenced the decisions that led to my quick deployment.

In a blog posting titled "Maximize Your Return on Luck," bestselling self-help author Mark Manson referenced a nine-year study on luck that sought to determine the reasons behind the success of certain global companies. Manson asked whether Bill Gates, for example, was luckier than others in building his enterprise. Did his competitors go under when Microsoft thrived because they succumbed to unpredictable events outside their control? In other words, did they suffer from less luck?

"The surprising answer is no," Manson wrote, pointing to the study researchers who "found after measuring 230 'luck events' over dozens of businesses, that the ultra-successful businesses did not receive any more lucky breaks than the companies that failed on average and vice versa. What set them apart is something they dubbed 'Return on Luck' (ROL).

All businesses and people, for that matter, experience both positive and adverse events. Those who succeed maximize their positive luck and minimize their negative luck. In other words, they take advantage of their ROL. When Bill Gates saw the opportunity to program an operating system from the original Altair, for example, he labored around the clock for weeks, often not sleeping for days. "He was able to recognize that it was a once-in-a-lifetime moment, and he had the wherewithal to push through and take advantage of it," Manson wrote. "That's a high ROL. Researchers found that ultra-successful companies regularly did this."

Successful people also do this regularly. I took advantage of my lucky opportunity and increased my ROL. Like my mother, I was hardwired to speak my mind, and that trait either got me results or in trouble.

Shortly after arriving on the ship, we collected our gear to fly to Spain to train with the Spanish Corps of Engineers in the mountains near Zaragoza. As the only platoon member not wearing a Trident, I presented a problem.

Before leaving, my leading petty officer pulled me aside, held out his hand, and a shiny new pin was in it. He said: "I spoke to the guys, and we know you don't have your 5326 qualifications yet, but we don't want anyone in our platoon walking around without a Trident, so wear it."

Snatching the gold pin in disbelief, the eagle's wings dug into my palm as I realized I cheated the system. They accepted me as a Team guy, and I wouldn't let them down. Thirty days in, my dream was realized: I was wearing the symbol that identified me as a Navy frogman and SEAL.

This is what the Teams were all about. Forget the rules and regulations; finish the evolution; complete the mission. Although an essential symbol of passage, it was still only a pin. There would be dangerous evolutions in front of me before I was official.

In the early 1980s, we weren't losing UDT/SEALs in war-time missions, but Team guys were dying in training accidents. We used live ammunition and conducted fire and maneuver drills at real-time speed. Within twenty-four months, two members of the 3rd were dead—Rick Horn was shot during a live fire exercise in a staged "shoot house," and Dan Langelier was killed in Puerto Rico while diving an MK-15 scuba rig.

We signed up for the danger and were regularly reminded in training, but it seemed unreal. I always envisioned myself finishing the mission and going home, wherever that was at the time. We'd gather at the dirt-floored Casino bar for every team guy loss and put a keg of beer on their tab. We toasted the lost frogman, drank his beer, and went to work the next day.

What do Team guys do when there's no war? We prepare for it.

23

HIGHS AND LOWS

I think the highest and lowest points are the important ones.
Anything else is just … in between.
Jim Morrison

I was living my dream, experiencing the wild and crazy things I'd fantasized about as a boy and doing them globally with the best in the world.

At only nineteen years old, could I have reached my potential? My entire life was ahead of me, yet there I was; I had the pin and the job. I should have been happy. By every measure, I was successful but remained restless, always anxious, and compelled to push myself to finish the mission and move on to the next evolution.

In his *After the Session Blog*, psychologist Robert Hill coined the term "pathologically persistent" in referring to the story of 70-year-old Alexander Doba, the Polish man who paddled across the Atlantic Ocean *not once but three times.* For Doba, kayaking this great distance was no feat at all. Instead, he described it as a personal eventuality. It was as if he was meant to engage and complete this task. It was his mission.

Giving up, or putting it aside, was not comprehensible to Doba. With no thought of dying, he felt almost pre-ordained to live his incredible journey. Hill considered whether persistence is the result of nature or nurture. He states, "We would like to think that persistence is learned, but the fact is that there is more to simply concluding that when a person does not persist that, they have been taught poor habits." Hill hypothesized that persistence was embedded as part of his fundamental DNA in Doba's case.

Are we born persistent? Doba's story compels this question. You might expect he died while traversing a great ocean in his kayak. No, he passed from a heart attack after climbing and standing atop Mt. Kilimanjaro in Africa. Doba's goal wasn't to be a kayaker completing daring voyages. Those were his evolutions. His mission—to complete them and then move on until he reached the top of the mountain—was his final act of persistence.

With an FNG mindset, when I was told to go for a ride in a helicopter, I excitedly packed my kit bag and got in, never considering whether things could go wrong. Once on the aircraft, I put my faith in the pilots, the crew, and the machine.

The platoon loaded into the bird on the helo pad on the fan tail (back of the ship), lifted off, and headed to a Spanish hillside. Thirty minutes into the flight, I gazed out the small portals, listening to the aircraft's rotors chopping through the air as the hilly green countryside passed below.

Leaning slightly nose down, we flew at a stomach-turning low altitude, zigzagging toward Zaragoza. The crew sat still, staring at the floor, waiting for us, their cargo, to unload at our destination, when I heard a "pop." The crew chief jumped up as I dodged a fluid stream shooting across the cabin.

"Shit, hydraulic leak!" he yelled into his headset. "We're going down. Prepare for a hard landing!"

How the heck do I do that? I thought. Grabbing the webbed seat's metal frame, the helicopter shook. The rotors stopped chopping at the sky and now made a "whoop, whoop, whoop" sound as the horizon zipped by the windows on our way to the ground. With a tremendous thud, the craft bounced, and we were thrown from our seats and strewn across the helicopter's deck.

We came to rest in one piece, and the chief called out, "Let's go. Everybody out!" The rear gate opened, and we ran down the ramp and out onto a baseball field.

The rotors slowed to a stop, and the pilot and crew abandoned the wounded bird, shaking their heads as they approached us.

"Fun ride, eh boys!" the pilot said with a snicker. "We lost the primary hydraulic system. That's how we control that thing. Lucky, we found this nice place to land."

Trying to gauge what to say and how to act, in a timid voice, I stammered, "Whoa, that was wild. Shit! Now what?" The crew was cool and collected like they'd crashed a thousand times before. My teammates walked away, cursing the craft.

"We need to pull our shit out of there,...fucking piece of shit Navy helos," scoffed Cowboy. "I'll take Marine choppers any day," he said.

Shaking, I wondered how, after nearly dying in a helo crash, their only thought was to retrieve our gear and make it to our rendezvous point. I couldn't help but think, how often does this happen, and why would I trust going up in another one? But I didn't say anything or ask questions; I was the FNG.

Within hours, we were back in the air on another chopper en route to Zaragoza as if nothing happened. Crashing in an aircraft makes most people nervous about climbing into another one, but SEALs are not most people.

Just as I'd forgotten, or repressed, the thought of our perilous night surf passage, our CH-46 crash landing became a distant memory as we continued our low-level trip across the countryside.

After our flight landed, we boarded 6x6 troop transports for the long winding drive up the mountainside to Mequinenza Dam to meet with the Spanish Army Corps of Engineers. We spent two weeks in the picturesque country with a hilltop monastery visible in the distance. Our camp, consisting of large white tents and Army cots, had a *Sound of Music*-like view and a crystal blue lake where we trained.

Members of the 3rd led classes using C-4 plastic explosives while our counterparts demonstrated their demolition expertise. Starting at a crisp 0700, we took a siesta from noon to 1500, worked again until 1900, and retired to the dinner tent. We were treated like royalty.

"Is this what every deployment is like?" I asked Bill, one of my platoon members.

"No way Brownie, enjoy it, but don't get used to it. This is as good as it gets."

Eating on long white-linen-covered tables and served by Spanish Army enlisted men, I enjoyed the magnificent service but reminded myself I had a job to learn. After weeks of blowing things up in and under the water and shooting every weapon in our arsenal and theirs, I completed my Personnel Qualification Standards (PQS) for demolition and weapons.

In the evenings, we sipped sangria and watched bullfighting on television at the only restaurant/bar in the village. We mingled with the town's women who came in to experience us, the oddity that descended on their hamlet, drank all their wine, and made a lot of noise.

Next, we traveled to Italy to train with their frogmen. The foreign naval special forces I encountered touted their abilities in briefings and stories, but once we got in the field, we learned they needed more practice to be efficient. The Italians and French swam the most complicated underwater scuba navigation courses without surfacing but couldn't find a corner drug store with a map and compass. There was a reason most considered us the best all-around special forces in the world. We proved it.

The days of the week blended; there were no weekends. Even the time of day was warped as early evening training evolutions continued to daybreak, and dusk operations lasted into the night. My dive qualifications were complete after five solid days of scuba compass courses.

Wasting no time, two days of parachuting between Italy and France on land, in the water, and at night gave me another qualification box checked, and with over ten static line jumps under my belt, I earned my gold Navy wings. The Army lead pin went into my shaving kit and was never seen again.

We didn't have access to large jet aircraft as in Airborne, so we borrowed a UH-1 Huey from a nearby Air Force base. Meeting at a remote inland field or abandoned airstrip, we schlepped our gear and freshly packed parachutes from the ship to the drop zone.

Sitting in the Huey's open door, my legs dangled as it powered up. Indeed, this was the best amusement ride on the planet. We lifted off, speeding across the terrain and up. The pilots pushed the machine hard to 1500 feet in altitude. Once there, we got the signal to hook our static lines to the floor D-ring and unclip our safety harnesses.

Now, the scary part for me. Without falling out, I needed to plant my feet on the skid (a metal bar below the aircraft resembling a Christmas sleigh). Inching my butt close to the doorway's edge, white-knuckled, I held on to the bulkhead (wall of the helicopter) and stretched my legs, but I couldn't reach the bar. I was too short.

Like the dirty name, I had to think my way around the problem, and I pushed myself out and hoped to land where my feet pointed. With hands on the Huey's floor, I launched, landing solidly on the skid. As I did, the crew chief grabbed me from behind, thinking I was about to fall out.

"Whoa, there, son! Are you okay?" he said.

Straining to see over my shoulder and past my parachute, I shook my head, "Yeah, I'm okay," as if I'd done it a thousand times. If he only knew I'd never jumped from a Huey before and that my skootch out of the helicopter was a huge leap of faith. Huey jumps were a combination of exhilaration and terror.

The jump master's hand tapped me on the back.

"Go!"

Leaning forward, I fell out. The experience was like falling off the Empire State Building. Rather than being blown around like a piece of paper at 140 mph in Airborne school, I dropped straight down, praying for the familiar static line tug pulling the parachute from my back. With a snap, the air caught the canopy, which inflated perfectly, a feeling that never got old.

Within the next year and between deployments, I attended a fourteen-day free-fall parachute course. Other Team guys taught us how to maintain control while falling at terminal velocity, 118 miles per hour. We also learned how to pack parachutes.

The more dangerous the situation, the odder the humor was for SEALs. My instructor, a former 3rd platoon member, last name Jackson, always said, "For God's sake, be careful" before we jumped out.

For God's sake, be careful. You've got to be kidding me, I used to think. We're throwing ourselves out into the sky, and now is when you say to be careful. You be careful when you pack your chute, put on your harness, and conduct safety checks. Being careful ends the second you decide to leap out; that's when it's time to be lucky.

Hearing that before flinging yourself into the atmosphere at 10,000 feet seemed preposterous. But he said it with a grin every time. He also reminded me that if anything went wrong, "remember to cut away and pull your reserve."

"Brownie, it's bad form to burn in without deploying your reserve," he said. This meant to hit the ground and die. "Don't do that, or you'll make me look bad."

The C-130 climbed until we passed the clouds. The buildings looked like dots, and the airfield was the size of a postage stamp. The cabin was hit with a frigid burst as the rear doors opened. The crystal blue horizon glistened against the drab green aircraft. Tightening my grip on the troop seat's webbing, I waited as Jackson threw his streamers to reveal wind direction and speed. With "Mr. Be Careful" close behind, I would be the final trainee out because I was the littlest. I thought my days of being sent to the back of the line were over, but it was better to jump last rather than have a heavier jumper crash into me from above.

The green light flashed, and he signaled us to stand and prepare. And to the little end, I went. The group's confidence was contagious and comforting as I repeated the jump procedures in my head.

"Go!" he said.

In a single file, jumpers leaped off the ramp and disappeared. With his hand atop my Pro-Tek helmet and a toothpick in his mouth, Jackson whispered, "For God's sake Brownie, be careful. Go!" As the plane roared through the sky with strength, its safety gripped me like a mother's hug, yet I ran down the ramp and threw myself off.

It was sheer uncontrolled terror as I flipped over onto my back, the "dying cockroach," as it's called, screaming toward Earth; I watched the aircraft fly away. "*Shit! Pull up, pull up, or you'll die,*" I thought as I plummeted. Arching, I pulled my arms and legs back and turned over, facing the ground with my eyes glued to my wrist altimeter, watching the numbers getting smaller. From appearing as a thin black line in the distance, the airport runway got closer and bigger…

5,000…

4,000…

…and finally, 3,000 feet.

After a waive-off signal, waving my hands back and forth, I yanked the ripcord from my chest strap, counting one, two, and *bam*! My chute opened, and I slid firmly into my harness with a smile.

In the 1980s, Ronald Regan became the President, and he loved the military. The Teams were flooded with money and new, mostly untested gear, and in the process, we received square ram-air parachutes. Capable of carrying more weight with a faster forward speed, we could jump from farther away and "fly" undetected to a target. I returned to air operations for my one-day familiarization and packing lesson to qualify with the MT-1X parachute.

The monster's 370 square-foot canopy had a 360-pound capacity. Perfect for an equipment-heavy tactical situation but putting a 120-pound person under that much nylon is a slow ride down.

After takeoff and with all our safety checks done, the jumpmaster gave us a ten-minute warning. Two massive hydraulic pistons lowered the C-130s large ramp as we neared the drop zone. At 13,000 feet, the crisp thin air needed to be consciously sucked in to my lungs to feel useful. The aircraft's crew, hugging their O2 bottles, monitored us closely.

The higher, the better was my attitude. The greater distance between me and the ground meant I had more time to fix any malfunction, something I preferred rather than bouncing off the earth in a tangled canopy.

The temperature with the open fuselage dropped below freezing. The sky was endless, and I thought I could see the edge of space above. With the green light, we filed out one at a time, only this time, I was the *very last* person, an ominous left behind feeling. As my instructor fell backward from the C-130, he mouthed, "For God's sake, Brownie, be careful!" Shaking my head in ambivalence, I hesitated momentarily, then bolted down the ramp.

As I reached terminal velocity, the problem started. My giant parachute bag hung over my sides, causing it and me to shake violently. The severe vibration blurred my vision and distorted my trajectory. This wasn't covered in our emergency procedures; it was my dilemma to solve instantly and what I was trained to do from my first day in BUD/S.

Pulling my arms back and pushing my feet out, I formed a delta. Flying forward like a 120-mile-per-hour glider, I screamed across the sky, and the shaking stopped. Unfortunately, I was speeding away from the drop zone and needed to improvise to survive at 10,000 feet.

As the last person out, no one was aware of what happened or where I was. I could see parachutes opening as the first jumpers reached 3,000 feet. If I opened while flying in a delta, my neck would snap forward and back like being hit from behind in a violent car accident. I had to slow my momentum. Pushing my arms out and bending my knees, the air resistance slowed me enough, allowing me to pull the ripcord without getting whiplash.

That square beauty came off my back so slowly that I turned and glanced over my left shoulder, expecting to see a malfunction. *Pop, pop, pop*, as each cell inflated. With the chute open, I happily steered the monster like a hang glider. I was flying like in my boyhood dreams with the air flowing over the parachute being the only sound. I glided over the runway, the parking lot, and back to the drop zone. A nylon wing replaced my cardboard cut-outs, and like my dreams, the ground slowly came up to touch my feet as I stepped forward for a soft landing.

Freefall jumping is liberating. It's art in motion, a sense of immeasurable vastness and total control in an uncontrollable situation. The excitement of the jump, the freedom of flying, and the satisfaction of a perfectly open parachute make the experience an emotional trifecta.

The 3rd platoon again boarded the *Trenton,* which sailed through the Suez Canal and into the Indian Ocean. All the ships in the battle group did "gator squares" for twenty days, delaying our arrival at the next port. We sailed without meaning as if were living The Rime of the Ancient Mariner, wasting away at sea:

> *Day after day, day after day,*
> *We stuck, nor breath nor motion.*
> *As idle as a painted ship*
> *Upon a painted ocean.*

With only PT, eating, sleeping, and sweating in the sweltering quarters, I grew older by one month. From the Spanish countryside dining on chef-prepared meals, we fell to the confines of a steel flotilla, consuming powdered eggs and drinking bug juice. If floating aimlessly near the equator was normal during deployments, I needed to consider the downside as much as the excitement and adventure.

I swear we etched permanent squares in the water as we inched between continents and toward Africa's east coast.

Going ashore, we met with Kenya's Naval Special Forces, who were ill-trained but were the most interesting group to work with. One officer described how his grandfather, a tribal elder, fought neighboring tribes. After conquering a tribe, they killed and ate their leaders, believing it would give them superpowers in battle. Their ancestor's battles and savagery were legendary, albeit barbaric.

But like other foreign forces we encountered, the Kenyan government sent their high-ranking, out-of-shape officers to train with us. The stop became an exercise in teaching fat officers how to scuba dive, cast and recover, and basic hydrographic reconnaissance.

During a hydro recon on a Kenyan beach, a CH-46 flew over, and the operation was canceled within minutes. From the beach, I could hear our leading petty officer yelling.

"Pull the line in, everybody out of the water, NOW!"

The helo's crew chief radioed that sharks had encircled our swimmer line. I spent days in the ocean and never came across a shark, maybe because I wasn't looking for one or probably because I didn't care.

Our deployment continued through the Suez Canal and to Spain before the last stop in Western Africa. With most of the platoon, I left the ship in Rota and flew back to the States via military airlift.

Roy, a member of the 3rd, and I made it back to UDT-21 after catching a flight from Rota to Dover Air Force Base in Delaware. He agreed to give me a ride to Mary's house on his way to Chicago.

Climbing onto his Honda 375cc motorcycle, we began our trek to Pennsylvania. Buzzing down the interstate with two backpacks, we rode the little bike to the Maryland border, where we were consumed in a cloud burst. Soaked, we pulled off the highway, found a laundromat, stripped off our clothes, and sat with our packs on our laps. Our soaked jeans, shirts, and jackets tumbled behind the glass circle as we chatted about the home cooking we'd soon enjoy.

Team guys got naked wherever and whenever the need arose. Stemming from BUD/S training, where skivvies were forbidden, we regularly walked around the barracks bare after dives and swims. We were so often wet that stripping off cold clothing became commonplace, with little thought or care about civilization's response to our nakedness.

Being desensitized to civilian culture helped us achieve our core objective of finishing the evolution and completing the mission, but it left some team guys with misguided notions of immunity for misdeeds—like the guy I replaced in the 3rd platoon.

Roy and I arrived on Chandler Street, where he met Mary and my extended family. But he had to finish his evolution and soon boarded his cycle, scooting his way to Illinois to see his girlfriend.

I'd been planning this day for months while traveling the world, jumping from airplanes and helicopters, blowing up hillsides and beach fronts, shooting machine guns, and throwing grenades. Pulling out an emerald ring I purchased from a street vendor in Mombasa, Kenya, I knelt and asked Mary to marry me. This time, she agreed. We held the wedding in the church across from her house with a family reception of homemade Polish food at a local club. Reluctantly, my mother and father traveled from Florida to attend the event they vehemently opposed.

"You're too young to get married," my mother said. "My God, David, she's from Miners Mills." But I was a stubborn son-of-a-bitch, as she branded me, and I had no intention of taking her advice.

Thinking back, I wish I'd had someone other than my mother to guide me. I needed a mentor, someone to trust who would have pulled me aside, not to change my mind, but to have me reflect on the bigger picture of love and life. My father wasn't that person; he never gave me counsel on relationships, sex, or money. I stumbled my way through life, tripping, falling, and learning. Oscar Wilde, an Irish playwright and poet, said it best: "With age comes wisdom, but sometimes age comes alone."

Despite what my mother said, I didn't think being raised in Miners Mills was terrible, but as much as I understood who I was professionally, I was still only nineteen years old. I thought I was an expert on relationships and my future. My single-minded, naïve view of the world rationalized that if I couldn't outwit a problem, I would beat it into submission.

With my new wife, a new family car, and my first mortgage, Mary and I moved to Virginia Beach, where she began her new life as a Team guy's wife, a challenge almost as difficult as going through BUD/S.

24

4TH PLATOON AND SEAL TEAM 4

I feel the need to endanger myself every so often.
Tim Daly

Upon my return, UDT-21 felt unfamiliar. The people I met six months earlier were deployed, reassigned, or out of the Navy. The entire 3rd lined up for muster only a few times before being dismembered by transfers, reassignments, and ending enlistments.

One 32° F morning, the XO came over, called me out from our formation, and pinned a shiny new Trident on my blue, hooded UDT-21 sweatshirt.

"Congratulations, Petty Officer Brown, you're officially a frogman," he said. The experience blew past me like the wind.

I would love to relive that moment again, to appreciate the road, the sacrifice, and the people along the way. What a terrible heritable trait I acquired. My parents didn't celebrate my accomplishments; why should I? And I didn't. Doing nothing, I didn't call or tell anyone. My family didn't understand what I did in the Navy until years later, when SEALs began writing books and making headlines.

Typically, the hazing that followed someone awarded their Trident was severe. Team guys were tied up in cargo nets, ink was thrown on them, and some were pissed on while held down. So, knowing the platoon was coming for me, I got myself ready and took a fighting stance. Surrounded, the 3rd effortlessly picked me up, carried me across the courtyard, and threw me into a frozen dive-ops dunk tank.

Waiting for the hose, ink, or even pee, I peeked over the tank's lip and watched them walk away. Huh?

"Brownie," they said, "you've been wearing that Trident for five months. You getting that pin today is no big deal to us." With the air freezing, dressed in nothing but UDTs and a hooded sweatshirt, and not wanting to be wet and cold, they left me in the metal tank and walked away. The hazing was over before it started.

Was I successful? Did I reach my potential? Those things were still always a day away.

Spending the next quarter in administrative status, I didn't waste a moment. I attended night college courses and free fall, dive master, intel, and photography schools. Soon after, I was transferred to the 4th platoon, which was in rotation for a six-month trip to Central and South America in support of UNITAS, a multinational maritime exercise conducted annually in Atlantic and Pacific waters in that part of the globe.

My new platoon consisted of enlisted men from broken-up platoons, strays from admin like me, and one or two FNGs. Our Officer in Charge, Lieutenant William McRaven, unknown at the time, would later reach world-renowned status for planning the raid that killed Osama Bin Laden. His assistant was Lieutenant Junior Grade George Coleman, a fellow Smurf. As a petty officer and no longer an FNG, I gathered intelligence, took photos, supervised dives, and drew hydrographic charts. I was also the point man.

Two platoons and I was always the point man, which was a bit like being the guidon in boot camp. Our leading petty officer, Steve Highfill said, "Brownie, you're so small no one will see you coming. You can kill them all before the rest of us get there," he laughed. The "point man" leads the platoon when patrolling. The rationale is that the smallest person isn't likely to be seen by the enemy, but it comes with a cost. The position's survival chance after contact was less than the other platoon's positions, but I was the littlest, so I was it.

Hopefully, I was more than just the shortest; I'd like to think I earned the job based on my radarman rating and land navigation skills. Each man in the platoon was required to be a professional in their craft, and I believed I was the best navigator. Another fun fact is that aside from potentially being the first person shot at, the point man is the first to encounter any obstacle.

I fell down hills, tried climbing cliffs, and was the first to walk into mud, water, thorns, and pickers. If I made it, the rest followed, and if I couldn't, they'd retrieve me, and we went in a different direction.

On the upside, I got to travel light, carrying only my gear and weapons. I wasn't bogged down with extra machine gun rounds or explosives. The tradeoff was worth it.

My second deployment involved more RDT&E, or what we called doing "stupid stuff." In my first experience in Puerto Rico, we tested the underwater plotting and navigation system. The complex equipment and the experiment proved exciting, but it didn't compare to what we would try in the 4th.

McRaven, a tall, attractive married man, was polished for a young lieutenant. He was calm and patient when we made mistakes, and I only recall him raising his voice to me once.

During the work-up to an amphibious landing in Ecuador, the platoon waited on the beach for hours for the craft to arrive. Concerned the operation wouldn't begin until after dark, Highfill sent me to the ship to retrieve red lens paper to cover our flashlights so we could direct amphibious craft in. Dripping wet in my swim booties and UDT life vest, I ran to the ship's Combat Information Center. As a radarman, I suspected they had the lens paper but was directed by the watch officer to go to the bridge. As I ran onto the bridge in my sandy, soggy booties, I was greeted by an angry officer who said, "What are you doing on here? You're supposed to be on the beach."

"We need red lens paper to cover our flashlights to guide the landing craft."

The officer said, "No, you don't. The operation will be completed before it gets dark."

Annoyed, I shot back, "The way this ship is run, it will be tomorrow morning by the time we get started, and I ran off in search of the thin red plastic. McRaven called me to his stateroom after the landing. In an elevated voice, he said, "Were you on the bridge yesterday?"

"Yes, Steve sent me to the ship to retrieve lens paper."

"Did you talk with an officer?"

Sheepishly I replied, "Yes, he was wearing a ball cap."

That's when he got mad.

"Did you notice all the gold leaf on his hat? That was the captain. You told the captain he didn't know how to run his ship, and he chewed my ass over it!"

"Oh shit, I didn't know, sorry Mr. Mac."

"Stay off the bridge, Brown! Now get out of here."

Lack of deference and lots of attitude got me in trouble every time.

McRaven was a young, up-and-coming officer who wanted to prove himself and us, and he pushed the limits of what and how we operated.

While conducting demolition operations at Fort AP Hill, Virginia, Mike Baker and I detonated hundreds of pounds of explosive hose when we were only yards away in a bunker. Crouching down next to the eighteen-inch-thick reinforced concrete wall, we heard a crackle over the radio.

"All clear."

As I keyed the handset, he said, "Fire in the hole," and turned the handle on the blasting machine. The massive explosion threw us into the air filling the bunker with dust and debris. My eyes and mouth were lined with dirt, and the intense ringing in my head muted every other sound. I sat stunned.

"Holly shit! Are you okay?" I asked Mike.

"Fuck, Brownie, it was like we were sitting on top of that shot!"

Spitting dirt, we fled from the room to find our teammates running toward us.

"We got blown up," I joked. "The thick concrete wall saved our asses."

As I did in BUD/S, I never questioned why we were doing anything; I just did it. Afterward, when I asked Highfill why we were so close to the ordinance, he said, "RDT&E Brownie, RDT&E." It was a scapegoat justification for what happened. It seemed we were the Navy's guinea pigs, testing equipment and techniques. Someone had to do it, and why not the very people who would operate in the most extreme conditions, UDT/SEALs?

We met a helicopter for cast and recovery soon after arriving in Colombia. With our swim fins tucked under our life vest straps, we went through the chopper's Hell Hole. The first was cast at fifteen knots forward speed and fifteen feet above the water. The helo circled, dropped the ladder, and we scrambled up and into the bird.

The next pass was twenty knots at twenty feet, a first at that speed and height for me. I watched the water zipping below the aircraft as we flew into position. One after the other, each man plunged into the ocean. Sitting down, I grabbed the bar and slid through the hole. I was falling for what seemed like forever then... Bam! Slicing down, down, down into the Pacific and popping up seconds later. Crazy! I listened to the platoon whooping and yelling at the thrill.

But we weren't done.

The ladder came by, and once again, we climbed in. We all cheered like fools.

"More, more, more! Higher, higher, faster, faster!"

Some idiot screamed, "Thirty for thirty!" and we all said, "Hoo-yah! Thirty for thirty!"

That's over thirty mph and thirty feet in altitude. Indeed, we'd lost our minds. We were exactly how the Navy trained us.

The bird circled, and we came in for our final drop.

Go! Go! Go!

With the ocean flying by underneath and so far away, I didn't dare think about what was about to happen. One by one, the others went through the hole. Taking my position, I grabbed the bar and again slid through. Pointing my toes, I concentrated, fixating my eyes on the helo above as I knifed through the air. Hitting the water at fifty mph evoked the terror I experienced being thrashed by the giant wave in our final Night Surf Passage.

I spun and tumbled, not knowing what was up or down. The ocean tore off my mask and fins. My feet ripped through my swim booties, now wrapped around my calves. My life vest strap ripped from its mount. As I made it to the surface, my only concern was to complete the mission and spot the chopper coming back for my pickup. Scanning the area for my equipment, I found nothing. As we trod water, the yelling down the line started.

"Holy Shit! All my shit's gone!"

Circling back, the helo flew in, and I grabbed the ladder and climbed into the cabin. Talking and laughing about our missing gear, we were sure we had experienced the upper limits for helicopter cast and recovery.

In my research for this book, I spoke with George Colemen to confirm my recollection of that fateful day. He recalled the incident and the loss of all the gear but said the thirty-for-thirty drop was a mistake by the pilots.

"We never intended to go that high or that fast," he said.

My version may be more likely a wishful memory of UDT guts and glory. But regardless of *why* it happened, it happened. Somehow, we survived.

In pre-deployment training for our trip to Central and South America, we met the SSBN *George Washington*. This former ballistic missile submarine was now used to assist special warfare operations. Our mission was to train to exit, or "lockout," while underway, use inflatable rubber boats to attack a shore-based target, return at night, and lock back in.

My six-man crew launched in a Zodiac, an inflatable boat from a Key West beach at sunset. Traveling twenty miles at night through the shipping lanes off the Florida coast, I drove as the others relaxed, some dozing off from the outboard motor's mesmerizing buzz. Focusing on the compass to ensure we stayed on course, I intently zipped across the straits. The stars provided the only illumination in the black sky. Tim positioned on the bow, sat up straight and screeched.

"Ship!"

Scanning through the night, it came clearly into view; bearing down on us were the bow lights of an enormous freighter.

"Turn! Turn! Turn! Brownie," everyone now awake, screamed.

Spinning our tiny Zodiac, I hammered the small thirty-five horsepower motor throttle, hoping to speed away and prevent being run over or pulled under the massive vessel.

"Go! Go! Go! Brownie!"

Our rubber boat was invisible to their radar, and the ship's crew was oblivious that we existed. The sky blackened as the ship passed, and the men's faces on the bridge came into view as we watched them stare off into the night.

I prefer to be skilled, but I'll always take luck over death. As the enormous rudder sailed by, I slowed the motor to see six men who should have been terrified begin to laugh.

"Holy shit, that was a close one!" Tim snickered. "Alright, I'm on bow watch; let's find that sub, Brownie."

Had we been run over, no one would have known what happened to the seven SEALs who went to meet the *George Washington*. Each time we cheated death, it hardened our callousness toward it. Unphased but more alert, we continued our trek to our rendezvous point.

Once inside the submarine, we prepared to lock out the next day. In a forward compartment, we three climbed up the ladder into the rescue chamber: a driver, the guy who controlled the valves and the riggers, me, and Bob. Locking the watertight door under our feet, the driver flooded the chamber to a level just above our chest, leaving an air bubble for us to breathe. Opening the waist-high hatch to our side gave us access to the ocean. Diving with twin 72s, Bob and I left the boat's safety and swam across its deck.

As I cleared the pressure hull, the sun's rays penetrated from the surface, casting scattered blue-green light beams onto the submarine's hull that faded into darkness. In front, the sub's black nose sliced through the water as the sea sweeping over the bow tugged at my mask, a familiar feeling. My exhale produced bubbles that darted backward, surrounding the conning tower that rose from the hull like a cross.

Our working depth ironically matched my scuba certification dive at Lake Wallenpaupack years earlier. It seemed a tremendous feat then; now, the surface was one breath away. Living my boyhood dreams in the depths, I became the character my mind created: Jacques Cousteau, with a machine gun, clinching onto a nuclear behemoth, speeding through the Caribbean.

Like conducting a spacewalk, we prepared the rigging, always conscious of the giant spinning black propeller waiting for us if we lost our grip. Holding tight to the deck's tracks, I pulled the lines from the conning tower towards the bow.

Pssst! CO_2 from a cartridge filled the buoy connected to a line next to the hatch and shot to the surface. It was our lifeline that transported our equipment to boats above. Repeatedly, we stuffed the trunk with gear and men and floated them in preparation for the night's mission.

As I sucked the steel tanks nearly empty, I cast off the sub's deck. Stealing the last bit of air, the silent gargantuan ship slid below me. A snapshot in time never forgotten like the long-ago wreck resting on the bottom of Harvey's Lake.

Picked up by the trailing safety boat, I returned down the bow line, holding my breath and locking into the sub to do it all again. My underwater odyssey was not lessened by its grueling toll. I held onto that submerged boat for four hours, a task only another UDT/SEAL could accomplish.

In Second Phase, we were evaluated for our ability to operate under conditions we were sure to face, like bronco busting a submarine. There was no bell to ring or opportunity to quit, only missions to complete.

We trained in Colombia, Peru, Uruguay, and Chile during our six-month-long UNITAS deployment. We jumped from many military aircraft, both U.S. and foreign, and dove to complete hydrographic recons in southern Chile's spectacular, burning-cold, 28° F water. We blew up and shot things we were supposed to and a few things we weren't supposed to because that's a SEAL's life—achieving the unattainable and performing the out-of-the-ordinary.

By the time I deployed on UNITAS, I'd been in training mode for three years. The 4th platoon traveled together for nearly a year, enabling us to gel and operate like a well-oiled machine. Only a few months into BUD/S, I became numb to the instructor's warnings that we would risk death daily. The risk was embedded in our psyche, and our actions accounted for it. But the danger didn't always end well for our cross-training partners.

In Colombia, we lost our first ally in a helo cast and recovery exercise. After the helo's first pass, inserting a mixture of SEALs and Colombian Marine swimmers into a brackish river, one of their men failed to surface. After search passes and a short, unsuccessful rescue effort, we found no body. The Colombians concluded that a crocodile consumed their serviceman.

The Chilean Navy suffered the second UNITAS casualty during an ocean parachute jump. A mile off Valparaiso's coast, one of their special forces sailors released his harness early, lost his grip on his leg straps and fell 800 feet to his death. Ironically, I was in the aircraft documenting the exercise and photographed the victim as he took his final leap.

In 1983, UDT-21 became SEAL Team 4. SEAL Team 4 moved into a new facility with SEAL Team 8, which specialized in classified, mini-submarine training.

We'd been back in the new Team 4 compound for a month, and after our 0800 muster, we were stretching for our usual weekly four-mile run in Virginia Beach. As the bus pulled past the barbed wire security gate, I heard someone say, "Hey, do you still suck at running?"

I spun to see Ron looking at me with a huge grin.

"Dave, you son-of-a-bitch! I told you I'd see you in the teams. Well, here I am, buddy."

Running over, I picked Ron up, hugged him, and said,

"You piece of shit, what took you so long? I want to hear all about BUD/S and your Hell Week."

"Get on the bus," I said, "and I'll show you how shitty a runner I am when I smoke you on this 4-mile run."

On that picturesque, Virginia Beach run, Ron again ran me into the ground yet somehow made me feel good about it.

He did as he said he would. Ron had persistence and completed the mission. He and I celebrated the promise from more than three years before to see each other in the Teams. He was wearing the telltale FNG woolen socks and was still shittin' BUD/S chow, and I was never happier to have someone beat me on a run.

25

INTO THE UNKNOWN, INTO SUCCESS

The hero's journey is not a summit to reach but a summit that,
when you get it, shows you new summits in front of you,
waiting to be conquered.
Victor Hugo Manzanilla

Soon after deploying to South America, I received the news that Mary was pregnant. She was twenty years old, living away from her Pennsylvania childhood home for the first time with her husband deployed somewhere in the world, risking his life daily. That is the life of SEAL Team wives. She worked full-time, took care of the house and our finances, went to medical appointments alone, and considered herself lucky to have a phone call with me once or twice a month.

"Hello, this is an international operator. Will you accept a collect phone call from Mr. David Brown?"

If we connected, the conversations were brief; problems were discussed and hopefully solved. My location then or upcoming couldn't be revealed, and exactly when I would be home was classified. I was doing so many exciting things, yet there was no time or place to tell the stories.

Sharing the ridiculous tales to our wives—like drawing loaded semi-automatic weapons from the hip to see who would win the gunfight or wanting to jump from a 200-foot suspension bridge into a river or locking out of a WWII submarine whose escape trunk had to be pried open with a crowbar— those conversations simply didn't happen.

If this book were about SEAL adventures, there would be another twenty-five chapters of mishaps and misdeeds, near-death experiences, and encounters with women worldwide. But our escapades were never written or told. The relevance seemed left behind as time passed, and the places and faces faded from our memories.

Performing warrior missions as if they were scenes from action movies, we lived dangerously while our wives suffered, wondering about the unknown. They mostly stood by us, for better and for worse. And when we returned home, sometimes it was worse.

With personalities fueled by adrenaline and with our fight trait dominant, some could be explosive. I rarely displayed anger or fought with Mary. If our conversation escalated and became heated, I shut down and repressed my emotions, leaving vast gaps of unsettled personal matters unaddressed and unsolved.

Concealing my feelings, I said nothing, standing there expressionless as she poured her heart out over her daily trials and concerns.

As I suggested, not all of us were great husbands or dads. I had moments when I could have been more loving. I should have cried seeing my daughter born, but I didn't. Taking my wife out on date nights and making her feel loved should have been my priority, but that never happened. Doing things only for a reason, I failed to do the most important thing: make myself a better person. Somehow, Mary and I managed to stay together. We had a baby to raise and were both young, naïve, and immature.

Defaulting to my training, everything was an evolution, and every task was a mission to complete. My first re-enlistment date approached, and I soon had to decide whether to remain at SEAL Team 4 or transfer to shore duty for three years.

Living in constant pursuit fits my definition of the pursuit of happiness. It was a selfish way to view life, but my world revolved around challenges. I climbed that mountain. My mission was complete; what was the new one?

Most Team guys left the Navy after their first enlistment. Everyone had their reasons for staying or going. The command master chief told me about an unheard-of billet in Pensacola, Florida, teaching water survival to aviators and that piqued my interest.

Being in the Teams wasn't exactly everything I thought it would be. Sure, it was exciting when we were operating, but doing SEAL stuff meant training for months and traveling before, during, and after. In between, we didn't have much to do but wait around, and we waited a lot.

We waited for helicopters, boats, planes, trucks, buses, and cars. We weren't at war but had to be ready for one. While I've never been in combat, I assume that adds a new intensity level to training and operations—a risk we craved, but as any combat veteran will attest, a risk you don't want.

Logic and instinct told me to move on and that there must be more to do beyond the Teams. My situation fueled my decision, so I transferred to Pensacola to have family time and earn a college degree.

Assignment to shore duty is a natural progression in a Navy career. Sailors spend a prescribed number of years at sea and afterward are relocated to a shore command. It's designed to allow sailors to spend a few years going home every night and live a "normal" life.

Shore billets for SEALs are limited. Our training didn't translate well to doing other jobs, so some Team guys never went, and some lasted only a short time before returning to the Teams out of frustration and boredom.

For me, the move would be a stepping stone. With a college diploma, I'd either apply for an officer's commission or leave and land a civilian job. My identity was being a SEAL, and I had to find a way to justify leaving.

Rationalizing, I concluded I was still a SEAL while teaching because I kept my special warfare qualifications. Jumping from helos every three months and scuba-diving daily I convinced myself I was still an operator even if I wasn't operating.

With only two years to accomplish what took most people four, I went to the educational counselor on base who told me, "It's impossible for you to earn a bachelor's degree in two years."

He didn't realize who he was talking to.

Stationed at Training Tank One, NAS Pensacola, I taught water survival to enlisted and officer flight crews during the day, and at night, I attended college. I tested-out of my undergraduate requirements and focused on my major courses to graduate on time.

From my first day in the Navy, I took pride being a 4.0 sailor and did everything possible to maintain that distinction. Character traits can be good or bad depending on how they are applied, and my lack of deference got me in trouble more than once.

As the only SEAL on base, I was unique, and that led to me testing the command chief's patience. To raise his ire, I had Mary perm my hair tight and curly. Spending hours underwater as a safety diver, I surmised that a short-curly-do was a no-fuss solution to a frizzy mop. Showing up for work with my new hairdo, the Chief called me into his office. "What the hell did you do to your hair, Brown?"

"Mary permed it," I said.

"It looks ridiculous. Cut it; it's not to Navy standards," he said.

"I think it's within the standard," I said. "Tell you what, if I pass the division inspection this week, I'm keeping it," and I walked out.

Later that week, I stood tall for inspection in my blue instructor collared shirt, UDT shorts, and sneakers as the Division Officer walked by me, not saying a word. That afternoon, I went in to see the Chief.

"See, I told you, I passed with my curly hair." In my subsequent evaluation, I received a one-tenth of one percent deduction for military bearing and lost my 4.0 sailor distinction. In the end, I won the hairdo battle, but the Chief won the war.

216

I wish I had taken the lesson to heart, but I was too stubborn to see the significance of missing a perfect 4.0 grade over a stupid haircut. My mother called it right.

I hid in the utility closet to do homework when I wasn't teaching. Escaping the chatter and activity in the training area, I studied under a seventy-five-watt bulb next to cleaning products and paper supplies. My textbooks lay open on floor wax containers and disinfectant as I wrote English term papers and memorized constitutional law. Curious, Mary asked me one day, "Why do you always reek of Simple Green?"

To graduate on time, I took night and televised courses for a semester, leaving me with only Sunday to be a husband and father. For three months, my days resembled a BUD/S training schedule: up at 0500, work, school, and return home at 2130. to eat, sleep, and do it again. I had to complete my mission.

In June of 1987, I graduated magna cum laude from Troy State University with a 3.75 GPA and a degree in Criminal Justice, just sixty days shy of my end-of-service date.

That spring, during my arduous schedule chaos, I sat in my living room on a Sunday morning, playing with my daughter Alexis and drinking coffee. I asked Mary, "So what would you prefer? Should I go back to the Teams or go into law enforcement?" It didn't matter what her answer was; I'd already decided.

Going back meant I would deploy overseas for four to six years. Operating was exciting, but it was peacetime, and there wasn't anyone to fight. We trained and practiced for war but never had the opportunity to test our skills in combat.

Restless to draw the gun I carried, I needed to move on. I didn't want to shoot someone; I wanted work where altercations were possible, and I could take advantage of my Sheepdog trait.

Wanting to protect society from criminals, as I'd protected the country as a SEAL, I thought becoming a federal law enforcement special agent was my next career.

Mary's answer?

"Do what you want to do. I married you, knowing I'd have to follow you and your career. I'm a cosmetologist; I can get a job anywhere."

Everyone faces difficult life decisions. Choose the path of least resistance or take that chance and proceed into the unknown. Instead of being Jaques Cousteau with a machine gun, my new plan, objective, and mission were clear.

I would wear a suit and carry a gun like James Bond.

The FBI, the Drug Enforcement Administration (DEA), and the Naval Investigative Service (NIS), now NCIS, were all on my list of opportunities.

NIS interviewed me in their offices on base. In my green inspection-ready uniform, sharply cornered hat, and displaying my Trident, I walked into a conference room with four men in suits seated at a table with one woman. The questions began immediately without introduction, which seemed strange.

Seeing the woman, I asked, "Are you an NIS special agent?"

"Oh, yes, I should have introduced myself" she said.

"I didn't know NIS had female agents."

My naivety and immaturity shined through with my brash comment.

Later during the interview, one of the men asked, "Can you handle yourself in a fight?"

I found the question odd since I was wearing a Trident, and it pissed me off a little. I said, "Would you like to step outside and find out?"

He said, "No, that's okay, I believe you."

Again, not the best response. Afterward, I was sure I had no chance of getting a position.

I took the FBI test and was told by the Panama City Field Office Special Agent in Charge that I didn't score high enough for a white male. My FBI application went in the trash. I also interviewed with the DEA, which seemed interested.

Much to my surprise, NIS offered me a job the following week and I was to report to the Federal Law Enforcement Training Center in Brunswick, Georgia, exactly one month after I left the Navy.

Energized, I prepared with the same intensity as I did for the BUD/S screening test. The idea of being a special agent fueled my imagination. I fantasized about busting in doors on search warrant raids, buying and selling drugs while deep undercover, and taking down the bad guy in his dirty business dealings.

Moreover, I was tickled to be free from the military's confines and restrictions. At twenty-four years old, I'd traveled the world and thought my life was perfectly planned. I realized my strengths, and I pursued them relentlessly. What I should have done was mitigate my weaknesses.

Confidence is a powerful drug. I didn't need a to-do list, self-help suggestions, or recommendations from a life coach to tell me how to be successful, nor do you. You know more about your abilities, and if you take the time to pay attention to yourself, you will recognize your weaknesses, something I took for granted.

Becoming a SEAL doesn't qualify me to give advice, and I won't. I wouldn't take life advice from another SEAL because I know too many. If you've learned anything from this book, you must realize that we, and I'll stereotype "we" as Team guys, are a hot mess. Our personality traits are off the chart; we run good and bad in extreme ways. I can no more provide specialized advice than Elon Musk can tell you how to become a billionaire. It simply doesn't work that way. Instead, consider science and advice from the experts.

Some of the best advice, in my opinion, comes from Dr. Jordan B. Peterson, an author, psychologist, online educator, and professor emeritus at the University of Toronto. Peterson has a lot to say, but fundamentally, he professes that you should learn about yourself. Understand your personality, strengths, and weaknesses, then work to be your best person.

In his book *12 Rules for Life*, Peterson propounds deep and valuable principles for building a meaningful life. He says to get your house in order before criticizing others. Peterson doesn't profess that you will be successful by merely following a checklist or rule book. Instead, he challenges us to look within ourselves and extract personal meaning from his 12 Rules.

After selling our house, the movers swooped in, packed, and stored our things. Mary and Alexis moved back to Pennsylvania to live with her parents while I attended federal law enforcement training in Georgia. I was on to my next evolution and intended to finish the mission at any cost.

My story of chasing success and happiness didn't end. My life's journey wasn't to become a Navy SEAL. Like Doba, that achievement was my ocean to cross, an inevitability, something that I was destined to do.

26

RAPE, SEXUAL ABUSE, AND AUTOPSIES

The price one pays for pursuing any profession or calling,
is an intimate knowledge of its ugly side.
James Baldwin

Not reenlisting in the Navy was a significant risk. My military salary was nearly $30K, a massive sum in my mind, while my special agent pay started under $18K. Like most people, I had bills to pay, but contemplated that if I excelled, I could more than double my income in three years, and I set my sights on doing just that.

In October 1987, my Investigations Basic Course at the Federal Law Enforcement Training Center (FLETC) in Brunswick, Georgia, began with a class of seventy-three and ended with seventy-two, an easy day for sure.

After retrieving Mary and Alexis, I was excited to show them our new house. It was more roomy and nicer than any place we had before, and the rent of $350 per month fit our tiny budget. Driving down the two-lane road to Beaufort, Mary talked less as she noticed the dilapidated houses and poor living conditions in the South Carolina Low Country.

"Does it get better, David?" she asked.

"Absolutely, it does. It's much nicer by the Marine Corps base, which is where most of the officers live."

But it didn't, and we passed shanty after run-down house until we were in our housing development. The last few miles, she started to cry.

"Oh, my God," she said, "I can't believe we have to live here."

I reported to the Naval Investigative Service (NIS) Resident Office at the Marine Corps Recruit Depot. "Where It All Begins" was the tagline for boot camp. I discovered that it was where all the crime began.

Neil Robins was the best boss a newbie agent could ask for. No nicer person loved the job more and knew every sentence in every NIS manual. He used to say to me, "There's not enough paper in the world to explain why you didn't follow the manual, David."

So, I read it and memorized the essential parts taking his advice. He was a true mentor, and a by-the-book guy is what I needed. He did love to brag. He'd say, "You know David, I'm the youngest Resident Agent in Charge, GS-13 in NIS history."

I would say, "That's great, Neil; one day, you'll be working for me."

"That will never happen, David, never happen." He laughed. In our tiny office on a pier next to the Beaufort River, I shared a room with Chris Compel, my FLETC roommate, and Kevin Marks, who graduated six months prior. Kevin was a good-looking fellow, a preacher's son type, with jet-black hair and standing over six feet tall. A former schoolteacher, he was blessed with southern charm but cursed with condescending undertones. Cock sure in his abilities, he spent afternoons lurching over my desk detailing his awesomeness. The reality was we had no idea how to solve crimes. In my first weeks, Neil sent me out on a break-in at the cobbler shop to investigate shoe polish theft. He had me interrogate Marines over government coleslaw and blanket misappropriation. I lifted fingerprints, processed crime scenes, and conducted interviews as if a murder had been committed.

Neil would say, "It's better to screw up missing coleslaw than an armed robbery." On a Sunday morning, one month later, I received a call reporting an actual homicide. I pulled into a dirt driveway at a single-wide trailer in a small housing area. The base police and a Marine Corps Criminal Investigation Division (CID) agent were on the scene. With police tape across the entire area restricting access, the scene was like a television crime show.

"What have we got?" I asked the CID agent.

"Caucasian female, early twenties, married to a staff sergeant, no kids, shot through the roof of the mouth. A small caliber revolver was on the living room table when we arrived."

I'd never seen a dead person, had little investigative experience, and was scared shitless. But as the senior person on site, it was my investigation to command, and I walked into the trailer like an investigator with ten years on the job. The putrid smell of death filled the room; the victim, untouched, lay in a small pool of dried blood. Her body fluids stained the couch where she remained stiff and ghost white with her eyes partially open. A revolver was positioned some two feet away on a coffee table.

Turning to the CID agent beside me, I asked, "If she committed suicide, how'd the gun get on the table?"

"Haha, I see they train you well at FLETC. Excellent question," he said. "What do you want us to do, SPECIAL AGENT Brown?" He crossed his arms over his chest.

There were two ways to handle this situation. I could act like a big shot in charge and make a major mistake or do what I did. "Man, I have no idea. I've been on the job four weeks and sure can use your help," I said.

Smiling, relaxing his shoulders, he pulled out a checklist and said, "I was hoping you'd say that. I'll take care of it but let me show you how it's done." We spent the day processing the crime scene; we swabbed the victim for gunpowder residue, took photographs, and lifted fingerprints. My new friend, Steve, the CID agent, collected the evidence and arranged for an emergency autopsy. With an encouraging punch to my shoulder, Steve said, "She's all yours, buddy," as the ambulance drove away. "You need to attend the autopsy." Jumping in my government car, I followed the ambulance to the Medical Examiners' office.

The exam room in a historic building had high vaulted ceilings, the walls were covered in white ceramic tile, and the temperature was a dank 62° F. The body lay stiff on a stainless-steel table as a man in a white lab coat sat at his desk completing paperwork and inhaling the final bites of a sandwich. "I'm Doctor Bronson, the medical examiner. Are you the investigator?" he asked.

"Yes, but it's only been a few hours." I nervously blurted.

"A few hours for what?" He looked over, puzzled.

I stood flat-footed, unable to gather a single intelligent thought.

"What do you know?" he asked. I explained the investigation up to that point, and he shook his head and said, "Well, this should be easy enough to determine if it's suicide." Bronson began his autopsy and sliced and diced her body using huge knives, clamps, and trays to hold the parts he pulled out. Overpowered by the stench, I nearly vomited.

"There's a jar of Vicks on the shelf; rub some under your nose," he advised. "Don't feel bad; you have to get used to it." After sawing her head open, he took two long stainless-steel rods and shoved one through her mouth and the other into her brain, showing where the bullet bounced off her skull and eventually landed in the base of her neck. "Come here," the doctor ordered. "You see the angle that bullet traveled?"

"Yes," I said.

"There's no way someone stuck a gun in her mouth at that angle and pulled the trigger. I've been doing this for a long time. This was suicide, I'm certain." It was nearly 9 p.m. when I finished at the examiner's office and drove home. I hadn't eaten since breakfast, yet food was the last thing on my mind. After the autopsy, the thought of eating meat was repulsive. It took weeks for me to get over the autopsy's disturbing images. The forensics revealed gunpowder residue on her left hand. Interviews revealed that after finding her shot on the couch, her husband grabbed the gun from her hand and put it on the table. I solved my first homicide. Over the following six months, I had two more homicide investigations—which was two more than I wanted.

Neil was promoted out of the Parris Island office and replaced by the new boss, Bob Robbins. Bob was as friendly and competent as

Neil and sent me back to FLETC for advanced training investigating child and spousal abuse, which seemed rampant in the Laural Bay military housing area.

After training, Bob gave me every abuse allegation to investigate, and soon my entire caseload was filled with rapists and child molesters. It is an honorable and righteous field working to catch and prosecute those who prey on the weakest, and the ideology went hand-in-hand with my Sheepdog traits. While I was highly successful at obtaining confessions, guilty pleas, and convictions, the subject matter weighed heavily, probably because Alexis was the same age as many of the victims.

Coming face-to-face with the aftermath of beaten or sexually abused children became daunting. I interrogated a Navy corpsman for sexually assaulting a dozen children under six years old in his wife's daycare and worked a solid weekend investigating a double rape. The courts served justice, but I sometimes wanted the punishment to be more severe, more medieval.

With so much education and training, I was drawn to more intellectual crime, and that's when I realized it was time to change disciplines and go to white-collar/fraud school.

Because he had no one trained to do fraud investigations, Bob was happy to send me to Norfolk for the month-long class. And like every other opportunity, I attacked it and returned to Beaufort, ready to catch my first fraudster.

We'd been in Beaufort for less than a year when my mother called and told me my father had a stroke and the doctors didn't think he would make it. The family descended on Sarasota to pay our last respects before the hospital removed him from life support.

I'd never attached a feeling when someone I knew died. Sure, Team guys were killed in accidents, and we honored and toasted them. I'd seen homicide victims but never experienced any emotion associated with the death. Emotions surrounding death were tucked into that little box, along with the fear of failure, never to be seen or displayed. And that's what I did. I didn't cry or allow myself to be

225

vulnerable or human. My father was gone at fifty-five years old, and I returned to work the next day to finish the evolution.

Kevin loved "general criminal" investigations and immediately pranced into my office laughing after learning I was going to white-collar fraud school. He pompously announced, "Dude, there's no fraud on this base. You will be doing stolen check cases the rest of your career." I set out to prove Kevin wrong.

Soon after, I landed my first significant white-collar investigation. A small company, Emerald Oil, was suspected of substituting used oil for the virgin crude they were contracted to supply to the depot boilers. The boilers kept breaking down due to the dirt and debris in the fuel, leaving no heat in many buildings.

From locking out of submarines to scanning bank statements, my world could not have been more different, but I was the same. While most agents sat behind their desks rummaging through paperwork, I recruited informants and went undercover to catch the fraudster in the act. After reviewing the contracts and the stacks of delivery receipts at the contracting office, I identified an Emerald Oil subcontractor near Atlanta. The subcontractor was a recycler who picked up used oil everywhere, from restaurant kitchens to Jiffy Lube shops. I was certain I had found the weak link. In Atlanta, I met with the reclaimed oil company president who assured me he did not know the delivery specifications.

"If you didn't know you were supposed to deliver virgin crude, prove it," I said. "Call the president of Emerald Oil and tell him NIS is investigating your deliveries, and you want to know the truth. And let me record the conversation."

When I called Bob to ask for approval, he was energized. "I can't believe you got him to consent! Great job, and good luck."

During the consensual call, Emerald's president admitted he didn't disclose the specifications and apologized. The recording provided probable cause, and I obtained and executed a federal search warrant for the business. With the mountain of evidence I collected, the Emerald Oil president pled guilty, and the Parris Island office reported its first white-collar prosecution. My work earned me the Regional Director's award, and Bob nominated me for Agent of the Year.

Knowing Kevin had yet to earn a single federal conviction, I taped a copy of the plea agreement to his door.

I'd done all I could at Parris Island and asked to be transferred to the Honolulu fraud unit. I was set on doubling my salary in three years and moved forward with a steady beat. My investigations took priority, leaving no time for vacations.

My success at work didn't translate to winning at home. Spending my twenty-four months at Parris Island working days, nights, and weekends gave Mary too much time to contemplate her what-ifs. She hated Beaufort the minute she saw it. Her tears of disappointment the first time we drove in were evidence. We joked, "The only thing to do in Beaufort is to count sand fleas and watch the swing bridge turn." But our path out was through my hard work, and I justified my absence from home by insisting it would all be worth the effort because we would all benefit from my success.

According to an article in *The Atlantic*, people sacrifice their links with others for their true love, success. They travel for business on anniversaries; they miss Little League games and recitals while working long hours. Some forgo marriage for their careers—earning the appellation of being "married to their work"—even though a good relationship is more satisfying than any job. Many scholars have shown that people willingly sacrifice their own well-being through overwork to keep getting hits of success.

As we landed on Oahu, Mary's face lit up with happiness. She loved the weather and our beautiful condo with a spectacular view of Pearl Harbor. To top it off, she found a great position as a chiropractor's administrative assistant in Honolulu. But I was there to work and make a name for myself, live up to my potential, and be successful.

I checked in as a GS-11 junior agent at the Pearl Harbor Regional Office, Fraud Squad. My boss, John DeDona, was a new GS-13 supervisor. John had an excellent reputation for conducting high-speed investigations in Okinawa, and we hit it off. He was a guy I could learn from, and I did. While the other agents sat behind their desks, I recruited sources from the community.

As the junior agent, I was given old, stale leads and cases that had languished for years. A senior agent, Keith Houston, threw a file on my desk. The label on the front read "Techno Engineering," and "AKC" was written across the front in bold black.

"Here you go, new guy," he said.

"What's A.K.C. mean?" I asked.

He replied, "American Kennel Club, dude. The case is a dog!" He laughed, turned his back, and walked away.

But I was a Doba, pathologically persistent.

It wasn't long before I recruited Ed Major, the General Construction Manager for Techno Engineering. After collecting years of contracts, employee time sheets, and thousands of certifications, I uncovered a pattern of salary fraud, a clear Davis Bacon Act violation. The Act required government contractors to pay prevailing wages, something Major and Techno knew and didn't do. I just had to prove it beyond a reasonable doubt to a jury.

Luke McGranaghan, a former Marine Ranger and my regular field partner, and I tailed Major into his Honolulu high-rise parking garage. Pulling behind his pick-up, blocking him in, we jumped from the car.

Holding my badge, I asked, "Are you Ed Major?"

The tall, hefty, white-bearded man stood stunned.

Wanting to speak, he stopped, stammered, and said, "What took you guys so long?"

He provided documentary and testimonial evidence against the company president. It took me a year and a half, but Techno Engineering was indicted on federal fraud charges.

But that wasn't my only fraud investigation. At the same time, I was working on a case involving Cummins Diesel for knowingly providing a substandard generator to the Naval Supply Command. This million-dollar fraud jeopardized the Navy's operational readiness to supply ships and bases in the Pacific. Sitting with a judge in Honolulu, I reached into my pocket and pulled out a bottle of

"White-Out" and a copy of the engine's specification sheet. Dabbing the white masking liquid over a few numbers on the page changed the engine's capabilities to appear as if it would run continuously versus intermittently.

"This is how the Cummins Diesel's engineer falsified the documents he gave to the Navy," I told the judge. My presentation was so convincing he signed the warrant.

After gathering the fraud squad members, we swooped in to execute the warrant. While searching the engineer's desk, I found the original falsified white-out documents. The Oahu Cummins Diesel distributor owner came flying into the office yelling when he heard about our raid.

"You can't come in here and take whatever you want," he said to me.

Handing him the warrant, I said, "Yes, I can."

As he was being dragged from the building, he cried, "You guys are Nazis!"

As I prepared for that warrant, I received a call from my mother in Florida. Every time my mother called, it was bad news, and this was no exception. She told me my sister Bonnie passed away unexpectedly.

"What can I do?" I asked.

"Nothing, you just need to know," she said. My priorities and perspectives were clear.

The next day at work, John came into my office and expressed his sympathy for my loss.

"You need to take a few days off," he said.

"I'm not flying back to Florida for the funeral," I told him. "I have to finish the search warrant affidavit." And like my Team brothers' deaths, I toasted my sister and remembered her life, then went on to complete my mission the next day.

After three years in Hawaii, I single-handedly accounted for 70% of all the recoveries, indictments, pleas, and convictions from my squad of five. John nominated me for government employee of the year, and the NIS Headquarters Director for Fraud traveled from Washington, DC, and took me to lunch in Honolulu.

"Dave, you're doing one hell of a job out here. We could use a talent like yours in HQ. It's not exciting, but you could help develop policy, and it would set you up for a promotion to GS-13."

I appreciated the director's visit, and I said yes, never thinking of asking Mary what she thought or wanted. All I could think about was Neil Robins, a GS-15 in HQ, and how I was catching up with him.

Four months after I arrived in DC, I returned to Honolulu for the three-week Techno Engineering federal trial. The jury found the company's president guilty, and he was sentenced to thirty-three months in prison, an unheard-of lengthy sentence for a white-collar crime.

27

WITH ONLY A SLING AND A STONE
1 Samuel 17:50 (NLT)

Like a hamster on a wheel, my assignment at NCIS headquarters in Washington, DC (The District) quickly became monotonous. In the office by 6 a.m. and never leaving before 6 p.m. was miserable, especially for a former skydiving, machine-gun-carrying undercover planning special agent. I longed to be back in the field, coming and going as I pleased in heavy pursuit of the bad guys.

The Environmental Protection Agency Criminal Investigation Division was growing with the advent of criminal statutes focused on environmental protection. US Attorney's Offices nationwide were excited to prosecute these flavor-of-the-month criminal cases, and I was happy to jump on their bandwagon.

Tired of sitting behind a desk, I arranged for an interview with Mike Catlett, a former Secret Service agent in charge of hiring at CID. Mike was friendly and invited me to his office at EPA headquarters in The District. As he read my resume, he paused.

"You're a former Navy SEAL?"

"Yes, I am. I served in UDT-21 and SEAL Team 4."

All he could talk about was my Team experience for the entire hour.

Afterward, I thought he didn't ask me one question about my investigative accomplishments. It didn't matter; I was sure he would offer me the job. If it was because of something I did ten years ago, I didn't care. I wanted out from behind my desk and out of DC.

The following day, Mike called.

"When can you come over? I have an Environmental Basic class starting at FLETC in two weeks. Can you make it?

"I want to be stationed where there are exciting criminal cases," I said. "That's my only request."

"Haha, don't worry about that. We can make that happen."

I said yes to his offer and again to a position change and move without asking Mary. With the decision made, I spent another two months away from home. After graduation, we moved to St. Louis, our fifth move in ten years.

Mary, Alexis, our dog Belle, and I loaded into a U-Haul in Burke, VA, and began our two-day drive to Missouri. I relished venturing into the unknown. We'd never been or knew a single person in St. Louis. Mike told me very little about the office but said it was connected to the agency's top as the Resident Agent in Charge, Steven Howell, was a longtime friend of CID Director Earl Devaney, a former Secret Service agent. In all my government moves, I never worried about the office dynamic of who was who. My only fear came from within: the fear of letting myself slip below the standard I set.

Arriving in St. Charles, outside St. Louis, I discovered our hotel was not pet-friendly. I was stuck, so I took a chance and called the first special agent on the St. Louis CID roster, Vic Muschler, and introduced myself.

"Hey Vic, this is Dave Brown, the new agent."

"Yeah, Howell said you'd be in town today," he answered. "He said you weren't his pick, and HQ sent you." Howell was less than enthusiastic about receiving a new agent and, worse, an unknown.

"That's true, but I have another problem. I have a Bassett Hound, and the hotel doesn't take pets. Can you keep her for a few days until we find a place?"

"Okay, sure, where are you? I'll be right over."

And that is Vic Muschler's story, a mid-western boy and former St. Charles County Sheriff's deputy who would do anything to help.

Vic and I quickly became investigative partners. Most mornings began with either Vic or me pulling our undercover car (nicknamed G-rides) into the other's driveway with a hot cup of coffee, ready to tackle the next big case. We spent days on the road crisscrossing Missouri, chasing down witnesses in the deadly downtown streets of St. Louis and the backwoods of the Ozarks. Without fail, Vic would charm a local barmaid or waitress into providing us with information or revealing the location of the witness we needed for our case. He inevitably "knew a guy" who could make it happen regardless of what needed to be done.

CID promised a promotion after my first year, and to their word, I became a GS-13 in twelve months. Catlett also kept his promise: St. Louis was the Wild, Wild West of environmental crime. Soon after I started the job, I got a call from a woman who reported concrete floating in a stream. That made no sense to me, so on my way into the office, I stopped by the city park where the floating concrete was on full display.

As I approached the five-yard-wide creek, there it was. Concrete slurry, fluffy, bubbly waste piles dotted the water's surface. Following the bank, I walked until I heard a truck off in the distance. Through the trees, I witnessed a truck back to the edge of an overhang and began dumping wastewater from its drum down the embankment and into the stream. Returning to my government car, I sped to the office to find the 35 mm camera.

Howell and Pat Flachs, an assistant United States Attorney assigned to prosecute environmental crime, were chatting as I flew through the door.

"Holy shit, I watched a concrete truck dumping in a creek north of Wilmore Park! I need the camera to take pictures."

Flachs laughed, "Who's this guy, Steve?"

Steve said, "Dave Brown, HQ sent him."

I chased concrete trucks all over St. Louis, taking photos as they cleaned out and polluted streams in every corner of the county. Setting up my criminal case, Flachs gave me grand jury subpoenas for several drivers. After one finished dumping, I parked my undercover car across the traffic lanes and got out. And like David with his slingshot and rock, I stood in the middle of the road with my badge and hand in the air and stopped the 28,000-pound truck.

Backing me up, Vic drew his Glock 9mm as I climbed onto the truck's cab, getting in the driver's face. After showing him my credentials, I said, "I'm an EPA Special Agent. I watched you dump into that creek. Here's your subpoena."

The stunned driver blurted, "They tell us to do it. 'Don't come back with anything in the drum,' they said. We have to get rid of it before we go back to the plant or get fired."

Environmental and fraud prosecutions are a lot alike. So many jurors see the violations as victimless crimes. The way to enhance a sentence is to find a victim. I canvased the county, evaluating every concrete batch plant owned by Breckenridge Materials, my target. After walking a quarter mile along the railroad tracks, I came up on the back side of a sizeable Breckenridge plant. Below a steep concrete-covered incline dotted with dead trees lay a toxic blue water lagoon where concrete trucks dumped their slurry. Near the gray wasteland's base, I spied a moving dot. As I got closer, the dot turned out to be a slurry-covered turtle, the victim.

The investigation lasted several more months, resulting in multiple convictions and the development of a national program to treat concrete waste by the American Concrete Institute.

As with every job before, I was busy running and gunning most days, nights, and weekends. Mary started a new position as an assistant to a wealthy insurance broker who lived at Lake St. Louis, very near us. Not the best influence, her boss loved to drink, and Mary was happy to go along. She often came home late, drunk from the happy hour gatherings they'd frequented. Mary's drinking problem spiraled out of control, and she didn't come home one night.

By midnight, I was frantic and called her boss.

"Janet, where's Mary?"

"David, she's not home? We were in a car accident; I was drinking and drove off the road into a field. She jumped from the passenger seat and ran, and I haven't seen her since."

"What the hell, why didn't you call me!"

"I thought you'd get mad at her. I thought she was home."

The front door swung open, and Mary walked in drunk and dirty from running through and falling in a farmer's field.

"How'd you get here?" I asked. "Janet said you were in an accident. Are you ok?"

"I'm fine," she said. "Someone saw me walking along the road and gave me a ride."

I demanded she seek treatment for her alcohol abuse problem. She said she didn't need counseling and could control her drinking.

But she couldn't and was arrested one night after leaving a bar and charged with DUI. The court reduced the charges thanks to Vic and his connections, and Mary avoided jail. Our relationship suffered between my work hours and Mary's drinking, but I refused to give up on our marriage. I took my vows seriously, for better or worse. And it got worse. Our marriage was fatally broken at that point, but my stubbornness refused to accept the failure. Still, in my "beat-the-problem-into-submission" Navy SEAL attitude, I neglected to devise a plan B, an escape route.

"Shortly after arriving in St Louis, Steve called me into his office, the only private place within the three-room CID confines.

"Have a seat Mr. Brown," he said as I closed the door. "Let me be perfectly clear: I didn't pick you or know you. Devaney said you're a former Navy SEAL, but that won't buy you a cup of coffee in this office. You have a lot of work to do to prove I can trust you." Not showing deference was my natural trait, but I also knew when to demure. "I hear you, Steve," I said, "but know this: If you ask me to do something and it doesn't get done, you better check the hospitals because nothing short of a serious injury or death will keep me from completing my mission." He sat back in his chair and ran his fingers through is white thinning hair, and said, "Humm...well, that's good to know."

The first investigation Steve assigned me after arriving in St. Louis was the Burlington Northern and Santa Fe Railroad (BNSF) investigation. A farmer in Cherryville, MO, reported that the men cleaning BNSF rail cars dumped debris on the ground, and the grass in his pasture was dying. The Missouri Department of Natural Resources investigator who referred the matter said, "It's been going on for years. We gotta convince them to stop dumping their trash and clean it up. It's a civil prosecution at best."

It didn't seem to be a civil case to me, and I began digging into the site's history and what the railcars were carrying. Two BNSF contractors operated the railcar cleaning facility. The cars traveled in a loop to pick up and dump lead ore from the Doe Run mine to its smelter in Herculaneum, MO. The cars made stops along the loop, and if any debris or waste was tossed into an empty ore car, that car was sent to the Cherryville railroad siding to be cleaned by the contractor.

The two cleaners may not have been high school graduates, but they devised an ingenious cleaning method to hoist a small front loader tractor into the railcar and scoop everything onto the ground. Over fifteen years, the debris began to build up, and BNSF forced them to remove it off-site.

Soil testing by BNSF years prior determined the build-up was mostly lead ore scrapped from the railcar's floor. The railroad environmental engineer never disclosed the hazardous site testing to their clean-up crew, and the contractors mistook the ore for innocuous fill, spreading the contaminant on properties around the county and poisoning residents.

The turning point in the case came months after BNSF turned over tens of thousands of documents in response to a grand jury subpoena. As I scanned every document for evidence, I found an envelope containing photographs of the car cleaning area. One photo depicted the two cleaners with their children, one playing in the contaminated soil. I identified the little boy and traced his tragic journey through a childhood destroyed by lead poisoning.

BNSF agreed to pay $10 million in fines and restitution and a further $9 million in remediation costs for hazardous waste discharges from the company's cleaning operation. The families affected by the illegal dumping sued the railroad and recovered undisclosed amounts.

EPA awarded me a Bronze Medal for my investigation, and while I thought I was a hot-shit investigator, I couldn't have done any case in Missouri without Vic. He and I were lethal partners to environmental criminals. We regularly dealt directly with defense counsels who often took our advice and worked plea deals for their clients.

The St. Louis CID office became the Regional Office, and Steve Howell became the Special Agent in Charge. Steve subsequently promoted me to Assistant Special Agent in Charge, a GS-14 position.

I was happy in St. Louis. Mary got help with her drinking and started a job as a dental assistant, and Alexis was attached to her friends and middle school. Happy I may have been, but I wasn't content. I hadn't lived up to my potential—to be the Special Agent in Charge.

Steve was satisfied as the SAC. Standing in his office doorway, I asked him, "Steve, do you have any plans after you retire from EPA?"

Without taking his eyes off his newspaper, he said. "Umm."

I enjoyed working for Steve; he became a father figure I respected despite his non-communicative communication style. He had an old-school cop mentality and demeanor and valued hard work, dedication, and loyalty. One of his memorable sayings was, "Why say yes when you can say no, and why say no when you can grunt." He grunted a lot.

David Montoya was my friend at CID and one-time peer, and then my boss as the Special Agent in Charge of CID. He moved over to be the Assistant Inspector General for Investigations at the Department of the Interior (DOI), Office of Inspector General (OIG). David was courted by the new DOI Inspector General, Earl

Devaney, who also came from EPA. In turn, David courted me to become the special agent in charge of the OIG in Sacramento.

My goal soon after I became an NIS special agent was to work my way up the ranks to be the special agent in charge. And here, the opportunity was at my fingertips. I was sure this would mean success. Once again, not giving my family a choice, I accepted the position and told Mary and Alexis we'd be moving to Sacramento, California.

When Alexis, who was in 9th grade, heard the news, she ran to her room and cried.

"Why do we have to move again, Dad? I don't want to leave my friends. We always move."

I assured her, "This is the last time, I promise. You'll make new friends, and you can finish high school in California. This is our final move."

I'd made it.

At thirty-nine years old, I was at the top as the Special Agent in Charge.

This mission was complete, and I was catching up to Neil Robins.

The greater Sacramento area was nice enough, but I wanted to live in the Sierra Nevada foothills, so we found a small house in the Lake of the Pines a few miles above Auburn. Mary got a great job as a dental assistant, and Alexis became a cheerleader. Everything seemed perfect.

Land prices in California were rising rapidly, and I took the opportunity to cash in and buy property and build our retirement home. We sold our house in Lake of the Pines twelve months after we moved in and rented a house in Nevada City while our new house was under construction in Penn Valley. But I kept my promise to Alexis, and she remained at the same high school.

As the SAC in Sacramento, I supervised offices in Billings, MT, Phoenix, AZ, and Guam. The billion-dollar DOI programs ran from Alaska down the west coast to the Pacific Island territories and several small island nations, such as the Marshall Islands and the Federated States of Micronesia.

The Sacramento office had only two agents, each with over fifteen years on the job, yet neither seemed to have much experience prosecuting criminal investigations. I quickly realized they were content hiding in their locked offices, doing everything they could to avoid speaking with each other.

Calling Montoya a week after arriving and assessing the region's challenges, I said, "Dave, what the hell? Why didn't you tell me I inherited the Island of Misfit toys?" He pleaded, "I know, calm down. This morning, Devaney told me: "Make sure Brown doesn't quit; once he finds out what he's got out there, he may jump ship." I told Dave, "Dude, you know me better than that, but I'm gonna have to make some changes here, so be prepared. The shit's gonna hit the fan."

"Ya, I hear you,"Dave replied, "but please, please, try not to kill anyone."

It took months to begin to straighten things out. I started hiring competent agents and opened another office in Portland. I was always in by 7 a.m. and left after 6 p.m.

My territory spanned across the international date line, and Monday in Guam was Sunday in Sacramento; as such, I often spent afternoons on the phone, resolving Guam's problems. Not exactly what I asked for, but it came with being the SAC. It was no different than hitting the surf in BUD/S, an unpleasantry that came with the job.

But I was glad to take the good with the bad. I traveled extensively throughout the Pacific. As a senior government official, I met with governors and top law enforcement officials in the US territories. In the Freely Associated States, independent Island nations, I met with their attorneys general and even the presidents. My position carried significant responsibility. Each island, much like American Indian nations, had distinct customs, traditions, laws, and regulations. My duty was supervising criminal investigations on these islands without antagonizing Montoya, Devaney, the Interior Department, or Congress.

But as fate would have it, I'd climbed the ladder so high that I climbed right out of doing the things I enjoyed and the reason I became a special agent to begin with.

Then, as I stood at the proverbial top of the mountain, the inexplicable happened. While I should have seen it coming, my personal and professional world began to crumble, and nothing I learned in BUD/S, SEAL Team, or the Special Agent Academy could prepare me for what was to happen.

Fast forward, two years later, I was driving down Interstate 80 to the office. Mary had filed for divorce, and my girlfriend was to be buried in a few days. Only moments before, I'd pulled away from the that gas station in Auburn, nearly tearing the nozzle and hose from the pump. With my bank account drained, my credit card maxed out, my shirt wrinkled, and my pants torn, my eyes welled up.

My thoughts flashed back to BUD/S and a horrifyingly familiar feeling. I'd been here, no worse. Running down the demo pit road with the pack pulling away from me and the ambulance on my heels, begging me to quit.

It's so easy to quit, throw your hands in the air and walk away. Quit your job. Go to your favorite bar and get drunk. Don't go to the gym and work out. And cheat on your wife when things get rough.

I refused to quit in BUD/S and had no intention of quitting now.

Arriving at the office, my Assistant Special Agent in Charge Mark Tinsley took one look at me and said, "Dave, you need to go home. I'll take care of things here." With that, my healing began.

I cried that day, all day, and at Dina's funeral that week. I cried for her and me. I cried to catch up on my forty years of emotional neglect and for everyone around me who suffered from it. I had a lot to make up for.

Eric Myers, a former English professor and volleyball coach, was given to me as a fresh-out-of-the-academy new agent. Very much like myself, reporting to Howell in St. Louis, Eric was untested and unknown. As luck would have it, he quickly became a prolific investigator and learned how to do the job not in years but in months. Sensing my despair, he left a sympathy card on my desk." In it, he wrote, "Let me know if you need to talk." When I thanked him for his card, he said, "Let's go out for a beer after work."

"Thanks, Eric, but I don't like beer."

"What! That's because you're drinking the wrong beer," he said. "We're going out, and I guarantee I will find you something you like."

Finally rejecting my perspective of being in the woods by myself with a K-Bar knife, I accepted his invitation, and he and I went to downtown Sacramento in search of the perfect beer. Eric had forgotten more about beer than I'd ever known. He listened in between me sampling copious little glasses of the fermented grain and yeast. He listened without judgment and as a friend— I could not have received a more perfect and valuable gift at that time.

I hadn't successfully completed a mandatory evolution. I was, in essence, rolled back in life to start over, and like in my Navy days, I needed to learn from my mistakes. It was the first day of the First Phase of the beginning of my new life.

I possessed the traits and talents to succeed, but that was not enough. I lacked a catalyst to express them adequately, and I finally got that. Her name is Sheryl. An unlikely match, she was the Marketing Manager at the local Public Broadcasting Station (PBS) in Sacramento. I am a die-hard Reagan conservative, and she was a liberal-minded, non-profit PBS employee. She loved art museums, community theater, and listening to jazz; I was ignorant of it all. With a calming personality and an inclusive perspective, she began to teach me how to manage my weaknesses.

Not only that, but she also owned a house and offered me a place to live for reasonable rent. Our differing perspectives converged over hours, days, and months, creating a new, more robust vision for me and my future.

Just because I decided to adjust my perspective didn't mean my problems disappeared. I was still in the middle of a divorce, and my relationship with my bosses in Washington, DC, was a disaster.

Never dampening my persistence and determination, Sheryl channeled the traits that made me successful as a SEAL and criminal investigator. Guided by a loving hand, I developed a strategy to succeed.

Instead of progressing through surprise and violence of action, I learned to influence through association and persuasion. The results were immediate and positive. My relationship with my employees improved, and I devised a path to success with my superiors.

It was the end of June 2004, and my divorce from Mary was finalized. Sheryl and I had been engaged for months, and we went back and forth about where we would have the ceremony.

Calling her at work. I said, "Hey, it's me."

"What's wrong?" she asked, "You never call me here."

"Can you get a wedding dress by Friday? Let's go to Las Vegas and get married this weekend."

There was silence on the phone. "Let me call you back." She hung up.

Damn, I thought, I did it again. I made a significant decision without discussing it with my hopefully future wife. I told Sheryl about my headstrong, persistent personality playing a negative role in my first marriage, and the first chance I got, I did it again.

But I was wrong.

Stephanie, Sheryl's twin sister, helped her find the perfect wedding dress. We drove to Las Vegas and were married on the 4th of July. I'd made another decision without discussing it with my family, but this one was more than appreciated.

With my family in mind, I continued to pursue career aspirations and was selected to attend the Senior Executive Service (SES) Candidate Development Program. After serving in an OIG SES position, the equivalent of a military flag officer, for eighteen months, I planted my flag on that mountaintop. The day after my retirement, I sat without assignments, deadlines, meetings, or titles. Sheryl stood in the doorway as I stared silently through our Victorian home's wavy single-pane glass at the massive oak tree and nesting Finch.

"Are you okay? she asked. It took a moment, but finally, I looked up, and with a happy, no-regret tear in my eye, I said, "Yes, finally... I am."

The final stone had been slung, and the most difficult battle won...the battle within myself.

EPILOGUE

BUD/S candidates have passionate reasons for wanting to be a SEAL and a mindset to never quit. The reality is that most do or are dropped from training for one reason or another. What separates those who quit or failed from those who didn't?

It's not determination, physical ability, or desire. Everyone who passes the screening test has those qualities and attributes. The formula for success begins with your DNA. Add your life experiences and how you react to and learn from those events. Factor in a bit of luck. That determines *why* someone will or will not become a SEAL or, for that matter, be successful.

Growing up, I had no idea the characteristics I embraced in elementary and high school would be what I would draw on in my most trying moments. Had I missed even one of those, I may not have solidified the will, determination, and confidence to endure BUD/S, the arduous missions in the Teams, and my later life challenges.

There are no shortcuts and no substitute for hard work, but you must understand one truth: The key to success is you. So, put away the lists and focus on yourself. Perfect your strengths and mitigate your weaknesses.

Dedication, long hours, and sacrifice are words from successful people who achieved and lived up to their potential despite their social or financial status, size, gender, or race.

There is a reason Norman Larsen, the inventor of the lubricant WD-40, called it WD-40 and not WD-1. He and his associates experienced 39 "failures" of this water displacement formula only to succeed, finally, on their fortieth try finally. Not seeing failure in each unsuccessful attempt, he realized he was getting closer to achieving his goal, to completing his mission. He refused to accept defeat.

It took me two attempts to make it through BUD/S. After training, I didn't grow six inches taller or increase my IQ. My family's societal status remained unchanged, and I didn't become wealthy instantly. Life didn't suddenly become easy. I had the same DNA I started with, but I learned to use my skills.

My potential didn't end with a Trident pin. Some guys stayed in the service for an entire career, and some, like me, left for other adventures. Some went on to be doctors, lawyers, financial planners, artists, cowboys, drunks, and inmates.

Why?

How can people with such similar powerful traits be so different over time? Prof. Carol Shumate of the University of Colorado provides one answer. In *A Vehicle for Mentality Change*, the professor writes:

"For almost a century, a debate has polarized the field of personality theory as to whether characteristics endure across the lifespan or whether they change. Does our genetic inheritance fate us to display particular personality traits, or can we escape our genetic bonds and change?" Decades of research have shown that about half of mental characteristics are inherited.

However, in 2020, an extensive cross-national study of twins found evidence that we are not doomed by fate to display the same mentality throughout life but that even inherited traits can change. This multi-generational study of more than 7,000 individuals suggested that 'heritability is not fixed' but that life experiences can change the given personality and its particular mentality."

After leaving the military, becoming a federal law enforcement special agent with the Naval Investigative Service was not enough. I moved to the Environmental Protection Agency Criminal Investigation Division, where I excelled, but that was still not enough.

Still, I clamored for more responsibility and changed agencies again. Finally, I was promoted to the special agent in charge for the Department of the Interior, Office of Inspector General. I completed my mission.

But where was my success?

In her paper "Jung's Model of the Psyche" for the Society of Analytical Psychology, psychologist Ann Hopwood opines on the work of Carl Gustav Jung, the Swiss psychiatrist and psychoanalyst who founded analytical psychology. Referring to Jung's groundbreaking theory of "the collective unconscious," Hopwood writes:

> "The theory of the collective unconscious is one of the distinctive features of Jung's psychology. He believed that the whole personality is present in potential from birth and that personality is not solely a function of the environment, as was thought when he was developing his ideas, but merely brings out what is already there. The role of the environment is to emphasize and develop aspects already within the individual."

Have you defeated your Goliath, and are you successful?

Only you have the right to judge, because only you know what you are capable of. Excuses fuel mediocrity, and we live in a world of fabricated hurdles telling us why something cannot be done or achieved. The reality is that *we* create the reasons everything *can* be achieved.

After a lifetime of chasing money, titles, certificates, and certifications, the thing I failed to do was to forgive. Forgive myself for the many mistakes and shortcomings, both personal and professional. My pathological persistence drove me to the next and the next fabricated achievement, leaving only a feeling of emptiness and longing for more artificial success. A success that everyone but me envied and held in high regard. It wasn't until it nearly disappeared that I realized what success was, which was my biggest achievement.

I retired from the federal government at fifty-two years old. I went on to a successful community theatre acting career, volunteering, becoming a community activist for public safety (my Sheepdog trait), and being the best husband and father I could be. Ultimately, I was able to slay my biggest Goliath and discover true success.

"Forgive yourself for your mistakes and shortcomings and understand them not as failures but as stepping stones to the greatness you can achieve. Without exception, everyone in their own right is destined to achieve greatness. It is in our DNA, and as DNA is unique, no two success stories are alike. As Norman Vincent Peal said, "Shoot for the moon; even if you miss, you'll land among the stars."

ABOVE: David and his sister Bonnie, at Harvey's Lake cottage in the summer of 1968. (Leo Brown Sr.)

BELOW: Third Grade class photo, 1970. David is second from left in back row. Albert Kita is fifth from left in the back row.

ABOVE: Preparing to dive as part of a winter SCUBA certification class. On the shore of Lake Wallenpaupack, Pennsylvania, 1979. (David Brown) BELOW: The pontoon boat pushes off into Lake Wallenpaupack, Pennsylvania, as a snowstorm approaches. (Leo Brown, Sr)

ABOVE: David holding the company flag and flanked by his boot camp classmates. (David Brown)

BELOW: Boot Camp Company 934, 1980. David with the company flag is in the front row on the right.

ABOVE: David and his red Triumph, Dam Neck, Virginia. (Ron Blackburn)
BELOW: BUD/S Class 114 head shaving party, 1981.

ABOVE: Preparing for a two-mile timed ocean swim. BUD/S Class 114, during the First Phase, 1981. (David Brown)
BELOW: Box lunch time during twelve-mile third phase compass course at Camp Pendleton, California, 1981.

ABOVE: David and his mother, Jean, between BUD/S classes 114 and 1115. Coronado, California, 1981. (Leo Brown)

ABOVE: David and his father, Leo, between BUD/S classes 114 and 115. Coronado, California, 1981. (Jean Brown)

ABOVE: David practices on the O Course during BUD/S. 1981.
BELOW: David approached the "horizontal ladder" on the O Course during BUD/S. 1981.

ABOVE: David tackles the "slide for life" on the O Course during BUD/S, 1981.

ABOVE: David on the obstacle course during BUD/S Class 115.
BELOW: Captain Flynn presents David his graduation certificate on completion of BUD/S Class 115, 1981.

ABOVE: Rappelling training with 3rd Platoon, UDT-21. Spain, 1982.
BELOW: 3rd Platoon, UDT-21, onboard a naval vessel in the
Mediterranean, 1982. David is in on the far right.

ABOVE: David and Lt (jg) Coleman preparing a closed circuit dive in Purto Rico, 1983.
BELOW: 4th Platoon, UDT-21, conducting cast and recovery operations off the coast of Colombia, 1983. (David Brown)

ABOVE: 4th Platoon, UDT-21, crossing "Jacob's Ladder" to board their Seafox. Off the coast of Chile, 1983. (David Brown)

ABOVE: 3rd Platoon, UDT-21, while training in Spain, 1982. David is front right.
BELOW: First group photo of SEAL Team 4. Little Creek, Virginia, 1983. David is on the far left in the second row.

ABOVE: Lieutenant McRaven (left) instructs David before house clearing training. 4th Platoon, SEAL Team 4. Ecuador, 1984.

BELOW: Casting from the rear gate of the Seafox for hydro recon. 4th Platoon, SEAL Team 4. Peru, 1984. (David Brown).

ABOVE: Point man training with a suppressed MAC-10. SEAL Team 4. Ecuador, 1984.

ABOVE: David, armed with an FN-FAL, during cross-training with Peruvian Naval Special Forces. SEAL Team 4, 1984.

BELOW: David's promotion to Petty Officer, 1st Class (E-6). Pensacola, Florida, 1986.

NCIS Bulletin

Volume I   United States Naval Criminal Investigative Service   Edition 2

October 1994

THEY'RE HERE!

9MM'S ISSUED TO NCIS

(Photo by Gary M. Crawford)

In This Edition . . .

Soft Body Armor Vest Passes Durability Test	**Investigative Specialists Assist Special Agents In Overseas Offices**	**24 Attend Foreign Counterintelligence Course at NCIS HQ**

ABOVE: David as poster boy for the NCIS rollout of the Sig Sauer.

ABOVE: David while working as an undercover special agent for the EPA. Lake St Louis, Missouri, 1994. (Mary Brown)

BELOW: David and his team when he was the Special Agent-In-Charge for Investigations' Western Region Office in Sacramento, 2008. (Bryan Brazil)

ABOVE: David playing the lead role in a production of "Dracula" at the Navasota Theatre Alliance. Navasota, Texas, 2016.

In 1980, **David W. Brown** attended boot camp at the Naval Training Center in Great Lakes, Illinois, where he was selected as the Navy League award recipient. Afterward, he became the Radarman School Dam Neck, Virginia honor graduate. David graduated from Basic Underwater Demolition SEAL (BUD/S) training in Coronado, California, class 115 in December 1981, then completed Army Airborne training in Fort Benning, GA. He served with distinction at Underwater Demolition Team-21 in Little Creek, Virginia, and SEAL Team 4 until 1985, participating in operations across the Americas, Europe, the Middle East, and Africa. David transferred to shore duty at Naval Air Station Pensacola and taught Naval Aviation Water Survival while attending night school at Troy State University.

In 1987, having obtained a bachelor's degree in criminal justice, David transitioned from active military service to a civilian role as a Special Agent with the Naval Criminal Investigative Service (NCIS). His career path led him from Beaufort, South Carolina, where he worked at the Marine Recruit Depot Parris Island, to the Naval base at Pearl Harbor, Hawaii. His exemplary work in Hawaii resulted in a promotion and transfer to NCIS headquarters in Washington, D.C.

David's journey continued at the Environmental Protection Agency Criminal Investigation Division in St. Louis, Missouri, where he advanced to the position of Assistant Special Agent in Charge of Region 7. He later took on the Special Agent in Charge role at the Department of Interior Office of Inspector General in Sacramento, managing operations across the western United States, the Hawaiian Islands, Pacific Territories, and Freely Associated States.

After 35 years of federal service, David retired as a Senior Executive. He lives in Sanford, Florida, where he proactively advocates for public safety in his community.

In addition to his Bachelor of Science degree in Criminal Justice, he graduated from the Center for Creative Leadership and the Federal Executive Institute. He has attended leadership courses at the Kennedy School of Government, Harvard University, as part of the Senior Executive Service Candidate Development Program.

Robert H. Gettlin, a journalist, author, and national bestseller, has left an indelible mark in his career. He has held various roles, from a newspaper reporter to a magazine editor, and a senior communications officer in Washington, D.C. His expertise spans national politics and government at all levels, and he has spearheaded numerous investigative journalism projects. Bob's ability to distill complex and contentious subjects into lucid, persuasive prose has earned him acclaim. He is also a seasoned public speaker and instructor, imparting his writing skills to diverse audiences.

Bob's literary achievements are significant. He co-authored the nonfiction hit *Silent Coup: The Removal of a President*, a groundbreaking investigative tome that brought new perspectives to the Watergate scandal and enriched the narrative of Richard Nixon's tenure. The book's impact was profound, securing a 12-week presence on *The New York Times* bestseller list in 1991 and featured on other prominent national charts.

Bob's professional journey has been enriched by a decade-long friendship and professional camaraderie with Dave, a testament to their shared values and mutual respect. He and his wife Arlene live in Woodstock, Georgia, outside of Atlanta.

DOUBLE‡DAGGER
— www.doubledagger.ca —

DOUBLE DAGGER BOOKS is Canada's only military-focused publisher. Conflict and warfare have shaped human history since before we began to record it. The earliest stories that we know of, passed on as oral tradition, speak of war, and more importantly, the essential elements of the human condition that are revealed under its pressure.

We are dedicated to publishing material that, while rooted in conflict, transcend the idea of "war" as merely a genre. Fiction, non-fiction, and stuff that defies categorization, we want to read it all.

Because if you want peace, study war.

Printed in the USA
CPSIA information can be obtained
at www.ICGtesting.com
LVHW011508270824
789403LV00016B/811